Managing
Hispanic and Latino
Employees

Managing Hispanic and Latino Employees

A Guide to Hiring, Training, Motivating, Supervising, and Supporting the Fastest Growing Workforce Group

Louis E. V. Nevaer

Berrett–Koehler Publishers, Inc.
San Francisco
a BK Business book

Berrett-Koehler Publishers, Inc.
235 Montgomery Street, Suite 650
San Francisco, CA 94104-2916
Tel: (415) 288-0260 Fax: (415) 362-2512   www.bkconnection.com

Ordering Information

Quantity sales. Special discounts are available on quantity purchases by corporations, associations, and others. For details, contact the "Special Sales Department" at the Berrett-Koehler address above.

Individual sales. Berrett-Koehler publications are available through most bookstores. They can also be ordered directly from Berrett-Koehler: Tel: (800) 929-2929; Fax: (802) 864-7626; www.bkconnection.com

Orders for college textbook/course adoption use. Please contact Berrett-Koehler: Tel: (800) 929-2929; Fax: (802) 864-7626.

Orders by U.S. trade bookstores and wholesalers. Please contact Ingram Publisher Services, Tel: (800) 509-4887; Fax: (800) 838-1149; E-mail: customer.service@ingrampublisherservices.com; or visit www.ingrampublisherservices.com/Ordering for details about electronic ordering.

Berrett-Koehler and the BK logo are registered trademarks of Berrett-Koehler Publishers, Inc.

Printed in the United States of America

Berrett-Koehler books are printed on long-lasting acid-free paper. When it is available, we choose paper that has been manufactured by environmentally responsible processes. These may include using trees grown in sustainable forests, incorporating recycled paper, minimizing chlorine in bleaching, or recycling the energy produced at the paper mill.

Library of Congress Cataloging-in-Publication Data

Nevaer, Louis E. V.
    Managing Hispanic and Latino employees : a guide to hiring, training, motivating, supervising, and supporting the fastest growing workforce group / Louis E. V. Nevaer.
        p. m
    Includes bibliographical references and index.
    ISBN 978-1-57675-945-5 (pbk. : alk. paper) 1. Hispanic Americans--Employment. 2. Personnel management. I. Title.
    HD8081.H7N484 2009
    658.30089'68073--dc22
                                            2009039763

First Edition

14   13   12   11   10   10   9   8   7   6   5   4   3   2   1

Author Photo: Jonathan Conklin   **Cover Image:** © Krzysztof Slusarcyzk/123RF   **Cover Design:** Irene Morris Design

*This book is dedicated to Gonzalo Guerrero,
who, in the sixteenth century,
saw the future and embraced it;
and Patrick J. Buchanan, who, five
centuries later, saw the same future
and recoiled.*

Contents

A Note on the Nomenclature

Many years later, as he faced the firing squad, Colonel Aureliano Buendia was to remember that distant afternoon when his father took him to discover ice. At that time Macondo was a village of twenty adobe houses, built on the bank of a river of clear water that ran along a bed of polished stones, which were white and enormous, like prehistoric eggs. The world was so recent that many things lacked names, and in order to indicate them it was necessary to point.

Gabriel García Márquez
One Hundred Years of Solitude

Since time immemorial people have tried to understand the universe in which they live. This involves, first, giving names to things, and, second, grouping things to make sense of relationships. At times this can be innocuous: we can divide people into those who are left-handed and those who are right-handed, mindful that there are some who are ambidextrous. A more obvious way to categorize humanity is by gender: male and female. Then again, it is prudent to bear in mind the transgender: those among us who are of one sex but identify with the opposite gender, or those who have the anatomical features of both sexes, but identify with one specific sex. There are also ways of looking at the world that can be charming in their innocence: anthropologists, for instance, classify societies based on the principal carbohydrate in their diets. The world, to them, consists of societies that eat corn (found in the New World), or consume rice (found on the western shores of the Pacific Ocean or the northern shores of the Indian Ocean), or those that subsist on wheat (Europe, the Mideast, and most of Africa).

In the United States, "identity politics," the natural outgrowth of the ideas championed by the nineteenth-century philosopher and misanthrope Herbert Spencer, rule the day: if Darwin sought to classify every creature into scientific families of genus and species, Spencer insisted that humans also be classified into groups that defined and constricted through orders and disorders. "Hispanic" is as much a product of Social Darwinism as is "Latino."

Terms evolve over time, of course, and nomenclature to describe those in the United States who are immigrants from Latin America, of Spanish ancestry or the descendants of these groups is no different. "Spanish Americans," used widely in the nineteenth century, gave way to "Spanish-speakers" and "Spanish-surnamed" for most of the twentieth century before "Hispanic" was introduced officially in 1970 by the Nixon administration, out of respect for the fact that the Spanish-speaking world, after nine years of deliberations, adopted, in 1935, the word "Hispanidad" as a universal affirmation of identity, which is commemorated on the "Día de la Hispanidad," an international holiday celebrated each fall.

"Latino," which, by using the Spanish word for "Latin," can be viewed as inherently condescending—would we call Americans of Italian ancestry "Italianos" or those of French heritage "Français"?[1]—emerged as a politically correct term in the 1990s. It has, in fact, replaced an array of words used to describe *Hispanics born in the United States:* Chicano and Mexican American, for instance, are now seldom used.[2] The same is true, of course, of other groups who have seen terms evolve over time: one can empathize with the staff of the National Association for the Advancement of Colored People and the United Negro College Fund: who calls people of color "colored people," and who calls blacks "Negros" this century? Those organizations, unfortunately, are stuck with terms that have fallen into disuse.

A simple way of remembering the difference is this: *though every Latino is a Hispanic, not every Hispanic is a Latino.* Hispanic is the more inclusive term.

Of course, many people prefer to be identified by nationalities: Puerto Ricans like to be called Puerto Rican, and Cuban Americans prefer almost always to call themselves "Cuban." Some new arrivals eschew a "Mexican" identity for their ethnic origins: Maya immigrants from Chiapas and Zapotec immigrants from Oaxaca see themselves preferably as "Maya" or "Zapotec" first; then, as a second choice, they embrace "Mexican."

For the purposes of this book, these are the definitions used:

Hispanic: a person of Latin American or Iberian ancestry, fluent in Spanish. It is primarily used along the Eastern seaboard, and favored by those of Caribbean and South American ancestry or origin. English or Spanish can be their "native" language.

Latino: a U.S.-born Hispanic who is not fluent in Spanish and is engaged in social empowerment through Identity Politics. "Latino" is principally used west of the Mississippi, where it has displaced "Chicano" and "Mexican American." English is probably their "native" language. "Empowerment" refers to increasing the political, social, and spiritual strength of an individual or a community, and it is associated with the development of confidence of that individual or community in their own abilities.

Latin: an abbreviation for "Latin American," or "Latinoamericano" in Spanish (written as one word), a Latin is a person who was born in Latin America and migrated to the United States. Regardless of his or her immigration status, a Latin is a foreign-born worker for whom English is a "foreign" language and who lacks the cultural fluency taken for granted by those born and raised in the United States. Spanish, Portuguese, or an indigenous language is their "native" language.

These words are not interchangeable, notwithstanding what Hispanic and Latino groups might want to mislead themselves into thinking. The following sentence is true: Hispanic culture had a huge impact on Aztec society. The following sentence is false: Latino culture had a huge impact on Aztec society. For marketing and political reasons, however, the terms are often used interchangeably. The "National Association of Hispanic Journalists," for instance, uses "Increasing the influence of Latinos in U.S. newsrooms" as a slogan. Shouldn't that be the job of the National Association of *Latino*

Journalists? The otherwise sensible Pew Hispanic Center—a Washington, D.C.-based think tank that provides information and conducts research on issues, perceptions, and trends affecting the Hispanics in the United States—joining the linguistic fray, uses "Hispanic" and "Latino" interchangeably just as one finds the random corporate use of "his" and "her" to create the appearance of gender-neutrality.[3] The Pew Hispanic Center is not only intellectually lazy by resorting to such a cop-out, but awkwardness results in almost every report they issue, because words are consistently used incorrectly.

There is something to be said for good form, with market-based caveats. If you were to ask me, I'd prefer that you'd say, "You haven't seen anything yet." But if you tell me that, for marketing purposes, you settled on the slogan "You ain't seen nothin' yet," I would understand your reasoning: it may not be grammatically correct, but it ain't gonna kill me to put up with slang.

It should also be pointed out that there are classist connotations to these terms. In the same way that the phrases "blue collar" and "white collar" telegraph certain generalizations about individuals, so do the terms "Latino" and "Hispanic." It's possible to criticize the use of code words to convey certain attributes, but, factually, a blue-collar worker is more likely to bowl and a white-collar employee is more inclined to play golf. Such is the way of the world. In this manner, a "Latino," for the most part, is likely to be working class, did not graduate from college, a Democrat, would like to be a member of a union, is paid by the hour, and is not fully assimilated into the mainstream of American life. A "Hispanic," on the other hand, is middle class, a college graduate, inclined to vote Republican, a salaried (professional or management) employee, and more likely than not to be acculturated to American society. Finally, many find the use of "Latino" when speaking in English to be both patronizing and a linguistic abomination, but it's a crowd-pleaser, particularly among the politically active.

This all said, Hispanics, Latinos, and Latins are distinct individuals, who, at times, loathe one another, and, on occasion, seethe when grouped together. Say "Latino" to the wrong person, and an unintended insult results. Say "Hispanic" to the wrong person, and you will be dismissed as being "prejudiced." It is important to remember that "Hispanic" and "Latino" can each be considered a pejorative, depending on the listener's sensibilities. What can be said with certainty is that, intellectually, "Latino," used when speaking in English, is the *name* given to the *children of the Hispanic diaspora in the United States*. For now, in terms of nomenclature, it remains challenging, and there are no absolute rules; terminology is still evolving as this century unfolds. With this caveat, be forewarned: terms used in this book mean distinct things, and please refer to this Note for clarification.

Louis E. V. Nevaer
New York, New York

Preface

This is the first management book published about Hispanics in the workplace since the election of Barack Obama, who, in his first news conference after being elected, referred to himself as a "mutt."[4] After centuries of vilification, "miscegenation" has been accepted on the public stage of American life. The ascendance of Hispanics, Latinos, and Latins is as fraught with emotion as it is sweeping in scope. To be sure, changes that alter the course of a society's narrative cause tremendous apprehension. Towns that became ringed by tenements on their way to becoming cities were overwhelmed by waves of human migration during the Industrial Revolution. Men lashed out at women, resisted and resented their arrival in offices throughout the nation, working their way through management and into executive positions.

Achievements were hailed as landmarks—the biggest city, the tallest building, the highest industrial output. Accomplishments were hailed as firsts—the first female CEO of a Fortune 100 company, the first woman in space, the first female to sit on the U.S. Supreme Court. There are scores of organizations, government agencies, and public policy institutes that monitor accomplishments of Hispanics, Latinos, and Latins in this country.

The discussion presented in this book reflects almost a quarter century of hands-on experience working with Hispanics and companies pursuing opportunities in Latin America and with the growing Hispanic, Latino, and Latin consumer market within the United States. This reflects both my personal history and my professional life. It provides an interdisciplinary approach to the management challenges organizations throughout the United States are facing as they come to terms with the ascendance of Hispanics, Latinos, and Latins in the workplace. The undeniable, and unstoppable, force of demographics is fast-transforming the American labor force, as the hues of the faces of high school students across the country demonstrate.

This book offers a road map on how to face these challenges; develop healthy relationships with Hispanics, Latinos, and Latins in the workplace; and implement strategies that will deliver success as the economy evolves in the years ahead. The controversies—immigration, language, academics who bemoan the emergence of "two cultures"—are alluded to, only as they are relevant to helping managers, supervisors, and other administrators understand their impact on labor relations in the workplace. Written in an approachable manner, with case studies and specific "action items," the discussion attempts to offer insights and make specific recommendations. This descriptive and proscriptive approach is one that balances the competing tugs of offering instructive information and providing action items that management should implement.

There's much to cover, so let's begin.

Introduction

Once every century a singular event transforms the American workforce. In the nineteenth century, industrialization gave rise to the cities becoming the nation's economic engines, resulting in waves of migration from the countryside into urban centers. Farmers became factory workers, and in the process, America's rural character became an urban one. The social and cultural consequences of this transformation gave rise to new sociological and cultural forces: "bourgeoisie" and "proletariat" entered academia, and the benign egalitarianism of a rural existence was replaced by the more defined distinctions between social class and economic income. It was in cities where the consumption of the "haves" became more conspicuous to the "have-nots," who were relegated to the urban squalor of tenements, ethnic ghettos, and immigrant enclaves on the wrong side of the tracks.

In the twentieth century, the defining event was the result of the nation's response to the Second World War. As the nation mobilized to meet military challenges in Europe and the Pacific, the labor market was depleted of able-bodied men who enlisted in the armed forces, and labor shortages were filled by women. American women entering the workforce proved to be a dramatic, sustained, and irreversible social and cultural phenomenon. Whereas women comprised only 18% of the labor market in 1900—primarily as schoolteachers, secretaries, waitresses, nurses, and other "support" professions—by the time the war ended, they would hold 28% of all jobs in the country.[5] In the second half of the twentieth century, women would continue to increase their presence in the American labor force, holding 42.5% of all jobs by 1980.[6] Since then, depending on how the labor market is defined and how workers are counted by age group, women comprise 46–51% of all workers.[7] In consequence, gender equality, "glass ceilings," affirmative action, mentoring programs, and discussions of sexism in the workplace have all been issues that have defined the business culture throughout the American economy for more than half a century. Women, as the twentieth century drew to a close, held 39.3% of all executive, administrative, and managerial jobs in the nation.[8]

In the current century, it is not difficult to see the seismic demographic changes that are fast transforming the American workforce: the United States has become a bilingual consumer economy, where "Oprima 2 para español" almost always follows "Press 1 for English," on virtually every customer service telephone number. No law requires that companies reach out to their customers, vendors, and the public by providing Spanish-language operators, but they do: it is *economics*—the natural interplay of market forces as celebrated by Adam Smith—that is driving the spread of Spanish in the United States. This was first anticipated by Adam Smith. "It is not from the benevolence of the butcher, the brewer, or the baker that we expect our dinner, but from their regard to their self-interest," he wrote in *The Wealth of Nations*. "We address ourselves, not to their humanity, but to their self-love, and never talk to them of our necessities, but of their advantages." Spanish is how corporate America seeks to build market share and establish a competitive advantage. Recruiting Hispanic employees is how this is most efficiently achieved.

To be sure, the passage of the North American Free Trade Agreement, or NAFTA, accelerated the integration of the economies of the United States, Canada, and Mexico. This internationalization fueled trade, tourism, and migration among the three nations, and strengthened the spread of Spanish throughout the U.S. economy. Suddenly product labels had to be bilingual because a manufacturer in Chicago was selling to stores in New York and Mexico City. Of greater consequence, a shopper walking into a store in Miami or Los Angeles was more likely to be more fluent in Spanish than in English than in decades past. At the same time, local and state government realized that to fulfill their mandates, they had to address linguistic challenges: a child entering school for the first time who spoke little English, a 911 operator taking an emergency call from a Spanish-speaking resident, a public health outreach coordinator challenged by the need to provide medical information in Spanish to greater numbers of people.

The proliferation of Spanish reflects fundamental demographic changes that are reshaping the nation's workforce. This is occurring at a time when Hispanic ascendance in the workforce reflects several fundamental trends:

1. As Baby Boomers age, non-Hispanic Whites are retiring in greater numbers, leaving the workplace entirely.

2. For unknown reasons, the fertility rate of non-Hispanic Whites is falling; fertility rates among African Americans hover around the natural "replacement" level; and fertility rates among Hispanics continue to increase.

3. Hispanics are predominantly working age, meaning that they are overrepresented in the labor market.

4. These overlapping trends—the emergence of a bilingual consumer economy in the United States and the ascendance of Hispanics in the labor force—are creating an unprecedented challenge for American employers.

That sweeping demographic changes are transforming America's workforce is undeniable.

Consider two facts:

- Hispanics in 2005 comprised 14% of the nation's population, but constituted 22% of workers.[9] *That Hispanics are almost a decade younger than the population at large means that Hispanics, Latinos, and Latins, disproportionately, are of working age, either leaving college and entering the workforce, or well on their way to establishing their careers;* and

- Hispanics in 2050 will represent 32% of the nation's population, but will comprise 55% of workers. *As America's baby boomers and Generation X-ers mature and retire, Hispanics and Latinos, native born and Latin immigrant alike, will dominate the workforce.*[10]

These demographic changes are sweeping in scope, but they are no surprise to any manager, supervisor, or administrator who has seen the rapid changes in candidates in recent years. The closest phenomenon in *living memory* remains the entry of women in the workforce after World War II: women today constitute almost, if not, half of all workers currently employed. The obstacles this continues to pose for business—"glass ceilings," and gender equality on governing boards, directorships, and CEO suites—demonstrate both the power of demographics, and the need to manage these changes effectively, and how the repercussions of demographic changes reverberate across the decades.

American employers, for the most part, have successfully incorporated women into their workforces, and the lessons learned can be applied to the successful integration of Hispanics now. In fact, Hispanics are fast expanding throughout the American workforce at a time when there is an emerging literature documenting how proper management of the Hispanic employee impacts directly an organization's performance.

Hispanics today are what women were to management in the 1950s: a challenge that must be met because it is a reality that cannot be ignored.

This book gives managers, supervisors, and other administrators the knowledge and tools necessary to deal successfully with this century's defining demographic shift that will transform the American workplace in the decades to come. Make no mistake: as irreversible as the ascendance of women over the past half century has been, it is now an undeniable reality that the "Hispanization" of the U.S. labor force will transform the nature, character, and culture of the American workplace.

The ascent of Hispanics as a presence in the workforce, and the specific challenges the Hispanic, Latino, and Latin employee poses to managers, stands to be the defining labor trend in the United States this century.

Managers confront obstacles that arise from the ascendance of Hispanics in the workplace, and from the characteristics of the mosaic components that constitute these employees. For Nonexempt employees, as such workers are defined under federal law, managers have specific tasks: how can managers assume their proper role in the corporate effort to increase productivity and profits? What does the explosion of Hispanics in the workforce mean? What are the characteristics of the Hispanic employee that require dedicated strategies from managers? How does America's increasingly bilingual consumer economy impact and inform the working environment? Is the stereotype of the Hispanic worker as being "docile" a cultural misunderstanding of Hispanic "loyalty" and "patience"?

For Exempt employees, as such personnel are defined under federal law, managers additionally confront other issues: Is the stellar performance achieved by Hispanic women with graduate degrees indicative of the how Hispanics in general will transform corporate America's productivity in the age of globalization? How can managers cultivate the Hispanic employee for the benefit of both employee and the organization as this century unfolds?

How can employees who are members of the Hispanic diaspora, an "out-group" in American society, acculturate and move closer to being part of the "in-group" of mainstream American life? To this end, the discussion presented in this book is divided into three sections.

Part I is "The Hispanic Employee and American Demographics." The impact Hispanics are having on the nation's demographics—and the disproportionate impact on the labor market—is discussed. This section addresses the fact that there is now a bilingual, bicultural workforce transforming the American workplace. The chapters in Part I introduce the reader to the demographic changes that are transforming the American workforce. The ascendance of Hispanics in the labor market is a seismic event, fundamentally changing the workplace and the nature of management–labor relations. Who are the Hispanics, what do they expect from their supervisors, and how do they see their obligations to their colleagues, co-workers, and employers? Chapter 1, "The Changed American Workforce," examines the demographics transforming the American workplace. Chapter 2, "Who Is the Hispanic Employee?" explores the mosaic of peoples and cultures that constitute the Hispanic diaspora in the United States. Although they share the same fundamental cultural, social, historical, and linguistic "DNA," there is tremendous variation within the "Hispanic" identity. Chapter 3, "Management and the Hispanic Outlook," examines the survival of worldview and philosophies of the continent's First Peoples in Hispanic society, and how the perspectives of Native American sensibilities inform how Hispanics, Latinos, and Latins see the world around them, the society in which they live, and their approach to life and work.

Part II is "The Strategies and Skills for Supervising Nonexempt Hispanic Employees." Most Hispanics in the United States are hourly employees. These chapters explore their cultural, social, and other characteristics. Together, the section examines the strategies and skills for cultivating and empowering nonexempt Hispanic employees, whether these are found in factories, restaurants, hotels, agricultural production, retail operations, and so on. Throughout this section the winning strategies employed by successful firms are discussed and developed. Chapter 4, "Finding, Attracting, and Selecting the Best Hispanic Candidates," discusses successful strategies for recruiting Hispanic, Latino, and Latin candidates, which, because of their language skills, remain in demand even in periods of economic contraction, simply because the American economy continues to evolve into a more fully bilingual consumer economy. Chapter 5, "How to Evaluate the Hispanic Employee's Performance and Conduct," offers insights on better strategies for measuring and appraising the work of members of the Hispanic diaspora, which is critical because traditional performance review systems are under scrutiny and are falling into disfavor. The final chapter in this section is Chapter 6, "Hispanics, Managers, and Labor Relations." This chapter compares and contrasts how the collectivistic tradition of Hispanic society affects not only how exempt employees, but also how these cultural values are fueling the resurgence of unions, with nonexempt Hispanic, Latino, and Latin employees swelling union membership. In a value-neutral discussion, more successful strategies for labor relations are presented.

The final section is Part III, "The Hispanic Employee and the Organization's Future." From Miami to New York, Houston to Chicago, Hispanic executives are coming into their own, and their needs reflect the cultural, social, and business skills that they bring to the table. These chapters focus on the career needs of Hispanic, Latino, and Latin employees, discussing the Hispanic, Latino, and Latin employee in management positions. Hispanics as managers and executives are among the fastest growing segment throughout corporate America. Chapter 7, "How to Keep Hispanic Nonexempt Employees Challenged and Satisfied in the Workplace," offers strategies for nurturing the majority of Hispanic, Latino, and Latin workers, who are nonexempt employees. Chapter 8, "Nurturing the Hispanic Exempt Professional," examines how mentoring is the single most important tool for developing, cultivating, and nurturing Hispanic, Latino, and Latin employees for middle- and upper management positions in ways that speak to their cultural traditions and are consistent with the values of the Hispanic diaspora. Chapter 9, "Training and Development: How Successful Managers Nurture their Hispanic Workforce," approaches training from a culturally aware approach, where policies make "sense" to members of the Hispanic diaspora. The last chapter, Chapter 10, "Empowering the Hispanic Employee and an Organization's Future," examines medium- and long-term strategies for easing the transition to the demographic inevitability of twenty-first century America: a Hispanic plurality in the American workplace.

A Conclusion summarizes the discussion presented with a broad overview of the implications for the changed American labor market of the ascendance of Hispanic culture in the United States.

Part I

The Hispanic Employee and American Demographics

For reasons that are not well understood, fertility rates among non-Hispanic women in countries spread across the northern hemisphere are dropping. From Italy to Russia to the United States, these demographic crises threaten the nature and character of various nation-states. Italy, for instance, has the lowest fertility rate in the world. The United Nations reports that fertility among Italian women dropped from 2.5 children per woman between 1960 and 1970, to 1.2 today. As a result, the population of Italy is expected to decline by 28%, from 57.3 million in 1995 to 41.2 million by 2050.[1] The consequences for Italy are sweeping: "Venice is on course to become a city virtually without residents within the next 30 years, turning it into a sort of Disneyland—teeming with holidaymakers but devoid of inhabitants," John Hooper reported in the London newspaper *The Guardian*. "The register of residents, tallied every 10 years, shows that the population of Venice proper has almost halved—from 121,000 to 62,000—since the great flood of 1966."[2]

In Russia, the situation is not as grave, but it is still alarming. Russia's population peaked in the early 1990s (at the time of the end of the Soviet Union) with about 148 million people in the country. Today, Russia's population is approximately 143 million. The U.S. Census Bureau estimates that Russia's population will decline from the current number to a mere 111 million by 2050, a loss of an additional 30 million people, and a decrease of more than 20%. Russia loses more than 700,000 people annually, roughly the equivalent of losing the population of San Francisco, California, every year. For Russian leaders, this demographic reality is unprecedented in scope. Russian leader Vladimir Putin has characterized this problem as "[t]he most acute problem of contemporary Russia. It is a crisis, insofar as the integrity and future of that nation-state is threatened."[3]

This time, come tomorrow, there will be fewer Italians and Russians in the world than there are today.

In the United States there is a similar demographic phenomenon unfolding. "Non-Hispanic White women and Asian women 40 to 44 years old had fertility levels below the replacement level (1.8 and 1.7 births per woman, respectively)," the Census Bureau reported in August 2008. "The fertility of Black women aged 40 to 44 (2.0 births per woman) did not differ statistically from the natural replacement level."[4] The number of non-Hispanic whites in the United States will begin to decline, while the African American population will remain more or less unchanged, within a decade. It is the *higher fertility rates among U.S. Latinos and Latin immigrants to the United States,* in fact, that account for the *population growth* in the United States: "Hispanic women aged 40 to 44 had an average of 2.3 births and were the only group that exceeded the fertility level required for natural replacement of the U.S. population (about 2.1 births per woman)," the Census Bureau report continues.[5] It is clear that U.S.-born Hispanics are the principal catalyst for internal population growth, and were Hispanics *removed from the demographic equation,* the United States would, like Italy and Russia at present, be confronting the specter of *depopulation,* beginning in 2020.[6]

Chapter 1

The Changed American Workforce

The demographic role of Hispanics becomes more apparent when one considers that immigrants from Latin America account for almost 60% of all legal immigrants. In addition, there are an estimated 10–12 million people in the United States who have entered, or remained, in the country in violation of existing immigration laws. Most of these illegal aliens are Latin American. That the majority of these individuals—legal and illegal immigrants alike—are actively employed further strengthens the importance of Latins in sustaining economic growth, and the role of Hispanics as members of the American workforce.

These facts represent a demographic sea change affecting the American workplace in unprecedented ways. It is important to recall that as recently at 1990, the Census Bureau believed that Hispanics would not overtake African Americans to become the nation's largest minority until 2020. It occurred fully *two decades* sooner than experts estimated. When it happened, earlier this decade, it transformed the United States into the fastest-growing *Spanish*-speaking nation in the world, and it made front-page headlines around the world. "Hispanics have edged past blacks as the nation's largest minority group, new figures released today by the Census Bureau showed. The Hispanic population in the United States is now roughly 37 million, while blacks number about 36.2 million," Lynette Clemetson wrote in the nation's newspaper of record, the *New York Times,* in January 2003, documenting the federal government's official announcement of the seismic demographic shifts that defined the character of the United States in the first decade of the twenty-first century.[1]

Every year since then the Census Bureau, along with other federal agencies, has continued to document the structural changes in

the American workforce, changes that herald the ascendance of Hispanics—and the Hispanic employee—in ways that a mere generation ago were unimaginable.

Consider a few tantalizing facts:

- Hispanics are almost a decade younger (9.5 years) than
  the general population;

- More than a third of Hispanics are younger than 18 years
  old;

- Fertility rates of Hispanics are higher than the natural
  replacement level;

- More than 34 million Mexicans have a legal claim of some
  kind to seek to emigrate to the United States, which will
  be discussed later in the chapter[2];

- Hispanic women who attain graduate degrees earn 15%
  more than their non-Hispanic counterparts; and

- In September 2008 the United States replaced Spain as the
  second-largest Spanish-speaking nation in the world; only
  Mexico has more Spanish speakers.[3]

These changes have not unfolded without comment. "It is a turning
point in the nation's history, a symbolic benchmark of some significance," Roberto Suro, then-director of the Pew Hispanic Center,
said of the emergence of Hispanics as the largest minority, displacing the historic position held by African Americans. "If you consider how much of this nation's history is wrapped up in the interplay
between black and white, this serves as an official announcement
that we as Americans cannot think of race in that way any [longer]."[4]
Other voices have been raised in acknowledgement—and alarm. "The
persistent inflow of Hispanic immigrants threatens to divide the
United States into two peoples, two cultures, and two languages.
Unlike past immigrant groups, Mexicans and other Hispanics have
not assimilated into mainstream U.S. culture, forming instead their
own political and linguistic enclaves—from Los Angeles to Miami—
and rejecting the Anglo-Protestant values that built the American

dream," Samuel Huntington, of Harvard University, wrote in the pages of *Foreign Affairs*.[5]

These demographic changes are also of profound socioeconomic consequence, simply because, unlike other immigrant groups, Hispanics have reached a "tipping point," economically mandating that Spanish be one of the languages of business, and through higher birth rates, fundamentally changing the character of American society in this century. It is not news, for instance, that, during the second half of the twentieth century, certain American metropolitan areas struggled to remain economically viable in the face of sustained population losses. Buffalo, Detroit, and Chicago are three cities that experienced sustained—and debilitating—population declines beginning in the late 1950s. Only one, Chicago, was able to *reverse* this trend, and is now in the throes of an urban relative revitalization that is the envy of the Midwest.

A closer examination of how Chicago achieved this turnaround is instructive: "After half a century of seeing its population dwindle as people abandoned the core of the city and moved to the suburbs, Chicago has finally rebounded," Pam Belluck reported in March 2001, after the Census Bureau released data from the 2000 census. "For the first time since 1950, the city's population grew, and by a larger number than demographers and historians had been expecting. . . . The growth is primarily the result of an influx of immigrants, especially Mexicans and other Hispanics. . . . The biggest change in Chicago's population mosaic is the increase in Hispanics, up more than 200,000 from 1990. While partly the result of better counting efforts, demographers say there has been a rapid stream of Mexicans coming from Mexico and from other American cities, and a growing influx of immigrants from El Salvador, Guatemala, Colombia and other countries."[6]

If only Buffalo were this fortunate, it might reverse its sustained decline.

What this means, however, is that there are more Hispanics than ever before, that they are younger than the general population, and they are entering the ranks of the employed in greater numbers. Non-Hispanic whites, whose numbers are declining, are also older, which means they are leaving the workforce: "Happy Retirement" parties are held, primarily, for non-Hispanic white and African American employees, while the "New Employee Orientation" programs administered by human resources professionals are generally geared for new Hispanic and Asian (Indian, Chinese, and Korean immigrants) employees, with a minority of new workers entering the workforce being non-Hispanic whites or African Americans.

In consequence, there is a continuous change in the character of American society: this time, come tomorrow, there will be fewer non-Hispanic employees in the American workforce than there are today, all other economic considerations notwithstanding.

The fact of this undeniable reality, too, has not unfolded without comment, and controversy. The debate over illegal immigration is as much about the failure of the federal government to control the borders as it is about the apprehension and fear that Americans sense as they witness, in the course of their routine workdays and their personal leisure, how communities across the country are changing. Hispanics are everywhere; Spanish is heard more often on the public stage of civic life.

The impact of Latin immigrants on "Native Born"—U.S. Latinos included—cannot be characterized as either negative or positive. Their impact depends on a variety of factors, including the economic circumstances of individual states, specific industries, and the conditions of local labor markets. In the most comprehensive analysis available, the Pew Hispanic Center sought to analyze, state-by-state, the impact of all immigrants (Foreign Born workers) on the economic opportunities of American workers, including U.S.-born Latinos (Native Born workers). The results, when plotted on a matrix, demonstrate that there is no single answer to that complicated question.

To understand the overlapping and interrelated dynamics of these demographic changes, however, consider New Orleans. In the aftermath of Hurricane Katrina, many residents decided not to return to that city, and as a result, the population remains just over half of what it was before the storm struck New Orleans. In the resulting absence of "Native Born" workers, industries—from construction

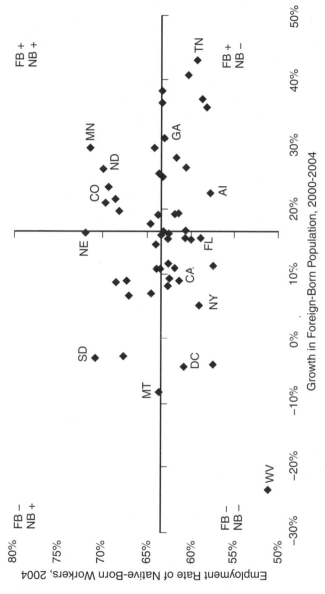

Growth in the Foreign-Born Population Is Not Related to Employment Rates of Native-Born Workers by State, 2000–2004

Center point is the average of growth in the foreign-born population and the average employment rates   + denotes above average   – denotes below average to hospitality, restaurant to health services—have desperately sought to find employees, regardless of national origin, or even immigration status. Latin immigrants have filled that vacuum, swelling the ranks of that city's workforce.

"First came the storm. Then came the workers. Now comes the baby boom," Eduardo Porter reported in December 2006. "'Before the storm, only 2 percent [of babies born in New Orleans] were Hispanic; now about 96 percent are Hispanic,' said Beth Perriloux, the head nurse in the department's health unit in Metairie." [7] The reality that New Orleans is becoming a Hispanic city is undeniable. "The demographics of the health units used to be 85 percent African American, who had Medicaid, and 15 percent other," Dr. Kevin Work told the reporter. "When the clinics reopened, I started seeing the faces changing. Now 85 to 90 percent are Hispanic undocumented, and only 10 to 15 percent have Medicaid." [8]

How can one assess the "impact" of Latin immigrants on "Native Born" workers, when the former residents of New Orleans remain absent from their community? Can it be denied that New Orleans is fast-becoming a bilingual city, where the majority of "new" residents are native Spanish-speakers, and where Hispanic culture is changing the fundamental nature of that city's social, cultural, and economic character? Of greater consequence, if eight or nine out of every ten children being born in New Orleans and neighboring communities is a Latino child, what will the city look like in the future? Has city government made plans for the fact that, beginning in 2010 and 2011, children enrolled in preschool and kindergarten are from households where Spanish is spoken at home, and whose understanding of English may be little, or even nonexistent? Further down the road, come 2020, what are the high schools of New Orleans going to look like, as these youngsters become teenagers, that city's youth—that city's future?

In trying to understand the continuing polemics over Latin immigration and Latino workers, a basic understanding of how Hispanic demographics are shaping the United States is a fundamental necessity for all workplace managers, supervisors, and other administrators. The demographic realities of New Orleans are visceral and dramatic; evidence of changes is also closely linked to the emergence of the United States as a bilingual consumer economy. In no uncertain terms, what is happening in New Orleans—hailed as the "newest" city in "Latin America" by some Latin American intellectuals—foreshadows how the American labor force will evolve this century.

It is, in essence, as if "Latin America," through an unexpected seismic movement, shifted, and is now about 200 miles north of the Rio Grande. The result is nothing less than the "Hispanization" of the United States, in general, and the American workforce, in particular. These are the demographic facts of life that inform how the American society will evolve and change throughout the twenty-first century.

In Review

- Hispanics, through higher fertility rates and immigration, account for virtually the entire population growth in the United States as this century unfolds.

- Hispanics, U.S.-born Latinos, and Latin immigrants are almost a decade younger than the non-Hispanics, meaning they are at earlier stages in their careers and are disproportionately represented in the American workplace.

- Hispanics, in the same way that women swelled the ranks of the employed in the second half of the twentieth century, are on track to constitute almost half the nation's workforce by 2050.

Chapter 2

Who Is the Hispanic Employee?

The word "Hispanic" originates in the Latin word for Spain, "Hispania." Hispanic is the broadest and most generous term used to denote people whose common denominator are societies where (1) Spanish, or related Iberian languages, are spoken, and (2) mainstream society has its origins in Spanish culture and history. This definition is the substratum from which all other terms are derived.

In the same way that the term "European" encompasses people from the part of the world that is geographically and culturally defined as west of the Ural Mountains, east of the Atlantic Ocean, with the Mediterranean Sea to the south and the Arctic to the north, "Hispanic" covers the nations and societies that are of Iberian origin and were ruled by Spain or Portugal during colonialism. Europeans exist, although there is no "Republic of Europe," and Hispanics are identifiable individuals, even though there is no "Hispanic Republic." Indeed, in the same way that a "European" can be French or German, Italian or Hungarian, the "Hispanic" identity can be narrowed down to distinguish nationalities (Mexican, Argentine, etc.), or ethnicities (Puerto Rican, Catalan). It is this identity that is celebrated around the world October 12 each year (see boxed text).

The understanding that "Hispanic" is the most inclusive term is reinforced by common sense. There are, for instance, seven countries between Mexico and Colombia—Guatemala, El Salvador, Belize, Honduras, Nicaragua, Panama, and Costa Rica. But when we speak of "Central America," Belize is not included, simply because, as a former British colony, it is part of the British Commonwealth. It may be physically Central America, but it is not one of the Latin American countries of Central America. Thus, the Central American Free Trade Agreement, or CAFTA, excludes Belize. It is common sense to think

19

of Cubans as Hispanics, but their Hispanic identity is not shared by residents of the neighboring island of Jamaica; Cuba was formerly a Spanish colony while Jamaica was an English one. On the island of Hispaniola, shared by Haiti and the Dominican Republic, few people have trouble understanding that the Dominicans are Hispanic, but the Haitians are not. (The Dominican Republic is a former Spanish colony, and Haiti was once a French colonial possession.)

Common sense tells us that, once differences of nationality, race, or ethnicity are set aside, Hispanics share a common language and are the product of societies derived from Spanish culture and history. Common sense also tells us that it is odd for U.S. Latinos to claim that "Hispanics" do not "exist" when el *Día de la Hispanidad* is an official holiday celebrated in more than two dozen countries around the world to embrace "Hispanicity." "Latino" objections to the use of the word "Hispanic" often center on the fact that it was the word selected by the Nixon administration to denote people in the United States who spoke Spanish (or another Iberian language). The argument is thus made that it was "imposed" on "Latinos," constituting a form of "colonialism." What "Latinos" fail to understand, and this may be a result of their being uninformed, is that "Hispanidad" is the name given to the countries that share a common heritage derived from the Iberian peninsula; it is the name that was chosen by those members of humanity who commemorate a common heritage on the *Día de la Hispanidad*.

Indeed, if there are no "Hispanics," then there are no "Europeans," and in the broadest, most generous sense, there are also no "Americans." There is a familiar and inviting set of characteristics that define what it means to be "Hispanic." Although there may be differences in accents or words and phrases used when speaking, there is a standard Spanish as defined by the Spanish Royal Academy, the arbiter of proper Spanish usage; Hispanics all use the same dictionary, consistent colonial norms were adopted, and there are shared historical narratives and development models pursued. Yet there is also something that Hispanics—whether they are U.S.-born Latinos, Latin immigrants, or Americans of Hispanic ancestry who live in the United States—have in common: *marginalization derived from being a minority.*

"Hispanic Day"

Although there is no "Hispanic Republic," Hispanics around the world set aside one day to commemorate their common heritage.

First proposed in 1926 by Argentina, the idea was to recognize the common heritages shared by twenty-two nations around the world that were once part of the Spanish colonial empire.[1] To broaden the appeal of an international celebration, "Hispanic" was the word chosen, as a bold affirmation of identity. Over the course of almost a decade, representatives from the Hispanic community of nations met in consultations and negotiations to agree on a name to celebrate their identity and the day on which it would occur.

"Hispanic," and not "Latino," was the name universally adopted and embraced by twenty-two sovereign nations, representing today almost 400 million people in the world, whose citizens commemorate "Día de la Hispanidad" on October 12, the day that Christopher Columbus landed in the New World. Since 1935, "Día de la Hispanidad" has been an international celebration to honor the cultural, historical, linguistic, and social bonds that unite the Hispanic nations.

"Día de la Hispanidad" is a national holiday in twenty-two countries, and in Spain, the King of Spain, who, as head of state of the Spanish kingdom, is accepted as the "moral" leader of the community of Hispanic nations and peoples, presides over a parade that is broadcast around the world, where, in various ceremonies, the day is marked by political leaders in the participating Hispanic countries. In Spain, the holiday is also known as "Fiesta Nacional de España," doubling as Spain's national holiday, the equivalent of our Fourth of July. In the United States, this holiday is known as Columbus Day, combining celebrations of both the Hispanic and Italian Americans, and the holiday coincides with the concluding days of Hispanic Heritage Month, which runs from September 15 through October 15.

The countries celebrating "Día de la Hispanidad" are Argentina, Bolivia, Chile, Colombia, Costa Rica, Cuba, Dominican Republic, Ecuador, Equatorial Guinea, El Salvador, Guatemala, Honduras, Mexico, Nicaragua, Panama, Paraguay, Peru, Philippines, Puerto Rico, Spain, Uruguay, and Venezuela.

The Hispanic Diaspora

The moment a Hispanic enters the United States he or she becomes a minority. Once Hispanics leave the countries of their births—where the constitution is written in the language they first spoke; where the president addresses the nation in the language that their mothers sang to them as they cradled them in their arms; where the leading newspapers and news anchors delivered the leading stories and sports scores in the language in which they learned the alphabet and shouted to their friends in the playground during recess; and where the principal language heard on the public stage of civic life is their own—Hispanics become marginalized, their "otherness" magnified and evident, different from the majority, culturally subordinate to a "mainstream" that is not their own. Think of entering a conference room where you are the only woman in a room full of men, or the only white person in a room full of African Americans, or the only New Yorker in a room full of Angelenos.

By stepping across the border, regardless of your circumstances in your own country, your hopes for the future, for a better life, for the ability to provide for families left behind, all of it—everything—is tempered by one reality: no matter how successful you become, you will never be part of the mainstream, because the language, culture, and customs that define you are alien to the majority of the people of the United States. This is a difference, not of immigration itself, but of one's place in society. A Cuban may move to Mexico, or a Mexican to Argentina, but in these migrations, all of these three societies share common traits that make these immigrants part of the mainstream. Canadians who live in London, and Londoners who settle in New York may speak with different accents, or have certain preferences and practices that are at odds with those around them, but the essence of the English they use and the British-derived society makes it easier for them to negotiate life in their new homelands.

This is different for Hispanics, who, inevitably, become the *Hispanic diaspora* once they settle in the United States.

Diasporas are as much about banishment, self-imposed or otherwise, as they are about longing (see boxed text). In the United States, the word "Latino" has emerged as a bold affirmation of identity primarily by U.S.-born Hispanics, the children of Latin American immigrants, or Hispanic families that have lived in geographies where borders have crossed one way or another. "We didn't cross the border; the border crossed us," is a popular Hispanic mantra throughout Texas, the American Southwest, and California, where the founding families of all the principal cities, from San Diego to El Paso, were Spanish or Mexican. Gabriel Sheffer, an authority on diasporas, describes them as being of a "sociopolitical formation, created as a result of either voluntary or forced migration, whose members regard themselves as of the same ethno-national origin and who permanently reside as minorities in one or several host countries. Members of such entities maintain regular or occasional contacts with what they regard as their homeland and with individuals and groups of the same background residing in other host countries."[2]

Latino is the name for the *anguish* of the *Hispanic diaspora in the United States*. Presented as a word of "pride" and "empowerment," it is a political construct to turn a negative (being a minority, the "other" outside the mainstream of American life), into a positive (an affirmation and celebration of identity). It is, in many ways, a process of seeking out one's identity. "Tapping into the blood's memory," is how American playwright August Wilson describes this process of reclaiming one's personal history, particularly germane when the host country is often hostile. The Federal Bureau of Investigation reports that "Hispanics" are the most frequent victims of hate crimes in the United States this century.[3] The employee in your organization most likely to be the victim of a hate crime is Hispanic, Latino, or Latin. In earlier movements, feminists used the song "I Am Woman" by Helen Reddy as a rallying cry, African Americans used "Black is Beautiful" as an affirmation of identity, and "Gay Pride" became a political statement for the gay/lesbian/bisexual/transgender/queer (GLBTQ) community.

The Hispanic Diaspora in the United States

The world is full of displaced people, or peoples who are minorities because their cultural, ethnic, religious, or racial identities stand in contrast with the mainstream ones in the nations in which they live. Oftentimes these peoples are described as living in diasporas. Since the creation of the State of Israel, for instance, the Jewish diaspora now has a homeland, which means that, within the worldview of the Jewish people, Jews who are not in Israel remain in the diaspora. The Chinese, who have a long tradition of being merchants around the world, and establishing trading colonies, have a name for the Chinese who live outside China: huáqiáo. Mainland Chinese express concerns, and have developed outreach programs, to help maintain the linguistic and cultural identity of the Chinese diaspora around the world. Among the French, Paris is so concerned with addressing the needs of French expatriates living overseas that French expats vote for a representative to the French parliament who speaks for their concerns and looks out for their interests.

In rough figures, one in ten Hispanics lives the Hispanic diaspora in the United States. These are persons who identify culturally, ethnically, linguistically, or socially as "Hispanic" or "Latino," but happen to live in the United States. The most direct way of understanding the notion predicament of the Hispanic diaspora is this: if a Hispanic, Latino, or Latin person wakes up in a country where the constitution of that nation is not written in Spanish, or a related Iberian language, then he or she is living in a diaspora, which is a form of cultural estrangement.

To this, it is necessary to consider that how others see us is important, for it affects how we are treated and how we are judged. Israeli Jews, for instance, consider every other Jew in the world who is not in Israel to be *homeless*. So it matters not that Steven Spielberg looks over the Pacific from his estate in Malibu, or that Henry Kissinger admires his Nobel Peace Prize before laying down his weary head on his pillow in his home in New York, for although each man may consider himself to be perfectly happy, to Israelis, both Spielberg and Kissinger are homeless Jews, worthy of pity. What's more, many Jewish religious leaders believe that Jews outside Israel have the obligation to make Aliyah (a visit to Israel) as their religious duty. Similarly, Hispanic societies believe it is the duty of U.S. Hispanics to be fluent in Spanish, and to reject certain cultural values of the greater Anglo-Saxon Protestant mainstream society of the United States, as a moral obligation.

For Latinos, their state of perceived estrangement from the community of Hispanic nations is exacerbated by the knowledge that significant portions of U.S. territory were once New Spain; there is a lingering sense of loss at what is interpreted as a humiliation: the border crossed a segment of the greater Hispanic nation, severing U.S. Hispanics from the Hispanic peoples to which they rightfully belong. The concern, particularly among Hispanic intellectuals outside the United States, centers on the alienation of Latinos. This describes the obstacles that U.S. Latinos encounter in their lives from their inability to speak Spanish, knowledge of Hispanic history, fluency in Hispanic culture, and the ability to function effortlessly in both societies.

As such, when Latinos dismiss the word "Hispanic," it is a source of anguish for Hispanic society: it underscores how uninformed this community of the Hispanic family has become, and the disadvantage in which they find themselves.

What does this mean? For one thing, don't be surprised if the "Latinos" in your organization have never heard of "Día de la Hispanidad"—which is a measure of both their ignorance of the global Hispanic community, and their relative alienation from the mainstream of Hispanic society. There are several repercussions to these kinds of social and cultural isolation and alienation, which are well-documented by the U.S. government: Latinos lag in virtually every measure, from educational attainment level to higher risk for diabetes, from lower household income to greater likelihood for being the victim of violent crime.

To these documented social facts that speak to the state of the lives of U.S. Hispanics, there is another component: how Hispanics are viewed by non-Hispanic Americans. How other groups in the societies in which we live view us is an important factor in our emotional well-being, and impacts the civility in which communities live. In Germany, for instance, second- and third-generation Germans of Turkish ancestry remain alienated from the mainstream of German life—and by choice. Turkish-Germans (who are Muslim) view their fellow German countrymen, who are of Teutonic (Caucasian) ancestry, and Christian, with contempt. To the Turkish-Germans, their fellow countrymen are people who pollute their bodies with alcohol and pork, and who lack enough sense to accept Muhammad as the true prophet.[4] In a similar vein, non-Hispanic Americans view Hispanics and Latinos with suspicion: who are these short, brown-skin interlopers who have arrived in the country, refuse to learn English, assimilate into the mainstream of American life, and make demands on non-Hispanics to the point where it is impossible to dial any toll-free number and not be affronted by the "Oprima 2 para español" message that is as grating as nails screeching down a blackboard? And where are Homeland Security officers when you need them?

This is the unspoken hostility that U.S. Hispanics encounter by virtue of living in this nation's Hispanic diaspora. This is the inevitable consequence that members of all diasporas encounter around the world, which requires "displaced" peoples to develop strategies to overcome obstacles inherent in being minorities at the margins of the societies in which they live. Sometimes the truth isn't pretty, and the truth about diasporas seldom is anything but wrenching.

The Latin American diaspora, too, is also about "learning" what it means to be a minority once they arrive in the United States: adopting the ways of the mainstream society that are not your own. Consider the story of Marie Arana, the Book Editor for the *Washington Post,* who was born in Peru of a Latin father and an American mother. As a young child in the 1950s, on her first visit to the United States to visit her maternal grandparents, who were living in Wyoming, the family sailed from Peru to Miami, where they boarded a train bound for Denver. In Denver they would take a bus to Wyoming. This is how she describes a stopover in Missouri:

> In the St. Louis station, [her older sister] Vicki and I took off in search of a bathroom and came to a stop before two doors marked Ladies. One said Colored. The other said Whites. We puzzled over the words, wondering what they meant, but Mother came by, grabbed our hands, and pulled us through the second door.
>
> "Why does the other one say Colored, Mother?" Vicki asked.
>
> "Because only the colored are supposed to go through it," she replied.

"Colored?" my sister asked, revealing a rare lack of enlightenment.

"Yes. Haven't you noticed in the station, darling? Or on the train? The black people?"

"With black hair, you mean?" Vicki asked.

"No, dear." Mother answered on her way into a cubicle, latching the door behind her. "Not black hair. Black skin. You have black hair, but you're white. Your skin is white. So is mine."

I listened and looked down at my dark-olive knees dangling over the snowy commode. They were green. They were yellow. They were brown. They were colored. Never in a million years could they be called white. But when Vicki and I emerged from the bathroom and looked around the station, we saw what was meant. . . . Here in March of 1956, in the St. Louis train station, however, where black and white was spelled out so boldly—where colors were carved on doors with directives—I do believe that for the first time I feared a little for myself.[5]

A Cuban-born U.S. citizen, now a Cuban American living in Coral Gables, Florida, and who has amassed a fortune between $25–30 million, characterized the anguish of exile this way: "No one leaves their country because they want to, and no matter what they achieve elsewhere, it's never really their country: Home is always missing."[6]

The impulse, then, is to recreate home in the Hispanic diaspora. Julia Álvarez, the novelist and teacher, best known for her books, *How the García Girls Lost Their Accents* and *In the Time of the Butterflies*, describes the process she herself has lived. Born in New York, the child of Dominican immigrants who subsequently returned to the Dominican Republic, Álvarez struggled to find her voice and her place in the world, commuting between her coffee plantation in the Caribbean and her home in Vermont, where she teaches at Middlebury College.

In her book examining how Hispanic, Latino, and Latin families in the United States struggle to continue the traditional coming-of-age parties for their daughters, known as "Quinceañeras" which are, roughly, the equivalent of the "Sweet Sixteen" celebrations or "coming out" debutante balls common in non-Hispanic American society, she writes, "These cultural celebrations are also about building community in a new land. Lifted out of the context of our home cultures, traditions like the *quinceañera* become malleable; they mix with the traditions of other cultures that we encounter here; they become exquisite performances of our ethnicities within the larger host culture while at the same time reaffirming that we are not 'them' by connecting us if only in spirit to our root culture. In other words, this tradition tells a larger story of our transformation into Latinos, a Pan-Hispanic group made in the USA, now being touted as the 'new Americans.'"[7]

The Hispanic Diaspora in the United States: Mexican Hispanic and Caribbean Hispanic

The inevitable nature of Hispanics in the United States being a minority aside, there are certain ways of understanding the differences among U.S. Hispanics. In the United States Hispanics can be broadly divided into two distinct categories: *Mexican Hispanics* or *Caribbean Hispanics*. Managers, supervisors, and other administrators throughout the United States remain mostly unaware of the distinct cultural, social, and racial differences between "Mexican Hispanics" and "Caribbean Hispanics." "Hispanics" are not a homogeneous community, but are a mosaic of peoples who share certain traditions, languages, and histories. One of the purposes of this book is to expand the "Cultural Intelligence" of managers, supervisors, and other administrators in order to understand the nuances that inform the various Hispanic, Latino, and Latin identities that exist in the American workforce.

Mexican Hispanics, who are the vast majority of all Hispanics, comprising almost 80% of all U.S. Hispanics, Latinos, and Latins in the United States, can trace their ancestry to Mexico or Central America. They live, primarily, west of the Mississippi, do not hold a college degree, work for an hourly wage, and are in the working- and lower-middle class. *Caribbean Hispanics,* who comprise about 17% of all U.S. Hispanics, for the most part, live east of the Mississippi, are of Puerto Rican, Cuban, or Dominican heritage, have at least graduated from a community college, are likely to work in management, and are well represented in America's middle class. (Hispanics of South American or Iberian origins comprise approximately 3% of all Hispanics in the United States and their profiles conform mostly to those of Caribbean Hispanics.)

There is another important distinction between *Mexican Hispanics* and *Caribbean Hispanics:* racial heritage. Mexican Hispanics are almost exclusively of Native American (indigenous) and European descent. Caribbean Hispanics are primarily of African (black) and European ancestry. In other words, *as race is defined in the United States,* Mexican Hispanics are "brown" and Caribbean Hispanics are "white" or "black."[8] This racial distinction is an important one, for it means that the social and cultural legacies of Caribbean Hispanics are more familiar to mainstream American society, where the history of slavery, race, and racial relations resonates throughout the Hispanic countries of the Caribbean.

Characteristics of Mexican and Caribbean Hispanics

The Hispanic presence in the United States arises from two distinct patterns: immigration from the Caribbean island nations; and Mexican Hispanics, many of whom settled in what is now the United States prior to the Mexican-American War, and most of whom are engaged in crossing borders that crossed them. In the case of California, as Kevin Starr, state librarian and author of cultural histories of California, described the ascendance of Hispanics in that state, "The Anglos hegemony was only an intermittent phase in California's arc of identity, extending from the arrival of the Spanish. The Hispanic nature of California has been there all along, and it was temporarily swamped between the 1880s and the 1960s. But that was an aberration. This [Census 2000 report] is a reassertion of the intrinsic demographic DNA of the longer pattern, which is part of a California-Mexico continuum."[9] The following descriptions of the two distinct characteristics of U.S. Hispanics are compiled from various sources.[10]

The Mexican Hispanic

- 77% of U.S. Hispanics can trace their ancestry to Mexico.

- These Hispanics are primarily of European (Spanish) and indigenous (Native American) ancestry.

- Most have not graduated from college.

- Most are not fully bilingual.

- Most are hourly employees.

- Most live west of the Mississippi, with clusters in New York, Washington, D.C., and North Carolina.

- Racially, Mexican Hispanics are brown (*mestizo*).

The Caribbean Hispanic

- 17% of U.S. Hispanics can trace their ancestry to Puerto Rico, Cuba, or the Dominican Republic.

- These Hispanics are primarily of European (Spain and Italy) and African ancestry.

- Most have post-high school education (community college course) or college degrees.

- Most are bilingual.

- Many occupy salaried and management positions.

- Most live east of the Mississippi, primarily in the New York/New Jersey–Florida corridor.

- Racially, Caribbean Hispanics are black or white.

Hispanic vs. Anglo American Societies: Religion, Colonial Formation of Families, & Miscegenation and the Nature of Race

At this point, it is necessary to discuss certain differences between Spain's colonies in the New World and England's. Until now the common denominators among all Hispanics have been discussed in terms of "language" and "Spanish" culture and history. Spanish as a language is readily understood: all Hispanics use the same dictionary, because, regional accents and colloquialisms aside, there is a standard written and spoken Spanish that is used by publishers, broadcasters, public officials, and professionals when conducting business. When it comes to "Spanish cultures and history," however, there are three areas that are markedly different from the Anglo-Protestant mainstream American society that characterizes the United States. These differences center on religion, formation of families under colonialism, and miscegenation.

Religion

Hispanics are, if not Roman Catholic, then heirs to the inclusive nature of Catholic society. Whereas the English who settled New England came for the freedom to pursue their own religion, the Spanish who were sent to New Spain set out to convert the indigenous people to the Roman Catholic faith. The English, such as the Puritans, set out to create communities where they could be left alone to practice their faith in peace, mindful that the price for this freedom was tolerance: other Protestants were free to worship as they pleased. A culture of religious tolerance, where no one group could dominate the others, thus evolved, and "freedom of religion" encouraged the proliferation of many variants of Christian faith.

In New Spain, by comparison, the stated goal of government— Roman Catholicism was the state religion—was to convert the indigenous people, and prohibit non-Catholics from settling in New Spain. There was one "true" faith, and it was the faith as defined by the Pope and practiced by the king. Whereas the Puritans in New England set up their own communities, and let others alone as the price for being left alone, in New Spain, missionaries were charged with building networks of missions—in California, in Mexico, in New Granada (northern South America), and beyond. These are powerful tendencies that reverberate in our own time.

It is the difference between *exclusivity* and *inclusivity.* New England was a place where you came, built a community for you and your own, and everyone else was kept at a neighborly distance. New

Spain, on the other hand, was a place where everyone was expected to come in under the same tent. This difference has informed American and Hispanic societies: If the United States had a history of inclusivity, there would be no need for "diversity" training in the workplace, which is a way of making everyone feel welcome under the organization's same "tent." If Latin America had not evolved into inclusive societies under the tutelage of the Catholic church, it can be argued there would be unending race riots, given that there are so many distinct peoples living throughout the nations of the region.

These distinctions still are very much in evidence. If you, for instance, find yourself in Pennsylvania in Amish country, the Amish don't want you to stay; they want you to leave them alone. If you find yourself in any town or city in Latin America, you'll find Protestants, Evangelicals, Baptists, Mormons, and Jews, but looming high over all of them is the cathedral, casting its influence like a long shadow. The result, then, is that Latin immigrants to the United States and U.S. Hispanics come from societies where, their own contemporary faiths notwithstanding, it is the Roman Catholic churches that dominate the public squares of towns and cities throughout Latin America, and its moral teachings influence the national conversations on the issues of the day. The world is seen through the inclusive sensibilities of Catholicism.

Formation of Families Under Colonialism & Miscegenation

A crucial social difference between New England and New Spain centered on the family. It is important to recall the stark differences between the English and Spanish colonies in the New World. New England was initially conceived as a way of ridding England of undesirable communities of malcontents and fringe religious and political elements. The Puritans fit that category, and the English monarchy was intent to rid itself of entire communities: thus Puritan *families*—men, women, and children—were banished to New England. The Spanish Crown did not concern itself with exile or banishment because, by banning Jews and Muslims who refused to convert to Catholicism, it had already accomplished, to a large extent, creating, in religious terms, a uniform society. That New Spain was breathtaking in its geographic size made only one ambition foremost: material wealth.

The Spanish who arrived were almost exclusively men with one expectation: striking it rich and returning home wealthy, or being able to afford to bring a European woman to become his wife in the New World. But not unlike the 49ers of the California Gold Rush centuries later, few would make fortunes that would afford themselves lives of leisure back in Spain. Confronted with harsh realities, few had enough to pay for passage back to Spain, and those who did could not bear to return empty-handed. This was further complicated by the nature of life: without their countrywomen, Spaniards (and other Europeans who arrived in New Spain after petitioning the Spanish Crown) found themselves forming families with indigenous women, or women who had arrived from other parts of Europe, the Near East, or were brought over against their will from sub-Saharan Africa.

The first union between a European man and a Native American woman occurred in the early 1500s when Gonzalo Guerrero, who had been shipwrecked on the shores near present-day Playa del Carmen, south of the resort of Cancún, married a Zazil Ha, a Maya woman. When his countrymen learned that he had survived, they sent word to him of his impending rescue. To the astonishment of the Spaniards, Guerrero refused to rejoin his countrymen. "I am married and have three children. . . . My face is tattooed and my ears are pierced. What would the Spaniards say if they saw me like this?" he said to the messenger. His children are the first *mestizos,* the name given to individuals of mixed Spanish (European) and Native American (Amerindian) parentage. The majority of Mexican Hispanics are *mestizos,* and there are certain racial characteristics that distinguish Mexican Hispanics from Caribbean Hispanics. In the United States, Native Americans have an expression to identify another person who has indigenous ancestry: "skin." A close examination of a photograph of actor and activist Angelina Jolie, for instance, reveals facial characteristics around her cheekbones and shape of her lips consistent with traits of the First Peoples: she has "skin."[11]

To Americans, this remains fraught with emotion. "Mixed race" couples and "interracial" children constitute miscegenation, which was an affront to the sensibilities of the Protestant settlers of New England. What Protestants considered a "sin" against nature, Catholics accepted as the will of God. Throughout the next two centuries, as New England and New Spain evolved as distinct societies, miscegenation was used against the emerging Latin American nations by the English and white Anglo-Saxon Protestant Americans.

The British, who had greater contact with the people of New Spain through their colonial possessions throughout the Caribbean—and who were steadfast in keeping whites and blacks separate through the institution of slavery—were "disgusted" by the "degradation" of the Spanish who took "Indian" women and formed societies of "half-breeds." "A nation of mongrels," is how the British described nineteenth-century Mexico. In the United States Senate, as rhetoric against Mexico intensified in the 1840s, with eyes on annexing Texas and then the territories west of Texas to California, Mexicans were described as an abomination, a people who, through mixing the races, had come to embody "the vices of the white man" and the "savagery of the Indian." Abraham Lincoln, in his debates with Stephen Douglas in 1858, was typical of Americans of the period when he said, "the people of Mexico are most decidedly a race of mongrels. I understand that there is not one person there out of eight who is pure white."[12] He would, once in office, change his mind, particularly after he had dealings with Mexico's president, Benito Juárez, who was of pure Zapotec blood.

Americans were aghast when Vicente Guerrero, a black man, became Mexico's president, at a time when slavery in the United States was a contentious issue, tearing the Union apart. The year was 1829, and it would take the United States 179 years before it elected a black president, and when it did, of all the African Americans in the United States, it elected a black American who has absolutely no personal connection to the legacy of the institution of American slavery. The influential nineteenth-century Harvard professor Louis Agassiz famously argued that, "the production of half-breeds is as much a sin against nature, as incest in a civilized community is a sin against purity of character."[13]

"White man's burden" offered intellectual cover for the political rhetoric used to insult Mexicans, to justify the annexation of Texas and the launching of the Mexican-American War, and to vilify Latin Americans. The stigma of interracial marriages in the United States lingered throughout the twentieth century. "Privately, they guess at my troubled heart, I suppose—the mixed blood, the divided soul, the ghostly image of the tragic mulatto trapped between two worlds," Barack Obama wrote in *Dreams of My Father,* describing how in his youth, he was circumspect about disclosing to others that his mother was white.

The point remains that, absent the wholesale immigrations of entire families, and with the inclusive nature of Catholicism, the societies of New Spain never set up "reservations" for the Native Americans in their midst, but instead welcomed them into the Roman Catholic faith, and the families that emerged in these societies reflected the intermixing of peoples of various races.

The Nature of Race

It should then come as no surprise that survey after survey conducted throughout Latin America confirms the belief, among Hispanics, that there is "little" or "no" racism in their countries. Americans refuse to accept this, perhaps because of the tortured race relations in the United States and the legacy of slavery. But the fact remains that there is no "racism" in Latin America as "racism" is manifested in the United States. U.S. Hispanics are reduced to being but mere spectators to the traumata of "black-white" race relations in the United States, and for those who arrived in this country (or were born after 1960), there is little memory of segregation. Cubans who arrived as refugees in Miami were surprised that the Woolworth on Flagler Street near the Freedom Tower would not serve blacks, especially jarring because the Woolworth in Havana, across the street from the National Congress, served anyone. Mexican immigrants in Los Angeles, when told there was a time when blacks were forced to sit at the back of the bus, look at you with puzzled expressions, as if you're pulling their leg. When Hispanics learn that it was not until 1967 when the U.S. Supreme Court, in *Loving v. Virginia,* struck down a law prohibiting marriages between individuals of different races; that a film that addressed interracial relations ("Guess Who's Coming to Dinner," starring Katharine Hepburn, Spencer Tracy, and Sidney Poitier in 1967, which won an Oscar for best original screenplay) was considered "groundbreaking"; and that the last state to remove language prohibiting miscegenation from its state constitution was Alabama in 2000, they are dumbstruck, not knowing what to think of American society.[14]

If race relations are fundamentally different among Hispanics, this does not mean that there is no *discrimination*. But there is a difference between "racism" and "lookism." The former refers to a set of characteristics and assumptions based on a person's race. The latter, on the other hand, refers to discrimination based on appearances: a person's weight, height, age, and whether or not a person approximates society's ideals of beauty, or "ideas" of beauty as packaged by Madison Avenue or promoted by Hollywood. Women, who are subjected to men's gaze every day, are sensitive to this kind of objectification, even though this is a complicated issue, and men are also subjected to objectification.[15] Sociological studies confirm that the "fat," the "short," the "old," and the "homely" are subjected to discrimination every day in their professional, social, and private lives. These are the four categories that fall under "lookism," and Hispanics, as a demographic group, are shorter than non-Hispanics and have a greater disposition of being obese than the general population.[16]

There are times when "biases" overlap and it is only from a distance that one gains an instructive perspective. Janet McDonald, an African American woman who grew up in the projects in Brooklyn, attended Vassar, went on to law school, and moved to work in Paris, to the subversive nature of "lookism," not necessarily as a woman, but as a "black":

> In France, I was liberated. . . . No one judged me on specifics, and I had nothing to prove. The French saw me as just another American, though I didn't see myself that way at all. I viewed Americans as white patriots in "Love it or Leave it" T-shirts, with a flag on their lawns, who didn't want me in school with

their children. I was black, period. The French drew no such
distinctions, which meant I no longer had to worry about
making *African-Americans* look good. Or bad. Whatever I did
was attributed to Americanness, not blackness. What a
switch—a black person with the power to make white people
look bad.[17]

The full implications of what these experiences meant coalesced after
Cornell West gave a talk in Paris. Janet McDonald spoke to him about
how the French didn't see her as "black" but as "American"—and
how they subsequently treated her as "full" human being, instead
of a macabre stereotype of "blackness."

Cornell West suggested that it was because she was educated
and well-mannered and carried herself in a respectful and respecting manner. "But I wonder how welcome you would be made to feel
if you showed up with some of the girls from your 'hood," she quotes
him as asking her. "But if my girls from the 'hood in the Brooklyn
projects were treated differently than I'm treated," she wondered out
loud when interviewed on "This American Life" on National Public Radio, "then it's not about race, but about class."[18]

*Discrimination that Americans label as "racism," Hispanics call
bigotry based on social class.*

As Mexican integration into the economic and social life of
North America accelerates, "lookism" is emerging as an "issue,"
even when it is not properly identified as such. Anthony DePalma,
writing of an incident that occurred to an American businessman
in Mexico City who attempted to have his maid join his family for
dinner that underscores the prevalence of "lookism" in Mexico,
demonstrates how "racism" blurs into discrimination based on
"lookism":

Mexicans and their country are torn between the twin poles of
their identities, trying to be modern but falling back on ancient
ways of work, courtesy, and corruption. They are proud of
their Indian roots, but no number of statues of the warrior king
Cuauhtémoc or other Indian heroes can hide their shameful
treatment of today's descendants of the Aztecs. I saw this

firsthand when a friend, Henry McDonald, an American real estate executive in Mexico City, told me of his experience when he tried to take his family to dinner at an expensive restaurant in Mexico City not far from the monument to Mexico's Indian past. They were turned away because he had brought along his dark-skinned Indian housekeeper. It wasn't a sophisticated rejection, nor a veiled objection. The maitre d' simply told Henry that no tables were available at the time. . . . Mario Padilla, the restaurant manager, later told me quite openly that the restaurant policy was for the benefit of patrons, he said, most of whom have servants but would never bring them along. However, some people "lack discretion," he said, obviously referring to Americans like Henry who wouldn't know not to bring a maid to dinner at a fine restaurant.[19]

Is this discrimination "racism"—or a question of "lookism"? Had Henry McDonald arrived at a restaurant with another American—an African American—would his party have been seated?[20]

In the sixteenth century Gonzalo Guerrero knew that his countrymen would not understand his choices, and his decision to remain among the Maya, through our own time, when Americans are confronting, for the first time, Native Americans—*in the form of immigrants from Latin America who are indigenous people*—in the workplace is puzzling.[21] "Lookism" affects members of the Hispanic diaspora as a form of discrimination. If Julia Álvarez alludes to the topic in *How the García Girls Lost Their Accents,* what can be said with certainty is that "lookism" is how the main character on the television program "Ugly Betty" became "ugly."

Although Hispanics, Latins, and Latinos agree that there is much discrimination based on "lookism" and perceived social class, it is important to understand that the fundamental nature of Hispanic societies is such that "racism" as it is experienced in the United States is, for the most part, an unknown phenomenon. As a result, there is a certain insensitivity among Hispanics about the tenuous nature of black-white relations in the United States, simply because race relations fraught with trauma are not well understood.

Consider how a reporter covering the sudden—and unexpected—arrival of thousands of Latin immigrants in North Carolina describes how Hispanics inadvertently upset the South's black-white racial dynamics in this workplace situation:

> Standing in the hiring hall that morning, two women chatted in Spanish about their pregnancies. A young black man had heard enough. His small town the next county over was crowded with Mexicans. They just started showing up three years ago—drawn to rural Robeson County by the plant—and never left. They stood in groups on the street corners, and the young black man never knew what they were saying. They took the jobs and did them for less. Some had houses in Mexico, while he lived in a trailer with his mother.
>
> Now here he was, trying for the only job around, and he had to listen to Spanish, had to compete with peasants. The world was going to hell.
>
> "This is America and I want to start hearing some English, now!" he screamed.
>
> One of the women told him where to stick his head and listen for the echo. "Then you'll hear some English," she said.
>
> An old white man with a face as pinched and lined as a pot roast complained, "The tacos are worse than the niggers," and the Indian leaned against the wall and laughed. In the doorway, the prisoners shifted from foot to foot, watching the spectacle unfold from behind a cloud of cigarette smoke.
>
> The [white] hiring manager came out of his office and broke it up just before things degenerated into a brawl. Then he handed out the employment stubs. "I don't want no problems," he warned [as quoted by *The New York Times* reporter]. He told them to report to the plant on Monday morning to collect their carving knives.[22]

These situations pose their own set of obstacles for managers, supervisors, and other administrators, who, as we shall see, are asked to bridge the tensions that arise between Hispanics and African Americans in the workplace.

"Hispanic" versus "Latino"

For almost 75 years the descendants of nations that emerged from the Spanish empire have embraced the word "Hispanic" to give a name to the family of nations, comprised of almost 400 million people, who are united by the common bonds of culture, history, and language. In the United States this preference remains: despite the popularization of the term "Latino," U.S. Hispanics prefer the term "Hispanic" to "Latino" by a margin greater than two to one.

"The findings of this research are probably a little less comforting to those at *Latina* magazine, who have invested so much into their name, than say, Hispanic Perspectives," Diana Layseca, of Q & A Research, told reporters when the findings of *Hispanic Business* magazine documenting the preference of "Hispanic" over "Latino" were released. "[M]arketers and researchers, alike, who target Hispanics, need to be aware of [cultural and linguistic nuances] to ensure the success of their surveys. Far too often there is a sense that, to effectively execute research among Hispanics in the U.S., all you need to do is simply draft a survey in English and translate it. It is understanding exactly these kinds of cultural sensitivities that is required to effectively conduct Hispanic research and to avoid alienating or offending our research contacts."[24]

Poll after poll, and survey after survey, reaffirms the greater acceptance of "Hispanic" over "Latino" among U.S. Hispanics. Indeed, the only time when "Latino" appears to be more popular is when respondents are given three choices: "Hispanic," "Latino," and "Latin," and *in Spanish,* so that those who respond to "Latin," as in a shorthand for "Latin American," or "Latinoamericano," are counted along with "Latino."[25]

Non-Hispanic Americans are understandably confused, simply because it is a vocal minority of U.S. Hispanics—"Latinos"—who insist on voicing complaints and demanding that the term "Latino" be used over the more generally accepted "Hispanic" term. A minority dictating to the majority is not new, and the world is full of linguistic paradoxes: in American English, we drive on the parkway, but park our cars in the driveway. Similarly, "Latinos," who are least likely, statistically, to be fluent in Spanish, are the ones who insist on using a Spanish word to label themselves.

> In the end, it bears remembering that come October 12, almost 400 million Hispanics around the world will celebrate "Día de la Hispanidad," or "Hispanicity Day," which should be the final word on the matter. It won't be.

Hispanics, in general, and Latin immigrants in particular, encounter biases because of their accents. This is not surprising, because there are biases against regional dialects *within* the United States that subtly influence our perceptions (see boxed text). "The University of North Texas conducted a study that showed how easily we stereotype people with no more to go on than the way they sound. The study used a recording of 10 white men reading an identical 45-second passage. The wording, constructed in standard American English, contained no jargon or any other indicators of anyone's background. Each speaker, however, had a distinct accent common to specific regions of the United States," Diane K. Faulkner reports. "The recording was then distributed to HR directors and others responsible for hiring in a variety of companies. When asked to rate and comment on the speakers' 'attributes,' respondents' comments got personal. The listeners noted that speakers sounded educated or uneducated, intelligent or unintelligent, energetic or lazy, uptight or laid back, outgoing or withdrawn, and assertive or docile. Based on their overall impressions of the speakers, the executives gave the men with the nondescript Midwestern and Californian accents the highest ratings. Accents from Minnesota, Boston, and Texas followed, and the worst ratings were for the men with accents representing Louisiana, Georgia, and New Jersey.[23]

In Review

- Hispanics share a common language and are from societies that are derived from Spanish culture and history

- Hispanics in the United States constitute a diaspora, which sets them apart from other Hispanics throughout the world

- Hispanics in the United States can be divided into two groups, "Mexican" Hispanics and "Caribbean" Hispanics

- Mexican Hispanics comprise almost 80% of all U.S. Hispanics, and most live west of the Mississippi
- Caribbean Hispanics comprise about 17% of all U.S. Hispanics, are comprised primarily of Puerto Ricans, Cubans, and Dominicans, and live along the Eastern seaboard

- The Hispanic experience with Catholicism, the history of racial miscegenation, and how race is perceived among Hispanics informs a worldview that is in sharp contrast with the American experience

Chapter 3

Management and the Hispanic Outlook

The inclusive nature of Catholicism, coupled with miscegenation accepted among the settlers of New Spain, resulted in the survival of indigenous cultures into our own time. In consequence, Latin American societies have centuries of experience in dealing with significant numbers of peoples whose worldview stands in stark contrast to how Europeans see the world, and their place in it. Americans have little experience dealing with indigenous peoples, simply because the United States has sought actively to exclude Native Americans from the mainstream of the nation's life. Expelled, displaced, and relegated to "sovereign" nations, the impulse to exclude the "other" has been a driving force in American history, as much a result of philosophical tenets of American Protestantism as it was the desire to secure the vast resources of the lands across the vast continent that became the United States.

This book was written in New York and published in San Francisco. The original inhabitants—the First Peoples—of New York were the Mana-Hatta, hence Manhattan, and of San Francisco were the Coast Miwok. The Bureau of Indian Affairs does not recognize any Mana-Hatta, or Coast Miwok, living in either city. By comparison, it's impossible not to step outside the Maria Isabel Sheraton in Mexico City or the Swissotel in Lima and not encounter indigenous people within a few steps from the entrances of these hotels.

In many ways, the challenge Hispanics pose for Americans is that, for the first time, Americans are being forced, after three centuries of reluctance to do so, to come to terms with First Peoples. This realization is at the heart of the fear confessed when Harvard's Samuel Huntington asks: "Will the United States remain a country with a single national language and a core Anglo-Protestant culture? By ignoring this question, Americans acquiesce to their eventual transformation into two peoples with two cultures (Anglo and Hispanic) and two languages (English and Spanish)."[1]

There is nothing that anyone can do to change the past, and it is true that the First Peoples were systematically excluded in the nineteenth and twentieth centuries, driven from their lands, settled in "reservations," and denied the opportunity to enter the mainstream of American life. The fact that there is a Bureau of Indian Affairs means that there is a federal agency charged with "managing" Native Americans—would we tolerate a "Bureau of African American Affairs" to "manage" blacks? Would we tolerate a "Bureau of Women's Affairs" to keep women in their place? But in the here and now, we have to own up to our societal shortcomings: how many organizations actively recruit Apache, Cherokee, Coast Miwok, Sioux, Navajo, or Crow employees to join their organization? The Bureau of Indian Affairs reports there are no Apache, Crow, or Navajo living in New York: of the millions of Americans working in New York City, none are from these First Peoples nations. Why? Why is there no proactive recruitment effort to reach out to the Native American peoples and offer them the opportunity to enter the mainstream of American life? Thus, non-Native American Americans have almost no exposure to working and living among First Peoples in New York City. There is nothing preventing any organization in New York from being proactive and affording members of these communities, who are their fellow citizens, the opportunity to assimilate into the mainstream of American life.[2]

Contrast that reality with the fact that Asociación Tepeyac (a Mexican organization), the Mexican Migration Project, and the Consulate of Mexico give various estimates, but the consensus is that there are approximately 30,000 Zapotec and Mixtec now living in New York City. New Yorkers are now, for the first time, encountering Native Americans (from Mexico) in their daily lives, and as co-workers. American employers who have never been proactive and reached out to the First Peoples from the United States are now hiring the First Peoples from Mexico, and with it, the worldview and sensibilities of the Native Americans in entering the American workplace, offering a new set of obstacles. (The Korean Greengrocer Association in New York, whose members hire a disproportionate number of First Peoples from Mexico, has established a Code of Ethics and offers its members guidelines on how to work with Mexican Native Americans.) Few other non-Hispanic associations have been as proactive in reaching out to the First Peoples entering the American workplace.

To be sure, Westerners have, for centuries, attempted to "make sense" of how the indigenous peoples of the Americas look at the world. Anthropologists have written much about the "fatalism" of the "Indian" in Latin America, of their "passivity" and the "nonlinear" understanding of time and life. For our purposes, the closest Western philosophy that approximates the indigenous peoples' worldview—and subsequently informs the attitudes and beliefs of Mexican Hispanics—is Stoicism. Founded by Zeno of Citium in the third century B.C.E. in Athens, Stoicism teaches the importance of self-control and moral fortitude as a means of overcoming destructive emotions. As the Greek philosopher Epictetus said, "Freedom is secured not by the fulfilling of one's desires, but by the removal of desire." There is passivity and fatalism attached to such an outlook, where one accepts that he or she is incapable of destiny, but must submit his or her will to whatever life brings with serenity.

This passive view of the world has proved problematic for Europeans to accept, simply because it suggests defeatism, and evokes nihilism. During colonialism, Spanish missionaries were fascinated by the worldview of the First Peoples in their midst, and they were at a loss to reconcile their "fatalistic" philosophy with Western ideas. The best they managed to do was to conclude that there were simply two ways of looking at the world. There were "gente de razón," or "people of reason," which was to say, the Europeans on the one hand, and "gente sin razón," or "people without reason," which were the natives. People of Reason looked at the world logically, as active agents who were in control of lives, while People without Reason were enslaved to their passion, unwilling to take control of their destinies.

This sentiment was shared by other Europeans in the centuries that followed. When the French invaded Mexico, Emperor Maximilian believed that the indigenous peoples of Mexico would be his allies, because he wanted to champion their cause. In short order, however, he was forced to realize that there was, as he phrased it, "a nothingness to the masses of the Mexicans" that rendered them "passive in the face of the future."[3] Maximilian died before a firing squad, but the French remained fascinated by Mexico, and it would take them an entire century before they "solved" the riddle: Jean Paul Sartre declared the Mexicans to be *existentialists*.

Other Europeans were not so enamored by this form of nihilism. The English were particularly hostile to the worldview of this continent's First Peoples. "How tedious of the white [man] coming with the trick of salvation, to rub oil on the baby, and put poultices on it, and make you give it medicine in a spoon at morning, noon, and night," D. H. Lawrence wrote in one of his short stories about the indigenous people of Mexico. "Why morning and noon and night? Why not just anytime, any when? It will die to-morrow if don't do these things to-day! But to-morrow is another day, and it is not dead now, so if it dies at another time, it must be because the other times are out of hand."[4] D. H. Lawrence promptly left; he was not missed.

A more sympathetic Englishman is James Hamilton-Paterson, who puts a more benign interpretation on non-Western worldviews: "They [indigenous people] are mostly unconvinced by the idea of education, so are often unwilling to send their children to school. Nor do they seem keen to learn new skills. And as for taking part in any social or political activity, it has proved almost impossible to interest them. They suffer, in short, from an admirable lack of ambition."[5]

A remarkable lack of ambition does nothing to impress on one's résumé. Yet, it is this Western perception about Mexican Hispanics that has colored the opinions held by Americans. In pop culture, for instance, contempt for "shiftless wetbacks" is so uniform that it becomes the one point on which the antagonists in "Giant" agree. John Steinbeck, in his novel, *Grapes of Wrath,* muses over how the passivity of the Mexican Hispanics leads to their disenfranchisement in the United States:

> Once California belonged to Mexico and its lands to Mexicans; and a horde of tattered feverish Americans poured in. And such was their hunger for land that they took the land—stole Sutter's land, Guerrero's land, took the grants and broke them up and growled and quarreled over them, those frantic hungry men; and they guarded with guns the land they had stolen. They put up houses and barns, they turned the earth and planted crops. And these things were possession, and possession was ownership.
>
> The Mexicans were weak and fled. They could not resist, because they wanted nothing in the world as frantically as Americans wanted land.
>
> Then, with time, the squatters were no longer squatters, but owners; and their children grew up and had children on the land. And the hunger was gone from them, the feral hunger, the gnawing, tearing hunger for land, for water and earth and the good sky over it, for the green thrusting grass, for the swelling roots. They had these things so completely that they did not care about them any more.[6]

It is clear that worldviews affect how people live their lives, privately and professionally.

The Contemporary Hispanic Worldview

It is important to understand how worldviews lead to behavior in the workplace and how Latinos' and Latins' attitudes about professional careers affect their choices and decisions. If one can say with confidence that America's Puritan belief in self-reliance and independence led to the evolution of a "can-do" spirit of entrepreneurship, then one can see the direct relationship between philosophy and life. In the case of Caribbean Hispanics, who share a similar development model as mainstream American society, where European and African peoples created new societies, it is not surprising to find that Caribbean Hispanics are more readily understood by non-Hispanic Americans, and that therefore Caribbean Hispanics are more successful in the United States. By American standards, Puerto Ricans, Cubans, and Dominicans are more successful: they have higher levels of economic achievement, household incomes, home ownership levels, and educational attainment levels than do Mexican Hispanics. That Mexican Hispanics constitute almost four out of five of all Hispanics in the United States, however, gives their worldview greater weight; non-Hispanic Americans are more likely to encounter Mexican Hispanics than they are Caribbean Hispanics.

Within certain parameters, Hispanics, as a group, have certain outlooks that are grounded in their philosophical and cultural ideas about the world; and specifically, about the nature of work. The commingling of peoples and ideas suffused Latin American thinking, and Hispanic society has evolved to place certain importance on specific attitudes. In the same way that "independence" is an American value, one where self-reliance and individualism prevail ; where authority is challenged and the best thing is the next thing—whatever that happens to be—then among Hispanics, there are other values. Independence is replaced by interdependence, because a tenet of Stoicism is accepting the limits of the individual. Individualism is replaced by humility, and a willingness to solve problems communally, putting one's ambitions second to one's obligations to one's family. Whereas Americans challenge authority, Hispanics are more deferential, respecting both those who have power and those who are elder. Hispanics believe that the new may not be necessarily an improvement on the present, and ambition revolves on what is a superior societal outcome for one's family and circle of friends.

This is a breakdown of the philosophical differences in how Hispanics tend to see the world vis-à-vis the dominant Anglo-Protestant culture of the United States. When critics, such as Samuel Huntington, point to the "threat" that Hispanics represent, what he refers to is the apparent difficulty in reconciling such divergent worldviews. One way of expressing the differences between the Mexican Hispanic worldview and the mainstream American one is linguistically: Mexican

Hispanics speak in the subjective tense while non-Hispanics (and Caribbean Hispanics) speak in the indicative tense. These linguistic preferences reflect philosophical differences about life. Mainstream American society is *individualistic,* while Hispanic societies tend to be *collectivistic.*

Individualistic societies are characterized by the cultures in which the members are principally concerned about themselves, and where the individual is accountable for the consequences of the decisions he or she makes. The chief concern is the individual, for whom the costs, benefits, and consequences of his or her actions, decisions, and ideas are first and foremost. Although society expects the individual to suffer the consequences of his or her decisions, society also accepts the idea that there is no moral obligation to share gains and rewards with those who did not choose to incur that individual's risks. Individualistic societies foster self-reliance, reward individual initiative, and nurture economies that foster entrepreneurship.

Collectivistic societies, on the other hand, are ones in which individuals see themselves as part of a group, with far less individual autonomy when it comes to pursuing personal interests. The principal concern centers on how their actions affect their group, whether this is their family, professional colleagues, or neighborhood. In consequence, decisions tend to be made through consensus-building and in a communal fashion. Self-sacrifice for the well-being of the community is highly valued. In collectivistic societies, everyone feels an obligation for others, decisions are arrived at in a communal manner, and societal institutions strive for social approaches to problem solving.

These, of course, are broad generalizations, but they speak to cultural values that differentiate one society from another. There is always a danger, when using essentialist and reductionist frameworks, of crossing the line into stereotypes, but the purpose of discussing the "Anglo American" and "Hispanic" worldview is to underscore where people are coming from, in cultural terms. But there are some broad generalizations that hold true. A peculiar one, for instance, has to do with the fact that people in the nations that emerged in former colonies remain intimidated by the accents spoken by the citizens of the mother countries. Americans find British accents to be refined, a mark of class and upward mobility, which is why companies that want to convey luxury, refinement, and exclusivity employ actors and spokespersons who speak with a British accent. Latin Americans similarly perk up and take notice when someone speaks Spanish with the intonations of Madrid speakers. A more general observation that holds true, however broad it may be, is as simple as pointing out that Hispanics tend to be Roman Catholic while non-Hispanics in the United States are typically not Roman Catholic.

That said, consider the distinctions made between the Anglo American "Individualism" versus the Hispanic "Interdependence," the first contrasts in comparative worldviews listed in Table 1. In American society, one value is nurtured by the idea of the self-made man and the self-made woman. Horatio Alger cultivated the "rags to riches" ideal of America: where one could achieve anything through individual initiative, hard work, and determination. In more than 100 stories, his protagonists overcame adversity and triumphed, strong values for a society that was moving westward, expanding, and in need of entrepreneurship, whether it was in a newly industrialized metropolis, or a determined cowboy out on a ranch. These fables informed the "can-do" optimism of the American character.

In contrast, in Hispanic societies, there is a strong suspicion of the ability of the individual to reach lofty goals alone, without the support of many other people. The success of one is the accomplishment of many. To some degree, absent the Horatio Alger context, Hispanics are more collective in their approach to life, and understand that others are part of one's efforts. In the masterpiece of Spanish literature, *Don Quixote,* there is a man, alone, tilting at windmills, a futile narrative of life's disappointments; and even then, he is accompanied by trusted and hapless companion Sancho Panza. Americans understand this on a subconscious level: Oscar winners never step up to the podium and announce that they accomplished this all by themselves; they often rattle off a long list of the names of those, without whom, their achievements would not have been possible. This is the difference between the American fable of individualism and the Hispanic reality of the nature of life.

Table 1: Comparing and Contrasting American and Hispanic Worldviews

Anglo American Worldview: Individualistic

1. **Individualism**, based on Protestant, Puritan, and Calvinist values
2. **Independence**, where personal responsibility is highly valued
3. **Entrepreneurship**, where the individual is expected to stand out
4. **Ideal of the Nuclear Family**, where the post-World War II construct of family is accepted as desirable
5. **Value Self-Expression**, where making a name for one's self is a societal ideal
6. **Challenge Authority**, where a premium is paid on questioning the status quo
7. **Embrace of the Future**, where the emphasis is on the new
8. **Personal Ambition**, where self-realization comes first
9. **Problem Solving**, where one takes charge of his or her destiny
10. **Confidence**, where an egalitarian impulse discounts self-doubt

Hispanic Worldview: Collectivistic

1. **Interdependence**, based on Catholic values and the Stoicism of the indigenous peoples
2. **Dependence**, where obligations to family and society come before personal goals
3. **Communalism**, where "societies of shopkeepers" depend on familial support behind initiatives
4. **Ideal of the Extended Family**, where families live in multigenerational arrangements
5. **Value Humility**, where modesty is a societal value
6. **Respect Authority**, where a premium is paid on acknowledging social and cultural hierarchies
7. **Cultivate Tradition**, where the individual is seen as caretaker of generations-old customs
8. **Familial Responsibility**, where self-sacrifice for family comes first
9. **Passive Resolve**, where one accepts life's limitations with grace and dignity
10. **Self-Improvement**, where accepting one's shortcomings, and the need to overcome them, is valued

If we were to examine the second difference in comparative worldview, "Independence" versus "Dependence," a familiar narrative in literature, cultural myths, and social values is found. The American notion of "independence" embodies the ideals that champion entrepreneurialism, "can-do" attitudes, and the quest for new opportunities. In the nineteenth century the westward expansion was a cultural value, one in which the romantic ideal of the West included the kind of men and women—cowboys, prospectors, pioneer towns—who left their families and hometowns to embark on adventures. The values portrayed in the cowboy literature, augmented by a body of film in the twentieth century, are cultural expressions of the spirit of American independence. By contrast, in Hispanic societies, the notion of dependence is reinforced in cultural values and beliefs. There is value in self-sacrifice, in putting the family's well-being before one's personal ambitions. The classic example is that of the daughter that, through the dynamics that are unique to each family, ends up sacrificing her own dreams for the greater good of the family. Hispanic families are filled with spinster aunts who are the primary caregivers for the siblings' parents as they enter old age. Hispanic families discount the myth of the "self-made" man or woman, comfortable in the knowledge that all great achievements reflect the work of many. (This is why, Hispanics point out, no one has ever given an acceptance speech upon receiving a Nobel Prize in which no one is thanked.) Hispanic literature is filled with dreams deferred and sacrifices made for children, parents, and siblings. Whereas American soap operas are about money and power, Latin American *telenovelas* are about obligations and sacrifices.

These are broad approaches to life, but there are morals and stories that shape the view of the world. Objectively, one can see that if a glass capable of containing twelve ounces is filled with only six ounces of liquid, if one group of people say it is half full, while the other say it is half empty, both are factually correct, but how they interpret reality affects how they deal with the world. Hispanics may be conditioned to accept life and life's limitations (the cards one is dealt accepted with a *passive resolve*), while Americans may encounter the same situation and obstacles and see them as a

challenge calling that they can rise above (making one's own opportunities through *problem solving*). It is possible to go down the line
through the other eight remaining worldview differences and discuss how social, literary, and pop culture reinforce these differences
in ways that are reflected in the attitudes, stories, fables, myths, and
literature each society tells about itself.

That said, the same cultural predispositions summed up in the
preceding table reflect the various cultural values that separate Anglo
Americans and Hispanics. In the workplace, these differences are
manifested in three distinct Hispanic characteristics that inform how
Hispanic, Latino, and Latin employees see job, their colleagues, co-
workers, employer, and the relationships among these:

- *Simpatía* is an intrinsic value that favors collectivism and
  group cohesion.

- *Confianza* means more than confidence, or trust. It embodies the concept of emotional bonds that solidify the connection between that employee and the organization.

- *Superarse,* to better one's self. Implies "getting ahead" and
  the awareness of what one "lacks" in one's ability and outlook to do so.

These "cultural values" evolved over various centuries as a way of
creating a strong sense of identity and societal cohesion. In contemporary terms, the first two of these concepts are closely linked to "social
capital," the idea that connections within networks have value. First
proposed in 1916 by L. J. Hanifan, he defined "social capital" as:

> . . . those tangible substances [that] count for most in the daily
> lives of people: namely good will, fellowship, sympathy, and
> social intercourse among the individuals and families who make
> up a social unit. . . . The individual is helpless socially, if left to
> himself. . . . If he comes into contact with his neighbor, and
> they with other neighbors, there will be an accumulation of
> social capital, which may immediately satisfy his social needs
> and which may bear a social potentiality sufficient to the
> substantial improvement of living conditions in the whole

community. The community as a whole will benefit by the cooperation of all its parts, while the individual will find in his associations the advantages of the help, the sympathy, and the fellowship of his neighbors.[7]

The idea has gained new currency in the writings of Robert Putnam who, in *Bowling Alone,* argues:

Countless studies document the link between society and psyche: people who have close friends and confidants, friendly neighbors, and supportive coworkers are less likely to experience sadness, loneliness, low self-esteem, and problems with eating and sleeping. Married people are consistently happier than people who are unattached, all else being equal. . . . The single most common finding from a half century's research on the correlates of life satisfaction, not only in the United States but around the world, is that happiness is best predicted by the breadth and depth of one's social connections.[8]

Simpatía

The concept of *simpatía,* as it relates to the workplace environment, emphasizes that individuals are to be courteous and respectful in how they interact with one another; confrontation is to be avoided. It is one strategy by which "social capital" is enhanced among Hispanics in the United States.[9] *Simpatía* has its origins in the Spanish word *"simpático,"* meaning a person who is nice and charming. For managers, *simpatía* is cultivated through courtesy and knowing how to use small talk to establish rapport. In Latin American culture, "small talk," or *la plática,* is a way of nurturing social connections, empathy among individuals, and creating "social capital."

Unlike English, Spanish is a more flowery language, where "getting to the point," which is valued in business as being "succinct" or "brief," is culturally misinterpreted as being "terse" or "rude." These ideas are closely linked to the notions of "civic virtue" in mainstream American society. As Robert Putnam observes:

Whereas physical capital refers to physical objects and human capital refers to properties of individuals, social capital refers to connections among individuals—social networks and the norms of reciprocity and trustworthiness that arise from them. In that sense social capital is closely related to what some have called "civic virtue." The difference is that "social capital" calls attention to the fact that civic virtue is most powerful when embedded in a dense network of reciprocal social relations. A society of many virtuous but isolated individuals is not necessarily rich in social capital.[10]

The idea of sociability reflects linguistic and cultural norms, legacies of the chivalric age, when nurturing social networks was a mark of good character. In Spanish *amabilidad,* or amicability, is a highly valued trait. As children, Hispanic children are taught the importance of being complimentary to others and extending social courtesies. Hispanic and U.S.-Latino culture, more so than is evident in the Anglo-Saxon cultural norms of mainstream American society, uses *indirect and implicit communication styles.*

The traits that characterize this approach include the following:

- Hispanics communicate in ways that emphasize harmony; disagreements, especially in front of others, are not looked upon favorably.

- Statements are often made in a passive tense in order to avoid making someone else uncomfortable.

- Positive expressions, terms of endearment, and compliments are used to soften criticism.

Confianza

The notion of *confianza,* similarly, reflects group cohesion, particularly urgent in the Hispanic diaspora, where Hispanics are, by definition, marginalized. The desire to build communities where one can do away with the burden of mistrust is all the more urgent among Hispanics who, as a group, have historically been vilified by non-Hispanic Americans. The centuries of being denigrated by slurs—as "half-breeds" and "mongrels"—linger, and there is always the self-doubt of what mainstream American society thinks that cast a shadow among Hispanics.

Consider this gem of an anecdote about how Latino pride is easily wounded by virtue of living in the Hispanic diaspora: "In 1988, when [George P. Bush] was 12, he was an unwitting participant in a short-lived hullabaloo about the way his grandfather, then the vice president, introduced him and his two Mexican-American siblings to President Reagan," Frank Bruni reported in *The New York Times*. "Vice President Bush affectionately called them 'the little brown ones.'"[11] Twelve years later, one of the "little brown ones" was interviewed by an anchor for Univision, the Spanish-language television network. "Even the Bush family has not escaped racism and discrimination," Jorge Ramos, the interviewer, would write years later. "During the 2000 Republican National Convention in Philadelphia, George P. Bush, son of Florida governor Jeb Bush and his Mexican wife, Columba, told me he had been a victim of discrimination. 'I have encountered a lot of discrimination in my life,' the young man, then twenty-four years old, told me. The statement caught me by surprise. 'A member of the Bush family was a victim of discrimination in the United States?' I replied. 'Of course,' he said, 'because in our society, unfortunately, people judge you by the color of your skin. I have encountered discrimination my whole life, all around the country. . . . With words like wetback, or ugly words like tar baby that people say to Latinos,' he responded, without losing his composure, as if this were the more normal thing in the world."[12]

In whom can Hispanics place their trust?

It would enhance the work environment if their immediate supervisors were included as people Hispanic employees trusted. As Robert Putnam states:

> A society characterized by generalized reciprocity is more efficient than a distrustful society, for the same reason that money is more efficient than barter. If we don't have to balance every exchange instantly, we can get a lot more accomplished. Trustworthiness lubricates social life. Frequent interaction among a diverse set of people tends to produce a norm of generalized reciprocity. Civic engagement and social capital entail mutual obligation and responsibility for action.[13]

Superarse

The Hispanic chant of *superarse, superarse, superarse,* improving one's self, improving one's self, improving one's self is a mantra of the Hispanic diaspora. With the exception of the majority of Cuban Americans and many Puerto Ricans, all other Hispanics groups, and Latin immigrants, have lower educational attainment levels than non-Hispanics. What is as important, however, is the reason for this effort: true, one improves one's self for personal fulfillment, but the principal reason for so doing is to be able to fulfill one's obligations and responsibilities to others. A Latina in Los Angeles wants to finish her college education so she can get a better job to provide for her children and parents first and foremost.

As the Census Bureau reported, Latinos' educational attainment levels "remain lower than levels for non-Hispanic Whites, Blacks and Asians."[14] The same is true of Latin immigrants: "The percentage of the foreign born with a high school diploma (67 percent) was dramatically lower than that of the native population (88 percent) . . . Foreign-born Hispanics, in contrast, had a smaller proportion with a bachelor's degree than the native population . . . The low educational attainment of foreign-born Hispanics, who compose more than 50 percent of the Hispanic population, contributes to the low attainment levels of the entire Hispanic population."[15]

In light of these dismal figures, it is not difficult to see how Latinos and Latins, especially, feel self-conscious about their lack of educational attainment, and why these two groups of Hispanics are the ones who stress the need to "improve one's self." As Robert Putnam explains, "precisely because poor people (by definition) have little economic capital and face formidable obstacles in acquiring human capital (that is, education), *social* capital is disproportionately important to their welfare." More to the point, this is a reality of the Hispanic diaspora since the Great Depression in the United States.

This is how Peter Hamill describes how Henry B. González, who served in the House of Representatives for thirty-seven years, sought to educate himself:

At the same time, young Henry B. [González] was coming up against the prevailing American bigotries of the era. He learned the hard way that some Americans thought of him and his father and his family as "greasers," or "messicans." His skin was brown, the color of the earth, and people with pink skins too often treated him as if he were dirt. . . . Schools were rigidly segregated. The use of Spanish was punished. Mexican customs were subjected to sneers. And on blazing summer afternoons, Henry B. and his friends were barred from public swimming pools. . . .

In spite of the derision, Henry B. began to forge an alloy of his Mexican heritage and his American identity, and followed the traditional path out of the ghetto. It was the same path followed by the American children of the Irish and the Jews and the Italians and all the other enriching streams of American immigration: education. From the age of eight, he haunted the public library.[16]

In this century, given the failures of the public school systems across the nation, Hispanics expect employers to recognize the educational obstacles Latinos and Latins continue to encounter, and to take proactive steps to help these Hispanic employees rise above their station in life through educational, continuing education, and similar learning opportunities.

It is true that all minorities, as well as newly arrived immigrants from Eastern and Southern Europe, confronted obstacles to educational attainment, but there is one important difference: Latin immigrants have arrived in such numbers that they have reached a linguistic "tipping point," where, through sheer numbers, they have transformed the United States into a bilingual consumer economy. Immigrants from other countries, whether Poland or Italy, China or Vietnam, have not arrived in such numbers as to be able to sustain national television networks that broadcast in their native languages, whereas Hispanics have Univision and Telemundo broadcasting from sea to shining sea in all major markets. This, coupled with the fact that Hispanics account for the entire population growth in the United States, means that the school systems across the country have to accommodate Spanish-speaking children arriving in disproportionate numbers at preschool, kindergarten, and first grade classes. These are undeniable factors shaping the linguistic marketplace throughout the country.

To be sure, there are other strong cultural markers, such as *Trabajar,* the notion that hard work is what is expected of everyone. This arises from Catholic teaching, where the observation made in the Book of Genesis, "By the sweat of your face you will eat bread, Till you return to the ground, Because from it you were taken; For you are dust, And to dust you shall return," is drilled week after week. Another strong factor is the notion of *Familia,* or obligations to family. The segregation by generation that is characteristic of mainstream American society is alien to Hispanics: multigenerational homes are the standard, and this has significant implications. MTV, the music channel, for instance, has MTV Latino that broadcasts in Latin America, but it also created MTV Tres for the U.S. bilingual Hispanic market, simply because they realized that in Hispanic homes, teenagers watch television with their grandparents, and MTV Tres designs programming that switches back and forth between English and Spanish, and between playlists that appeal to both teenagers and persons over the age of sixty. These ideas, however, are dealt with in the discussion of the societal impulse of Hispanics and Latins to value communal cooperation—*Colaborar*—as part of their civic duties to their communities at large.

Keys to Cultivating Simpatía and Confianza

Mindful of the role *simpatía* and *confianza* play in the Hispanic psyche, there are strategic steps that managers and supervisors can take to increase the "social capital" among their organizations' Hispanic employees.

Communication is often indirect or passive ("A problem has emerged in the department" versus "We have a problem in the department"). Hispanics may not volunteer information, particularly if it is unpleasant, critical, or conflicts with what the individual believes the manager wants to hear.

Directive, blunt, or "to the point" communication is often seen as abrasive and may be offensive. Be complimentary, even when there is a problem or disciplinary actions are called for in a situation. To Hispanics, compliments and praise for positive aspects show respect for the culture and individual. These can be simple, but should be sincere.

Small talk is valued, as a prelude to other business-directed discussions. "How is your family?" has greater cultural resonance than "How are you?" Conversations should have a slower pace, and how things are said is almost as important as what is said. "Would you please take a seat," is more effective than, "Have a seat," or "Just sit down for a minute," which come across as too informal.

Emphasis is placed on the personal supervisor-subordinate relationship. What you say is often less important than who you are and how a Hispanic employee believes you feel about him or her.

Personal space between individuals is shorter than among non-Hispanics in the United States and physical contact is valued, such as a hand to the shoulder. Managers should be aware that among Hispanics, and particularly among Latins (who are less acculturated to American norms relative to U.S.-born Latinos) hugs, kissing on the cheeks, and other displays of affection are seen as appropriate, among women of equal rank, especially at the beginning and end of conversations, which at times is in conflict to practices used in the American workplace to foster a hostile-free environment.

Respeto is essential. For Hispanics, like many other cultures, the concept of respect for authority often results in miscommunications and misunderstanding in the workplace. Employees may "agree" with supervisors and indicate an "understanding" of what is expected of them *in order to avoid being disagreeable.*

This "understanding" of being in "agreement" may not translate to compliance. "*Obedezco pero no cumplo,*" I obey but I do not comply, is a cultural norm that evolved over the centuries in Spanish America as local circumstances were modified to meet the realities unforeseen by authorities in Europe.[17] Managers should be aware of these cultural impediments, and should cultivate *sim-*

patía as a strategy for avoiding confusion or misunderstanding, maintain a mutual respect among staff, respect for authority, and a sense of agreeableness that will elicit compliance. This arose from the colonialism, when local authorities were, because of local circumstances, unable to comply with directives from Madrid. Consider instructions that, on the king's request, to celebrate the arrival of spring, children were to be allowed to collect flowers the first Sunday in April. An administrator in Argentina or Chile, where the seasons are reversed, would have no flowers blooming in the middle of winter, so he would report back that he "obeyed" with the directive—meaning it was his intention to carry it out—but he was unable to comply, because there was half a foot of snow outside. In this tradition, it is not uncommon for Latin employees to "agree" to come in on Sunday to finish up a project (whether it is finishing the foundation on a building, or an accounting report due on Monday), and then not show up. Come Monday, the "excuse" is that he or she intended to comply, but it was Sunday and between church services and familial obligations, he was unable to report to work. The employee knew about these obligations on Friday, but wanting to avoid being "confrontational," nothing was said at that time.[18]

CASE STUDY

Western Union Applies These Lessons

Mexicans working in the United States send almost $25 billion a year in remittances to family left behind. More than 70% of all remittances sent from the United States to other countries flow to Mexico.

This is an enormous business, and one of the dominant players is Western Union. This is counterintuitive considering the enormous effort commercial banks, such as Bank of America, Wells Fargo, and Citibank have made in reaching out to Latin immigrants and Latinos alike. For most Americans, Western Union is associated with telegraphs and wiring emergency funds under dire circumstances, such as sending money when normal banking transactions are not available for the recipient.

Western Union, by understanding the historic mistrust of banks among Latin immigrants, where initial deposit requirements made opening a bank account very difficult for most Latin Americans, has been able to build *confianza* among U.S. Hispanics. That Western Union also has a proactive recruitment and hiring program that zeros in on the *simpatía* that Latins expect from their employer, there is tremendous loyalty. Even as the consumer banks have sought to enlist the assistance of the Mexican government, and use ATMs to allow people in the United States to make deposits that can be withdrawn by their relatives in ATMs in Mexico, Western Union remains a dominant player.

"[T]he Mexican government has distributed about a half-million of the cards, known as *matriculas consulares* [in 2002]," Mary Beth Sheridan reported. "[T]he cards have been recognized as official identification by nearly 200 U.S. police departments in such cities as Los Angeles, Chicago and Houston, according to the Mexican Embassy. Dozens of banks and city governments accept them. . . . Supporters say the cards help hardworking immigrants who must present an official photo ID for basic necessities, from cashing a check to registering a child for school."[19]

In the remittance business, this David versus three Goliaths shows the importance of courting and selecting Hispanic employees. Western Union invested in learning the how's and the whys of the cultural preferences of the U.S. Latin and Latino customer, and it has paid off in the dominant market share that firm now enjoys. The strategies, throughout the 1980s and 1990s, transformed Western Union into a global financial leader.

Their success did not go unnoticed; consumer banks in the 2000s made significant strides in entering the remittance market, using IDs provided by the Mexican government to open bank accounts for Mexican immigrants and migrants. In fact, in the most comprehensive survey ever conducted, the Bank of Mexico in 2006, 70% of Mexicans sending money had bank accounts.

Nevertheless, because of its resonance with the cultural values of its employees and customers, Western Union remains the dominant firm Latin American immigrants use to send money to their families.

In Review

- The ascendance of Hispanics in the workplace is forcing organizations to confront attitudes and perceptions that are derived from the indigenous worldviews of the continent's First Peoples.

- The philosophical differences between Hispanics and non-Hispanics in the workplace are consistent with the anthropological differences between societies that are *collectivistic* and those that are *individualistic.*

- Three components of the Hispanic worldview are reflected in ideas that foster "social capital"—*Simpatía:* conveys the notion of empathy, in which the individual assumes responsibility for his or her group; *Confianza:* more than confidence or trust, it encompasses a communal approach to human relations, including a strong bond between the employee and employer; *Superarse:* recognizes the need for constant self-improvement in order to fulfill one's responsibilities to others.

- In the workplace, Hispanics favor a collectivistic approach, where they are an integral part of a team, working toward common goals in a structured, hierarchical manner that respects the contributions of all, while mindful of obligations to all members.

Part II

The Strategies and Skills for Supervising Nonexempt Hispanic Employees

In this section we look at the continuing challenges of attracting Hispanic candidates for nonsalaried positions. Insights into the cultural and linguistic obstacles that Hispanic job candidates encounter are analyzed. These chapters address reasons why their performance in interviews is weaker than that of non-Hispanics, with a particular emphasis on how to cultivate simpatía to Hispanic, Latin, and Latino employees. The Hispanic value system has different priorities; for a job offer to be attractive, specific benefits have to be presented in the total compensation package.

When supervising hourly Hispanic, Latino, and Latin employees, non-Hispanic managers are often puzzled by cultural differences:

What motivates Hispanics as workers?

Why are Hispanics reluctant to look you directly in the eyes?

Why are Hispanics hesitant to call managers by their first names?

Why do Hispanics say they understand directions when they don't?

Why don't Hispanics speak up when there is a problem?

Why are Hispanics often reluctant to wear safety equipment?

Why are Hispanics often uninterested in the firm's benefit plans?

The challenges posed by these cultural differences are addressed fully. So how do managers attract and manage the best-qualified Hispanics for non-salaried positions? What are the post-hiring management problems that non-Hispanic managers encounter? How can managers establish workplace policies that are readily understood by Hispanic, Latino, and Latin workers?

Chapter 4

Finding, Attracting, and Selecting the Best Hispanic Candidates

There are differences between salaried and nonsalaried positions in the American workplace. Salaried employees, almost always, have continued their education beyond high school. This higher education attainment level equips them with certain professional and social skill sets that allow them to exercise greater judgment in fulfilling their responsibilities to their employers, require less supervision, and manage their time and workload with a greater degree of independence. Nonsalaried workers, by comparison, have their time more closely monitored, simply because they are entitled to overtime pay as provided by law, their responsibilities are more clearly defined, and they are expected to exercise less discretion in how they perform their duties.

There are legal distinctions between the two categories of employees. The Fair Labor Standards Act of 1938, or FLSA, defines employees paid by the hour (nonsalaried workers) as "nonexempt" workers who are covered by the FLSA legislation and rules. Salaried workers, "exempt" employees, on the other hand, are not covered by the FLSA. The FLSA remains the principal legal framework for protecting the wages and rights of employees. It is, in legal terms, the difference between what we commonly refer to as "blue" and "white" collar work, the broader socioeconomic framework that differentiates "Latinos" from "Hispanics." Most Latino and Latin employees in the American workforce are nonexempt employees, paid by the hour, entitled to overtime pay and whose working conditions are covered by the FLSA, and oftentimes are also represented by unions.

Across the nation, the impact of this simple demographic fact—Hispanics, whose median age is 27.2 years, account for 35% of all people in the United States under the age of 18—is challenging employers as Hispanics disproportionately swell the ranks of the American workforce.

Despite their numbers, and natural obstacles imposed by the ups and downs of the business cycle notwithstanding, the continuing challenges of attracting Hispanic candidates for nonsalaried positions arise from the failure of employers (and human resource professionals) to understand the cultural differences that inform Latino and Latin thinking. The first chapter of this book described the demographic changes (disparate fertility rates between Hispanic and non-Hispanic women in the United States and the impact of sustained immigration from Latin America) transforming the American workplace. The next two chapters describe the broad categories into which the mosaic of identities that constitute the "Hispanic" in the United States fall. Building on this foundation, it is now possible to offer insights into the cultural and linguistic obstacles that employers encounter when they are recruiting nonexempt Hispanic workers.

How Do Employers Approach This Pool of Workers?

First, one of the more compelling public perceptions, and misperceptions, about Latin immigrants, who are portrayed negatively by the media, is that they are aliens who represent, to one degree or another, danger. The cable television shows, particularly the "Broken Borders" series on CNN's *Lou Dobbs Tonight*, have, over the course of this decade, vilified Latin immigrants, going further than xenophobic rhetoric of generations past, and almost bordering on "hate speech." There are no other "news" programs on the air today that have continuing segments dedicated to the vilification of any other demographic group the way Hispanics are targeted. Regardless of the journalistic merits of this programming, which blurs the lines between reporting, entertainment, and voyeurism, the social impact on American public opinion is clear, and is detrimental to the Hispanic community.[1]

"I live in Marin County, where a part of the community is fighting against the Latin American immigrants," Isabel Allende, the Chilean novelist, told *Mother Jones,* commenting on the resistance of many Californians to the immigration of indigenous peoples. "People are terrified because they see these dark men standing in groups waiting for someone to offer a job. That's very threatening. Because they don't know them and don't understand their ways or their language, they feel that these men are criminals, that they don't pay their share in this society and yet they benefit. That is not true. . . . They come here to do the kind of work that no American will ever do. You will not be able to stop them. . . . It's unavoidable: In 20 years they will be part of this society, just as the Jews are, the Irish, everybody."[2]

Second, reconsider the "us" versus "them" thinking that is widespread, with Harvard's Samuel Huntington being a leading example. Latin immigrants from Mexico and Central America, who are seen as outsiders, whose "otherness" instills apprehension, are, as we have seen, individuals who carry with them the traditional values and customs of indigenous societies. One aspect of the Mexican Hispanic worldview that is misinterpreted by non-Hispanics in the United States centers on the collectivist nature of community life. One manifestation of *simpatía* is the "town square" interaction that nurtures a sense of community and belonging. For many Latin immigrants, thrust into rural communities where Spanish is a minority language and they encounter the marginalized reality of being part of the Hispanic diaspora, the tendency is to recreate a "town square" for the sake of building "group cohesion." This manifests itself in Latin dayworkers gathering in the parking lots of bodegas, or larger establishments, such as Wal-Mart, Home Depot, or 7-Eleven, or where construction contractors or landscapers frequent. These are spontaneous developments: workers looking for jobs (labor supply) congregate near the stores and businesses where employers (labor demand) go to buy materials or sundries on their way to their projects.[3]

To non-Hispanics, who are not familiar with the communal nature of small groups of Latin men gathered together, with no apparent purpose, it appears as if these men are loitering. The perceived "idleness," even "tension," of these "Native American" social gatherings in public, coupled with the cultural assumptions of American society where men of color are seen as representing danger, creates tension between Latin immigrants and the greater non-Hispanic society in which they find themselves. Since the 1960s, when Latin immigrants were recruited in large numbers for the nation's agricultural, construction, and light industrial sectors, rural communities throughout Texas, the American Southwest, and California have seen the spread of Mexican Hispanics throughout the United States, with social conflicts arising from the lack of misunderstandings.

The cultural norms that are familiar to the indigenous peoples can often be seen as "threatening" by the greater society. In a similar fashion, once employed, performance reviews of Nonexempt Mexican Hispanic employees are weaker than those of non-Hispanics.[4] From an administrative perspective, human resource professionals and managers express frustrations. In almost two decades of working with employers, several specific issues contribute to inferior performance reviews, even at a time when the benefits of annual evaluations are being more closely scrutinized. Although these issues are more acute among Mexican Hispanics, they pose significant obstacles to most nonexempt Hispanic, Latino, and Latin employees.

To be sure, the societal "negatives" associated with Hispanic employees are alive and well, and there are stigmas to "walking while brown."

The Hispanic Employee and Immigration Status

It is impossible to discuss Hispanic employees without addressing the polemics of illegal immigration. Fraught with political land mines, the indisputable facts remain that labor markets in capitalist economies respond to supply and demand. Demand for labor continues to pull across the border during periods of economic growth and expansion, and when demand slackens, Latin immigrants return to their homelands. The economics laws of supply and demand trump immigration laws, and the emergence of a fluid population that ebbs and flows with the season is an inevitable part of the natural fluctuations in demand and supply of labor across the confluence of economies of North America. There are aberrations—a dam diverts a river, draconian laws render criminal natural labor movements—but a natural equilibrium between supply and demand in the labor markets struggles to find its balance organically. It is expected that, beginning with 2010, Mexicans immigrations officials will document a net return of immigrants to Mexico from the United States; and on the U.S. side of the border, the volume of remittances showed fewer individuals sending money back to their native countries, indicating fewer Latin immigrants.

Consider how the terrorist attacks of September 2001 interrupted the rhythms of the U.S. labor market. This is how Dan Baum described in *The New Yorker* the migratory pattern of labor between the supply in Mexico and the demand in the United States:

> As recently as five years ago, crossing the border was easy enough so that Mexicans could view the United States as a kind of high-wage zone of their own country. They would venture north for a few months to take jobs as roofers and dishwashers, and return home with presents at Christmastime. They'd continue the cycle until they'd earned enough cash to get married or to start a business in Mexico. Many had no intention of staying in the United States, or of becoming American citizens. After September 11, 2001, border enforcement grew more stringent; immigrants can no longer count on being able to go back and forth. The number of immigrants in the United States—overwhelmingly from Mexico—continues to rise (an astounding sixteen per cent over the past five years), and the new barriers to crossing the border seem to have changed their attitudes about staying permanently in the United States.[5]

The natural pattern—venturing into the United States for a season, or a permanent position—was interrupted, but as the U.S. economy entered into a recession in the fall of 2008, Latin migrants, primarily Mexican nationals, began to cross the border on a homeward-bound journey. While critics have long characterized Mexican immigration to the United States as an "invasion" of "illegal" aliens who take jobs from American citizens and burden local schools, hospitals, and public services, economists have simply pointed out that the ebbs and flows across the border reflect the natural interplay of supply and demand for labor, and their impact on local communities cannot be uniformly characterized.

Right-of-center critics have dismissed such assertions, claiming that once here, Mexicans stay here. Compelling evidence that economists, on this point, have been right all along, however, is irrefutable: Mexican officials are reporting that more than 1,500 Mexican nationals—most of whom entered the United States illegally—were returning to Mexico every day, beginning the month after the Wall Street crisis of September 2008. Enrique Flores López, director of Commission of Migrant Affairs (Comisión de Atención a Migrantes) in Sonora State, reported that almost 1,500 Mexicans began to return to Mexico through the border crossing in the cities of Naco, Agua Prieta, and Nogales. Most of these Mexican nationals were from Michoacán, Zacatecas, Chiapas, and Veracruz states, all in the south of the country.[6]

As Rubén Martínez chronicles in his book on Mexican migrants, Latin immigrants do return to Mexico:

> They come with the new clothes or still in the dirty jeans in which they picked the last of the crops or washed the last pile of restaurant dishes. They come back with billfolds thick with dollars or as poor as they left, perhaps even deeper in debt to the local loan sharks. Often they come in a car they just bought with cash, because most migrants don't have checking accounts or credit cards and hardly ever apply for bank loans. They have gassed up the car at fluorescent-lit pit stops on all-nighters down I–5, I–19, I–25, or I–35, the interstates that

> lead to San Diego, Nogales, El Paso, and Laredo. . . . This time
> no Border Patrol jeep will chase them. The [Border Patrol]
> does not patrol the highways' southbound lanes, because they
> know the migrants are heading home and thus deportation is
> unnecessary.[7]

Many returning Mexican nationals stated that the lack of jobs was the most compelling reason for their return. Others indicated that the strengthening of the U.S. dollar since this summer has made it possible for them to achieve their goals of saving enough money to return to Mexico, where they plan to use these savings to start their own small businesses. Some reported that they are themselves in need, having been unable to find day-labor work in the United States. The various reasons tell the story of individual success or failure, and flesh out the state of the American economy and labor market. An observation worth noting is that, although they are the category of workers who are at most risk and least compensated, illegal aliens tend to fare better in economic downturns: they perform the lowest-paying jobs, are seldom afforded health care or other benefits, and their work is crucial during "skeleton" work shifts.

"In past years, [the migrants] said, they had even gone home to see their families for the winter or, perhaps, traveled to Florida or Texas, where farm work could be found. But many said they were remaining in Seattle, because they could not afford to go elsewhere or because they were worried about security crackdowns along the border and in the United States," Sam Howe Verhovek reported. Feeling stranded during economic contractions, some migrants were joining the ranks of the homeless, homeless that, because of their immigration status, were especially vulnerable. "'Now I would do anything to just be able to go home,' Raúl [a Honduran national who declined to give his last name] said about the city where his wife and his son and daughter, both 6, live."[8]

In other words, while demand for workers falls during economic contractions, illegal aliens in the United States tend to remain in disproportionate demand vis-à-vis native-born and legal immigrant workers. That the United States continues to evolve into a bilingual consumer economy, regardless of where the nation finds itself in the natural business cycle, further increases demand for employees who are knowledgeable, if not fluent, in Spanish. This is a challenge, for U.S.-born Latinos and native-born non-Hispanic employees alike: if they are not bilingual, they are at a competitive disadvantage in the changed American labor market, which demands a linguistic skill set that is undeniable. For employers, the increased dependence on bilingual native-born workers and Latin immigrants, also changes dynamics: many immigrants arrive in the United States with the intention of supporting their families left behind in their home countries. Employers who recognize the inherent desire to *superarse* that this reflects, and who show *simpatía* for the aspirations of these employees are more likely to earn their *confianza*, which only strengthens their commitment to the organization, and their effectiveness in enlarging the potential candidate pool for future employees.

Recruiting Hispanic, Latino, and Latin employees, however, presents its own set of obstacles. Hispanic candidates do not respond to traditional recruiting methods, the availability of qualified candidates is distorted by geography, and educational attainment levels are quite disparate between Mexican Hispanics and Caribbean Hispanics.

Lack of educational attainment remains a challenge for Hispanics as a group, one that requires proactive management programs that encourage Hispanic youth to remain in school, enhance internship programs, develop formal mentoring within the firm, and facilitate continuing education. This is part of an organization's moral obligation to be a responsible corporate citizen and be involved in the community in which it does business.

Organizations are more successful if they establish their organization's credibility within the Hispanic community and nurture their firm's "brand" among Hispanic workers in order to increase the numbers of Hispanic candidates availing themselves to "Self-Selection," "Co-Worker Referral," and "Personnel Search Organization" recruitment avenues, which are consistent with employees already working for an organization encouraging others through word of mouth.

Subtle biases work against Hispanic hiring and promotion, which range from the fact that many Hispanics speak English with an accent, and the life experience of Hispanic employees are outside the mainstream of American society.

Interviewing Hispanic job applicants is more successful if it reflects the cultural distinctions that make Hispanics appear as weaker candidates relative to other candidates. Non-Hispanic managers and HR professionals mistake how Hispanics show respect for passivity and intimidation, which is commonly seen in the short replies Hispanics give to answers, their unwillingness to convey confidence by stating their answers with "I" ("I accomplished this" versus "This was accomplished"), and by the tendency of not making frequent eye contact with the interviewer. The use of formal scripts when conducting interviews can result in a more accurate assessment of a candidate's qualifications for the position. Blue-collar candidates may appear particularly "passive," "timid," or "indifferent" as cultural manifestations of how Hispanics of indigenous ancestry defer to authority figures.

Pre-employment screening and testing often does not reflect the cross-cultural realities of the life experience of Mexican Hispanics, and many Latin immigrants. Apart from testing for illegal substances, traditional pre-employment screening and testing are not as effective for Hispanic candidates as they are for non-Hispanic candidates. Management is better served if they tailor probationary periods as valid screens to assess the skills and job performance of Hispanics.

For Hispanics, attractive offers address their collectivistic value systems and reflect their familial obligations and responsibilities. Hispanics flourish under a more paternalistic relationship with their employers, wherein they "bond" with the organization, seeing their colleagues and managers as an extended family, and in which their managers and supervisors are sensitive to their wider social concerns and communal needs. Hispanics expect their employer to facilitate their development—*superarse*—through continuing education,

English-language and accent elimination courses, and seminars on cross-cultural issues, all of which are necessary, if not for Latin acculturation and Latino integration into the mainstream of American life, then at least for Hispanics to feel confident about their ability to navigate the greater American society around them. These are cultural norms: in healthy relationships both parties benefit, and in long-term relationships both parties grow. For Hispanic salaried (exempt) employees, company-sponsored committees for support and networking are crucial to their success within an organization; this can be as simple and cost-effective as providing a room where employees can meet once a week to discuss projects or activities that they want to do in a communal effort, whether it is repairing a baseball or soccer field in a nearby park, or organizing a project in their hometowns in their country of origin. For Hispanic non-salaried (nonexempt) employees, corporate support financial education, particularly in light of the role remittances to countries of origin through Hometown Associations (HTAs) continue to play, is important in strengthening the bonds between the Hispanic worker and his or her employer.[9]

Attracting the Best Latin and Latino Employees

There are cultural and acculturation factors that affect how Latin and Latino employees perform in the workplace. The Latin employee faces linguistic obstacles and may not fully understand the differences between how the work lives of Americans are organized vis-à-vis their countries of origin. Latinos, on the other hand, encounter acculturation issues that stem from the realities associated with being from less privileged socioeconomic backgrounds in the United States. For all Hispanics, also, there are certain values in place that impact work preferences and priorities. The emphasis on group cohesion and the cultural ideas that embody *simpatía,* for instance, suggest approaches that human resources professionals within an organization can emphasize to make their organization more attractive. It's important that the communal values of Latins and Latinos mean that "word gets around" within the community, and workers who feel their employer is making efforts to display *simpatía* enjoy a competitive advantage. For instance, all applications and orientation material should be in both English and Spanish.

In addition, employee orientation should clearly articulate the fundamental difference between the United States economy and that of many Latin American nations which include: "Social Security" is not analogous to "Seguro Social" in Mexico, a point that is confusing to some Latino and most Latin employees (see discussion in Chapter 5); there is no national health insurance program in the United States. (as this goes to press); wages comprise most of an employee's total compensation; apart from unemployment insurance, government does not administer "worker benefit" programs; In contrast, in Mexico there are extensive programs available to employees, such as Infonavit, which is a federal agency that facilitates the financing for the purchase of homes for Mexican workers, one reason Mexico was able to avoid the housing bubble that proved quite problematic in the United States; or SAR, which is a program to facilitate saving for retirement (roughly analogous to the Social Security Administration in the United States).

Also, management should take into account that efforts to make the workplace more "egalitarian" conflict with strongly held cultural values Latins and Latinos feel more comfortable in vertical hierarchies than in horizontal ones; immediate supervisors should be addressed with honorifics (Mr., Mrs., and Miss); uniforms are preferred over "casual" dress codes.

Benefits that prove more enticing address the aspirations of Latin and Latino employees to *superarse* and foster communalism and group cohesion. On-site "English as a Second Language," or ESL, classes for workers, recognizing that there may be resistance, and these objections usually arise from embarrassment: many Latin immigrants did not finish high school in their native countries, and are sensitive about lacking the "classroom skill set" necessary to be good students.[10] On-site "acculturation" workshops administered by human resources professionals, which include topics such as how to register children for school, how to determine the kind of health coverage each employee should have, a general orientation to community services (where parks, laundry facilities, libraries, local banks, and credit unions are located). On-site access for government and nongovernmental agencies to make presentations (fire department to conduct basic fire-safety presentations, the American Red Cross about their programs, motor vehicles departments about car registration and drivers' licenses).

The cumulative impact of these initiatives builds *confianza*, the perception that an employer is concerned about their employees and their families. These initiatives are specific benefits that have greater resonance in the total compensation package, and Latin employees respond enthusiastically.

Managers and supervisors who realize that, for Latins and Latinos, an employer is seen as a responsible corporate citizen by taking the steps necessary to overcome the cultural differences that make workplace communication more difficult than with non-Hispanic employees, stand to benefit. Most of the post-hiring management problems that non-Hispanic managers encounter can also be ameliorated through a proactive human resource program that nurtures a sense of community and builds *confianza*, and is also rather cost effective. In some ways, employers are required to envision their needs of Latin and Latino employees who are, in fundamental ways, *at-risk* populations.

"For the poor, the government can be central to their well-being, and for some even to survival. For the rich and the comfortable, it is a burden save when, as in the case of military expenditure, Social Security and the rescue of failed financial institutions, it serves their particular interest," John Kenneth Galbraith observed.[11] The investment in setting aside a conference room for the local librarian to talk about how to get a library card and the services offered, or for a representative of the American Red Cross to talk about basic disaster preparedness and the importance of donating blood, is small, but the value to the employees is great. Proactive management fulfills expectations many Hispanic employees have about the "communal" responsibilities of their employer.

CASE STUDY

The Demand for Illegal Immigration: Tyson Foods

"Tyson Foods Inc., the nation's largest meat producer and processor, was indicted . . . on charges that it conspired to smuggle illegal immigrants across the Mexican border to work in its processing plants," David Barboza reported in 2001. "The 36-count indictment, . . . accuses Tyson of arranging to transport illegal immigrants across the border and of helping them to get counterfeit work papers for jobs at more than a dozen Tyson poultry plants."[12]

This lawsuit stunned the nation, and it underscored the lengths to which corporate America was prepared to go in order to secure workers. The jobs were so exhausting, the hours so long, and the pace of work so relentless that the average employee lasts no more than a year. "Slaughtering swine is repetitive, brutish work, so grueling that three weeks on the factory floor leave no doubt in your mind about why the turnover is 100 percent," reporter Charlie LeDuff wrote of the Smithfield slaughterhouse in Tar Heel, North Carolina. "Five thousand quit and five thousand are hired every year. You hear people say, 'They don't kill pigs in the plant, they kill people.' So desperate is the company for workers, its recruiters comb the streets of New York's immigrant communities, personnel staff members say, and word of mouth has reached Mexico and beyond."[13]

Critics charge that the reason native-born workers are not interested in these jobs is because the pay is too low, and that foreign workers, who often do not know their rights under U.S. laws, are exploited. Company officials respond by saying that consumers are unwilling to pay higher food prices wage and benefit increases would demand, and were they to raise wages, foreign companies, primarily from China and Latin America, would undercut them, taking away market share. The impact of these foreign-born, at-risk workers is one of distorting American socioeconomic forces. "There has been an inverse relationship over U.S. history between union membership and the percentage of the population that is foreign born," Vernon Briggs, at Cornell's School of Industrial and Labor Relations, argues.[14] The merits of both arguments notwithstanding, as Hispanics continue to swell the ranks of the American workplace, the risks are many for both employees and employers. In December 2008 workers voted to bring in a union to represent them.[15]

For Hispanic employees, the subject of "wages" is often tied to the topic of "unions" and union representation. This arises from the fact that in most Latin American countries, unions are affiliated with government labor departments and work to "arbitrate" between the private sector and labor under the auspices of government oversight. In this country, this is an alien concept, because unions are not affiliated with government. This, in turn creates its own set of misunderstandings, and for Hispanics—and certainly Latin immigrants—there is the cloud of suspicion that perhaps they may be foreign-born, and if so, that they might be in this country illegally, and the fear that they will be exploited. "In 2007, the median usual weekly earnings of foreign-born full-time wage and salary workers were $554, compared with $722 for the native born," the Bureau of Labor Statistics reported.[16] Critics of immigration have long argued American workers ultimately suffer because employers can hire immigrants at lower wages than they would have to otherwise pay to U.S.-born American citizens. Federal statistics substantiate this view. In addition, for employers, there is the lingering doubt about the authenticity of paperwork—Social Security cards, ID documents—submitted by employees. Efforts to "regularize" workers in the United States illegally have stalled in Washington for more than a decade, and programs to launch "guest worker" programs face critics. "Guest worker programs create problems; they do not solve them—especially this one which will essentially turn people loose to find jobs anywhere and under almost any circumstance," Vernon Briggs argues. "Moreover it does nothing to address the continued violation of the nation's immigration laws, so what is the point?"[17]

These are challenging issues, even in times of economic contraction, and, particularly for Latin immigrants, there is the perception that they are under unfair scrutiny. This arises from cultural stereotyping, of course, much the same way that, as has been amply documented, African American males are angered by being disproportionately pulled over by police officers ("driving while black," is the phrase used to describe the phenomenon); or Asian American students who are presumed to be "brilliant" in math and science, and are "disappointments" to their instructors when they are "average" in those areas. For Latin immigrants, similarly, there is the perception that, if their English is not flawless, or once they disclose they were not born in the United States, questions will arise about their legal status and their right to be in this country. For employers, the failure of federal authorities to regulate and manage immigration to this country successfully means that burdens are placed on companies throughout the nation to "verify" the immigration status of their employees. Not only does this create bureaucratic challenges for human resource professionals, but makes it almost impossible for every hiring decision maker to be able to verify the authenticity of documents presented by a would-be employee. In many industries, such as meat packing, hotel and restaurant management, employers are overwhelmed, often unable to verify with absolute certainty that every person on their payroll is in strict compliance with U.S. immigration laws.

The nation's demographic changes, however, mean that the American labor market's dependence on Hispanic employees will continue to increase, both in periods of economic growth and during recessions. "The indictment of Tyson Foods Inc., the nation's largest meat processor, on charges that it conspired to smuggle illegal immigrants to work at its plants, is a sign of how dependent the American food and agriculture system has become on foreign-born workers, many of them here illegally," David Barboza reported.[18]

Tyson and its executives were found not guilty of engaging in a conspiracy to smuggle illegal aliens into the country. In a different legal action the firm was found guilty of hiring workers who were not authorized to work in the United States. The company argued that it is dependent on immigrant labor because U.S.-born employees are not willing to work for such low wages. This "dependence" on low-wage immigrant labor is fraught with risks for both employers and employees. The six Tyson executives indicted were found not guilty in March 2003.[19] Years later, however, immigration reform remains unresolved, constituting a continuing problem for American employers, who remain caught between the demands of the market economy and the contradictions in state and federal labor and immigration laws.

Despite these obstacles and challenges, there is an emerging recognition of and respect for the contributions of Hispanics in the American labor market. A patrician gentleman in New York who has been a family friend for almost half a century, when I was discussing this book with him, wanted me to make this point. As a point of honor and respect, he had made it a point to read the names of the fallen men and women in the Iraq War that is published in the *New York Times* as the names are released by the Defense Department. The names of American servicemen and servicewomen who have been killed, today, number in the thousands. "I continue to be surprised by two facts," he said. "By how young they are, foremost. But I am also struck by how many have Spanish surnames." The U.S. labor market where Hispanics are disproportionately represented includes the armed forces.

In Review

- The Fair Labor Standards Act of 1938, or FLSA, is the legal framework that distinguishes between hourly and salaried employees, between "blue-collar" and "white-collar" employees.

- The majority of Hispanic, Latino, and Latin employees are blue-collar workers, whose availability reflects the ebbs and flows of supply and demand in the labor market.

- Current immigration laws stigmatize Hispanics, subject them to greater scrutiny from employers, law enforcement, and media critics, oftentimes creating a social climate of hostility and a contributing to a hostile work environment.

- Tips for Hispanic employees:
  - Hispanic employees respond to employers whose policies reflect collectivistic values, not individualistic ones.
  - Latino and Latin employees consider their social and communal obligations and responsibilities in employment decisions.
  - Non-Hispanic managers encounter cultural obstacles in conveying *simpatía* and earning the *confianza* of job applicants.

- Hispanic, Latino, and Latin employees prefer work environments that reflect vertical organizations where "social
  capital" is valued.

Chapter 5

How to Evaluate the Hispanic Employee's Performance and Conduct

The previous chapter addressed the concerns of recent Latin immigrants and U.S.-born Latinos, primarily of Mexican and Central American descent, who comprise the majority of Hispanics in the United States who are employed in nonexempt positions. Critics may express concern about the generalization made when categorizing Hispanics in this discussion, but the differences between Caribbean Hispanics and Mexican Hispanics are significant, and encompass racial, ethnic, cultural, and political distinctions. Puerto Ricans, for instance, are Hispanics, and some may consider themselves Latin (in Puerto Rico) or Latinos (on the mainland United States), but the one thing that they can *never* be is an *immigrant:* Puerto Ricans are U.S. citizens by birth and can come and go as they please, with the only restriction on their citizenship being that, if in Puerto Rico, they cannot vote in presidential elections.

Cubans, similarly, are subject to the Cuban Adjustment Act of 1966, which means that any Cuban who enters the United States is entitled to political asylum, which grants them automatic permanent residency and benefits from various entitlement programs, including Social Security. Cubans can *never* be technical immigrants by virtue of being *political refugees.* (Those who doubt that the differences between Caribbean Hispanics and Mexican Hispanics can be discussed with definite certainty, consider the fact that it is virtually impossible for a Mexican to cross the border, claim to be a Cuban, and ask for political asylum. It just doesn't happen.) Dominicans, on the other hand, enjoy no special citizenship or immigration status or other migratory privilege; they are subject to immigration laws as any other immigrant.

Hispanics are sanguine about the paradox of U.S. immigration law, which attempts to sow divisions among Hispanics by having three distinct classifications: citizens (Puerto Ricans and U.S.-born Latinos), political refugees (Cuban), and all other Hispanics. The paradox is not lost on Mexican Hispanics: "No other immigrant group in U.S. history has asserted or could assert a historical claim to U.S. territory. Mexicans and Mexican Americans can and do make that claim. Almost all of Texas, New Mexico, Arizona, California, Nevada, and Utah was part of Mexico until Mexico lost them as a result of the Texan War of Independence in 1835–1836 and the Mexican-American War of 1846–1848," Samuel Huntington writes. "Mexico is the only country that the United States has invaded, occupied its capital—placing the Marines in the 'halls of Montezuma'—and then annexed half its territory. Mexicans do not forget these events. Quite understandably, they feel that they have special rights in these territories."[1]

This is the historical backdrop that colors attitudes among Hispanics about each other, and about the United States. There is, quite naturally, a certain level of resentment—Puerto Ricans and Cubans enjoy privileges denied to other Latin immigrants—but there are also the lingering tensions. Cubans feel compelled to fuel the "Cold War" as a way of justifying their special role in resisting global Communism. Puerto Ricans have to overcome the perception that they are "turncoats" to Hispanic culture—sellouts who, for the privilege of having a U.S. passport, gladly surrendered their sovereignty. Throughout Latin America Puerto Ricans are mocked as being "independent" only at the Miss Universe Pageant and the Olympics, where Puerto Rico is represented apart from the United States by its contestant or athletic delegation.

The narrative of the lives of Hispanics in the United States is informed by these realities, and it affects how Hispanics, Latinos, and Latins interact in the workplace. It isn't that there should be different standards that apply to the various subsets of Hispanics, but rather, management should be aware of the moral hazards that suffuse the work lives of Hispanic employees. This comes at a time when there are increasing questions about the value of the performance review processes developed and adopted over the past quarter century. As the American workplace has become both more diverse and globalized—with disparate functions performed in offices overseas—progressive organizations are rethinking how best to evaluate an employee's performance. Inherent in this process, of course, are considerations that center on the cultural intelligence of managers in a newly Hispanized American workplace.

This is less daunting if cultural situations are approached with mindfulness, and creativity. Consider the incident described by María Elena Lagomasino, the Cuban-born CEO of Asset Management Advisors LLC with more than $10 billion under its management, who formerly was president of the Chase Manhattan Bank's Private Bank. "A leader needs a vision of what they want to have, then they need to have the courage to make it happen," she says. "It's most important to have courage because you need to be able to communicate that vision to the people in your company. As you add others to your company and they see your vision, they will want to do what needs to get done to realize that vision."

When she was tapped to run Chase Manhattan Corp.'s Latin America private banking practice in New York in 1983, she succeeded because she found a mentor and an ally in Chase's then-chairman and CEO, David Rockefeller. Lagomasino recalls a groundbreaking incident that took place on a Chase trip to Monterrey, Mexico. She was traveling with Mr. Rockefeller and various Chase colleagues to attend a dinner featuring the top fifteen businesspeople in that city. Her colleagues didn't know how to include Ms. Lagomasino in the gathering, because she would be the only woman. "The guys in the bank were really uncomfortable," she recalls. But Mr. Rockefeller took charge and phoned the wife of the man hosting the dinner, asking, "Would you co-host the dinner with your husband tonight?" She did and the dinner turned out to be a success. "But it took Mr. Rockefeller to figure out a way to get this dinner to work."

"Making it work" is imperative. Hispanic, Latino, and Latin employees respond to different incentives, both in terms of "work/life" balance, and incentives in their careers where promotions, compensation, mentoring, and responsibilities/obligations are concerned. "Workplace surveys still register high levels of employee stress stemming from work/life conflicts. Large groups of women and minority workers remain unemployed or underemployed because of family responsibilities and bias in the workplace. And in too many cases, the programs have reached only the workers who need them least," Fay Hansen writes. "Many [managers and Human Resource professionals] acknowledge difficulty, however, in creating a culture that supports these programs, extending flexibility to nonprofessional employees, and building solid tools to measure results."[2]

The efficacy of the five traditional purposes of performance reviews continues to prove less satisfactory when applied to the Hispanic workforce, and as we shall see, the reasons are cultural in origin. Hispanics, through sheer numbers, are forcing managers and supervisors to greater levels of adaptability. Management approaches that proved successful for non-Hispanic employees throughout the twentieth century are proving less effective this century. Organizations that have greater flexibility, whose policies evolve to reflect new criteria, and who take proactive approaches to meeting the needs of their employees enjoy greater success. At this point, it is necessary to revisit the purposes of performance appraisals, which are as follows:

Coaching. For a variety of cultural reasons, Hispanics respond more successfully to mentoring programs than traditional, once-a-year performance reviews. Often there is a comfort level in being able to speak in Spanish with an employee or colleague who has been at the organization for a longer time. For non-Hispanic employees, it can be frustrating to see Hispanic or Latin employees speaking rapid-fire Spanish in hushed tones among themselves as they walk down the hall, or socialize in a cubicle or office. But this process, one of acculturation to an organization's distinct culture, remains the more effective way of communicating, educating, and teaching Hispanic and Latin employees.

Feedback. The expectation that performance reviews are an opportunity for managers or supervisors to elicit constructive criticism or commentary from Hispanic, Latino, and Latin employees is not a realistic one. The vertical hierarchy with which Hispanics view the workplace is similar to the Hispanic worldview in general, where family members defer to the wishes of the matriarch or patriarch, or supplicants respect the strict line of command in Catholicism. Hispanic, Latino, and Latin employees resist offering criticism to their supervisors, and this is particularly true of Hispanic females. This results in the compilation of performance reviews that have little value in terms of critical feedback that can benefit the organization.

Merit Raises. Performance appraisals have long been used to justify merit pay increases. The reluctance, particularly of Mexican Hispanics (more than Caribbean Hispanics), to speak in the indicative tense, means fewer are comfortable taking credit for accomplishments, or jobs well done. The use of "we" and "our team," rather than stating "I" or "my," makes it difficult for managers and supervisors to justify giving credit to an employee who defers being singled out for specific contributions. This runs counter to the idea of communalism that is so engrained in the worldview of the indigenous peoples that is an integral part of the Mexican Hispanic approach to work. The result can be frustrating for managers and supervisors; oftentimes Hispanics will not take credit for their own accomplishments unless another employee is improperly seeking credit for work performed by another. Unless there is the perception of a social injustice, assertive declarations that begin with "I" are few and far between—and when they occur, it is highly likely it is to correct an apparent affront to the sense of communalism.

Staffing and Promotion. It's clear to see how the Hispanic reluctance to be anything other than deferential in the work environment, and the cultural predisposition to defend the integrity of communalism, makes it more challenging to promote and staff a

department or division properly. This is where the cultural predisposition to daily interaction, observation, and commentary is
important if management can make correct decisions concerning
personnel. The absent manager, or department head who is not comfortable quietly observing and informed about the nuances of how
Hispanics interact with each other, is not as successful in ascer-
taining how promotions and staffing issues can be adequately
addressed.

Documentation and Poor Performance. The most cumbersome
aspect of performance reviews centers on the legal requirements that
human resources professionals establish. Documenting problems and
poor performance to justify personnel decisions is an unpleasant but
necessary task, one that, perhaps, is the only effective use of performance appraisals. The limitation, of course, remains that in a situation that is chronic and requires immediate action, "reviews" that
"document" actions for demotion, transfers, or terminations need
to be taken in a time frame that is less than allowed through annual
performance appraisals.

The cumulative impact of these cultural predispositions is that
it requires managers and supervisors to avail themselves to a different skill set in the evaluation of the performance of employees. This
is consistent with the emerging consensus among human resources
professionals that there are unintended consequences to traditional
performance reviews, and the limited information that can be derived
from them. It furthermore reflects the emerging consensus that greater
cultural sensitivity is required to nurture excellence among Hispanic,
Latino, and Latin employees. One of the more succinct descriptions
of the "cultural intelligence" this entails is provided by David Thomas
and Kerr Inkson in *Cultural Intelligence,* in which they describe the
three components as:

- First, the culturally intelligent manager requires *knowledge*
  of culture and of the fundamental principles of cross-cultural
  interactions. This means knowing what culture is, how cultures vary, and how culture affects behavior.

- Second, the culturally intelligent manager needs to practice mindfulness, the ability to pay attention in a reflective and creative way to cues in the cross-cultural situations encountered; the most important cultural indicator being looking down and mumbling a reply, which indicates either disagreement with what is being said by the manager, or a lack of understanding about what is expected from the employee.

- Third, based on knowledge and mindfulness, the culturally intelligent manager develops *behavioral skills,* and becomes competent across a wide range of situations. These skills involve choosing the appropriate behavior from a well-developed repertoire of behaviors that are correct for different intercultural situations.[3]

This book has presented a discussion that raises the reader's "cultural intelligence" of the Hispanic workforce in fundamental ways.

For managers, supervisors, and other administrators, book knowledge of Hispanic, Latino, and Latin culture can be acquired through reading. What is important, however, is *mindfulness,* which implies a *proactive* effort of awareness, watching how Hispanics interact with each other when they are among themselves. Only then is it possible to be perceptive, notice the subtle nuances, and learn about human interactions. In many ways, this is how life works: think back in your own life to the first time you became infatuated with someone: how did that manifest itself? There is a natural, almost insatiable, curiosity about the object of one's affection. Most people simply want to know as much as possible about the person with whom they are infatuated.

In a different way and on a different level, of course, the same mechanism is at work: managers should have the *presence of mind* to be curious about learning about the Hispanics swelling the ranks of the workplace. This stands in sharp contrast to the manager at the Smithfield meat packing plant quoted earlier in this discussion. When encountering a verbal exchange between Latin women and an African American worker, while another Caucasian employee looked on, calling the Hispanic women "tacos" and his black colleagues "niggers," all the supervisor managed to say, with apparent indifference was, "I don't want no problems," as he distributed carving knives to those he supervised.[4] Is it any wonder that, on average, all of the workers at Smithfield resign within a year?

"Cultural intelligence enables us to recognize cultural differences through knowledge and mindfulness and gives us a propensity and ability to act appropriately across cultures," David Thomas and Kerr Inkson explain. "The culturally intelligent manager draws on a breadth of experience and can make fine discriminations among subtly different behaviors that perfectly fit the situation."[5] Cultural intelligence, of course, is a two-way street, and with unexpected results.

In the wake of the election of Barack Obama as president, a survey among Hispanic voters conducted by Hispanic Economics revealed how indifferent Hispanics were to the unhealed wounds in the American psyche. A Latin immigrant respondent said, "I had never realized just how traumatized Americans still remained over the question of slavery; I felt sorry for a nation where something as *ordinary* as electing a leader who is a person of color was a 'monumental' event. It was a real eye-opener, almost like Holocaust survivors who still have nightmares about being in a concentration camp, or something. The American people, *pobrecitos*. [Poor little ones]."[6]

As a demographic group, Hispanics, Latinos, and Latins, who come from countries where blacks, indigenous peoples, women, and other minorities (Alberto Fujimori, of Peru who is of Japanese descent; Carlos Menem of Argentina, who is of Arab ancestry, etc.) are routinely elected to their nation's highest offices, do not fully sympathize with the raw emotions of how race is lived in the United States. That a significant number voted for Obama is unremarkable, and although the "Latino" vote was not indispensable for Obama's victory, it did widen his margin of victory over John McCain. This can foster unintended insensitivity among Hispanics, which creates conflicts in the workplace. For Hispanics, that Thomas Friedman could write in the *New York Times* that "[n]othing more symbolically illustrated the final chapter of America's Civil War than the fact that the Commonwealth of Virginia—the state that once exalted slavery and whose secession from the Union in 1861 gave the Confederacy both strategic weight and its commanding general—voted Democratic, thus assuring that Barack Obama would become the 44th president of the United States," and mean it, was a monumental commentary on the nature of American society that is breathtaking in its pathos.[7]

Acculturation is a two-way street, and this is an area where Hispanics need to show more *simpatía* for non-Hispanic society in the United States: empathizing with the continuing struggle over race in America. Members of the Hispanic diaspora are oftentimes culturally sensitive to the black-white traumata of the mainstream American society in which they live. For non-Hispanic managers and supervisors, on the other hand, to understand the job performance of Hispanics, greater cultural context is required. One cultural characteristic of the Hispanic, Latino, and Latin employee is that they become emotionally invested in their work; their co-workers become a *de facto* extended family. In consequence, there are several factors to consider: while they are fully invested in their job performance, they internalize criticism and often see it as a reflection, apart from the status, ranking and place and role within their family life, on their self-worth as an individual in the community at large.

In Hispanic culture, *confianza*, the notions of "honest boldness" and "firmness of opinion," is a word that describes the successful growth and evolution in interpersonal relationships. This has a definite place in a work environment, and in the training arena; the concept of *confianza* is an integral aspect to successful integration into the work environment. If *confianza* is absent between employees, managers, or supervisors, many Hispanic employees will "shut down" in how they see their managers or supervisors, and how their repertoire unfolds.[8]

When reviewing the work performance of Hispanic employees, one way of closing the cultural gap between Hispanic and non-Hispanics is to incorporate trust-building behaviors into the review process, and to have an adequate lead time that focuses on active listening, conflict resolution, team problem solving, and proactive decision-making in the months leading to a performance review. This allows for *confianza* to evolve and develop, which minimizes misunderstandings or conflicts that may emerge during the review process.

Successful managers are aware that Hispanics, Latinos, and Latins may be less able to distinguish between criticism of their work and criticism of them as individuals. When evaluating Hispanic employees, managers should use their "cultural intelligence" and consider, in a value-neutral manner, that:

> *Hispanic, Latino, and Latin employees are often unwilling to sacrifice family considerations for work*, meaning they are reluctant to agree to travel, incur extended separations, or accept definitions of family that include only nuclear family members and adult parent; balancing the family-versus-work dynamic informs how they view the totality of their work performance.

> *Hispanic culture has a more generous view of time*, one in which a sense of urgency can be equated with immaturity and impatience; there is a more methodological approach to delivering correctly than promptly, a trait that may not be conducive to meeting organizations' expectations.

> *Hispanic culture places value on long-term planning and long-term goals*. This can lead to conflict with management that seeks to deliver results for shareholders for the next fiscal quarter.

> *Hispanics place tremendous emphasis on a steady and sustained path to* "superarse," meaning that evaluation and per-

formance reviews are taken as a measure of "life progress." This can be at odds with the American workplace, since non-Hispanic management styles favor the "quick hare" over the "slow and steady tortoise."

The cumulative impact of these differences is one that reinforces the "communalism" of the Hispanic, Latino, and Latin employee. While mainstream American society believes in the myth of the "self-made" man and woman, among Hispanics, there is the belief that no one is self-made simply by virtue of the fact that everyone is dependent on the benefits afforded him or her by the community at large. Here, again, we see the conflict between the individualistic American view and the collectivistic Hispanic one. This situation is exacerbated by the nature of the Hispanic work force in the United States. As Pew Hispanic Center reports document over the past quarter century, there are certain generalizations that can be surmised about Hispanics in the American workforce. These generalizations are explained in the text that follows.

Hispanics are concentrated in nonsalaried professional service occupations, such as building and ground cleaning and maintenance and food preparation and serving. The representation of Hispanics in management and salaried professional occupations declined between 1990 and 2000. (Although Hispanics/Latinos are increasing in their numbers, few graduate from college; the pool of non-college Hispanic/Latino employees is surging, while, as a percentage, Hispanic/Latino college graduates continues to lag.) To a significant degree this has to do with discrepancies in the educational attainment levels between Mexican Hispanics and Caribbean Hispanics. Mexican Hispanics have lower "classroom skill sets" than Caribbean Hispanics, the majority of whom have completed a high school education. *That is to say, at a time when there are increasing numbers of Hispanics and Latinos in the workforce, there are fewer Hispanic or Latino management candidates. How do managers meet this peculiar cultural challenge within the Hispanic labor force?*

Occupations in which Hispanic workers are concentrated rank low in earnings, education requirements, and a general measure of socioeconomic status. The obstacles they face are not unlike those encountered by non-Hispanic employees, particularly African Americans and Caucasians from rural states, and resonate for all employees who are grouped together as "the working poor."[9] *In other words, why are so few Hispanics, Latinos, and Latins rising up through an organization's ranks, and what does this portend for a firm's future? How can management engage in fast-track programs for their Hispanic employees, and what are the benefits of mentoring programs within an organization?*

The occupational status of Mexicans and Puerto Ricans lags in comparison with the status of whites. Cubans and whites are comparable in occupational status. *How can management address the lingering reality that, time and time again, Cuban Americans are appointed to top positions held by Hispanics, when there is a cultural and racial gulf between Cuban Americans and Mexican Hispanics, who comprise the overwhelming number of Hispanics in the workforce?*

A measure of occupational dissimilarity reveals an increasing degree of separation between Hispanics and whites from 1990 to 2000. Whites increased their representation in salaried professional occupations while Hispanics trended toward construction and service occupations. When American women entered the workforce in the twentieth century, it is true that they were native English speakers, had basic educational attainment levels, and were fully assimilated into the mainstream of American life, but there was resistance from men to their entering the workforce, and there was sexist discrimination against women, who faced obstacles in hiring and promotion. It would take decades of "consciousness raising" and strong antidiscriminatory legislation to open opportunities, conditions that Hispanics now encounter: hostility to them and limited opportunities. *How can managers implement mentoring programs, similar to the ones developed in the 1960s and 1970s to help women achieve greater career suc-*

cess, to help Mexican Hispanics flourish in the American workplace?

Changes in the structure of industries, such as the rise of the technology sectors and the decline of manufacturing, diminished the prospects for upward occupational mobility for Hispanics in the 1990s. These shifts led to a decline for Hispanics in employment in several salaried professional occupations with high socioeconomic status. *In recent years there has been a paradox: with the devaluation and subsequent revaluation of the U.S. dollar and an increase in college graduation rates in Mexico, many firms are shifting middle-management positions to Mexico, while the United States, as a direct result of a sustained devaluation of the American dollar on world markets, is becoming a "low-wage" country.*[10] *The challenge, then, is to create opportunities that allow native-born Hispanics to become competitive on a global scale, ensuring that they will be able to have solid, middle-class careers in the United States.*

Education contributes to improving the occupational status of a worker but less so for Latins (foreign-born Hispanics). *Can managers address the "linguistic glass ceiling" that impedes the advancement of Latin employees? Are Latins the "new" Southerners—the Southern accent in customer service call centers continues to elicit prejudice from callers—held back because of their accents, which continues to be documented by researchers?*[11]

The length of time that Latins (foreign-born Hispanics) have been in the United States contributes to a narrowing of the gap in occupational status with respect to whites. Assimilation proceeds faster for the more educated and it is estimated that the less educated will never fully assimilate in occupational status. *Is there a proactive role that organizations can play to help Latin employees move from acculturation into assimilation?*

More recently arrived compatriots of Latin immigrants have lower occupational status than previously arrived compatriots even if they have the same level of education and experience. *Are Latin employees held back by their lack of fluency in English, and if so, how can managers address this obstacle to the ability of immigrant workers to advance within an organization?*

Looking just at the college-educated, Hispanics are found to be more likely to change occupations—either in the upward or downward direction—than other workers. Recently arrived immigrants and immigrants who do not speak English have a very high probability of switching occupations within five years. *How does management address the paradox confronting the U.S. labor market in a manner that conforms with the expectations of mainstream American society: whereas 80% of all Hispanics are Mexican Hispanics, only 20% of college degrees are awarded to Mexican Hispanics? The result is that Caribbean Hispanics are able to disproportionately rise up the ranks of an organization, but because of cultural reasons, are reluctant to make long-term commitments to employers west of the Mississippi.*[12]

These differences are the backdrop against which the narrative of Hispanic employees' job performance unfolds, and these are the distinct markers that can help managers understand how Hispanic, Latino, or Latin employees discharge their responsibilities and conduct themselves in the workplace.

A common element that transcends Mexican Hispanics and Caribbean Hispanics, whether they are U.S.-born or immigrants, is the cultural trait to become emotionally invested in their work. Unlike others who can compartmentalize their lives, often taking an "it's just a job" attitude, or making inviolable separations between their work and private lives, Hispanics as a cultural group, invest a significant portion of their identity and notion of self-worth in their jobs and careers. This has its origins, of course, in the Hispanic worldview that places a premium on dependence, communalism, and the propensity to cultivate tradition.

There are other factors as well, the more compelling of which is that in the United States, as a group, Hispanics have a lower educational attainment level than non-Hispanics. This results in a tremendous sense of pride and accomplishment in what Hispanics achieve in their work lives. It also transcends other considerations.

A Cuban refugee of my acquaintance who was a superintendent of schools in Havana displayed an enormous sense of accomplishment when, after arriving in Miami and working a string of blue-collar jobs, he was able to become fluent in English, study at night for a professional recertification, and then resume his career in the Miami-Dade public school system, becoming a principal at a high school. A Mexican immigrant in California similarly expressed pride in completing a two-year community college education, and rising to the ranks of being a foreman for a manufacturing firm in greater Los Angeles. An equal sense of pride was very much evident in a Latino youth in Texas telling the story that she was the first in her family to go to college, a dream that was only possible after a stint in the U.S. Army.

There is seldom nonchalance among Hispanics when it comes to the respect shown to educational achievement, which (incorrectly) is seen by many as an aspiration beyond their reach. Mexican Hispanics and Puerto Ricans, especially, devalue their ability to achieve graduate degrees: a Mexican American with a doctorate degree is as rare as a month without a full moon. This accounts for the emotional investment that Hispanics make in their work. (It also explains why Hispanics prefer to wear uniforms; are ambivalent about addressing supervisors, or being addressed by subordinates, on a first name basis; and how humility can, at times, undermine their career advancement because there is a cultural reluctance to display the kind of workplace bravado that is seen as assertiveness by non-Hispanics.) An observation that follows has for Hispanics, colleagues, and co-workers become a *de facto* extended family. A level of intimacy develops, particularly among Latin employees who, acculturating and assimilating into their adopted country, yearn for the warmth of befriending a fellow immigrant. In this setting, too, hopes and aspirations about how best to *superarse* strengthen the emotional bonds to others in the workplace.

Managers and supervisors conducting performance reviews encounter several obstacles. Foremost is the cultural propensity among Hispanics to internalize criticism more so than non-Hispanics. The emotional investment that Hispanics make in their work leads many to see their job performance as a reflection of their worth as an individual. For managers and supervisors, *how* criticism is phrased is more important than the criticism itself. The nature of *confianza* being fragile and tenuous, negative criticism is interpreted as a "vote of no confidence" in their job performance and their capabilities as an individual.

For many Latinos—and certainly many more Latins—another factor in this equation arises from the controversies surrounding illegal immigrants in the United States. Puerto Ricans are annoyed if non-Hispanics "forget" that Puerto Ricans are U.S. citizens, and Cubans are cavalier in their confidence as the last line of defense against Communist threats. The result is that Puerto Ricans and Cubans display a bravado that borders on definite brashness; such is their confidence in their status. For all Hispanics—U.S.-born Latinos included—there is always that cloud of suspicion: African Americans long resented the "driving while black" phenomenon, where black drivers are more likely to be pulled over by the police; and now, Hispanics and Latinos fear the consequences of "walking while brown."

That stereotype is in reference to the *mestizo* appearance of Mexican Hispanics; even Latinos whose families have been in the United States for several generations have come under suspicion from law enforcement and non-Hispanics of being in violation of immigration law by virtue of their appearance. The insidious nature of this Hispanic reality casts a shadow over the lives of most Hispanics in the United States. Certainly the United States has served as a social "safety valve" for Mexico, allowing multitudes of Mexico's poor, unemployed, and marginalized people to find employment, which has resulted in the "browning" of America, where the traditional "black" and "white" character of race relations is being supplanted by the ascendance of "brown," and nowhere is this more evident than in the American workplace, which is now confronting the tensions between "black" and "brown," and the suspicions between "white" and "brown." This is further complicated by "lookism," where racial categories become more ambivalent: where does "mocha" or "red" fit in?

Performance Reviews and the Nonexempt Hispanic Employee

A challenge for managers reviewing the performance of their Latino and Latin employees is the "passive" nature of Mexican Hispanics. The opposite side of the *superarse* coin, of course, is the implied lack of self-esteem. An employee who is self-conscious about what he is lacking does not convey the confidence about what he or she brings to the table. This is more the case when dealing with Latinas and *Hispanas:* lack of self-esteem undermines their confidence in the workplace. There is a reticence about speaking up when something is wrong, and about taking credit for a job well done. Performance reviews for female employees, in general, tend to underreport their contributions to the team and the department. For reasons that are not fully understood, this is especially the case for self-identified "Latina" employees who are Mexican Hispanics.

An orientation meeting *prior* to the performance evaluation should:

- Stress the importance of speaking in "I" statements: "I brought the team together to achieve this goal," "I was responsible for the department's success in this task"
- Encourage employees to bring supporting documentation to back their achievements, such as reports, work logs, and production/productivity summaries
- Highlight the importance of showing how constructive criticism of previous reviews has been acted upon
- Emphasize the role of performance reviews in giving promotions

- Accent the performance review as an opportunity to impress management

The natural existentialist impulse in the Mexican Hispanic in the United States is an obstacle to career advancement, and often is misinterpreted by managers, who believe it is a sign of either indifference by the employee, or lack of initiative. In consequence, as performance reviews as a management tool evolves, where Hispanic, Latino, and certainly Latin employees are concerned, appraisals are better suited if they: (1) Emphasize team/department results over those of individual contributions. The inherent reluctance of Mexican Hispanics to highlight their individual contributions and achievements, a form of cultural humility and deference to their immediate social unit in the workplace, means that indirect approaches have to be taken to elicit information about an individual's contribution. How did your department do this quarter? Was the team able to meet its goals? What was your role in this achievement? Do you think you could have done something differently to get better results? English is an "I" language: "I achieved my goal." Spanish is a passive language: "*Se logró la meta*," or "The goal was achieved"; and (2) Ask the employee to rank the members of the department, excluding that employee, in order of contributions to the team. If there are ten individuals in a team, a department, or a section, ask each individual to rank the other nine in order of contributions or value to the unit. When this is done with all ten individuals, the internal social hierarchical structure of the team or department is revealed. Oftentimes contributions to the team transcend title or position or seniority, and the respect an individual has earned from his or her co-workers is an apt indicator of value, contribution, and job performance to common goals. This information is not to be used for performance evaluation purposes, but it allows managers to understand more fully the internal dynamics of department members among themselves and the internal group dynamics.

In the decade after the implementation of NAFTA, time and again managers from U.S. companies encountered "problems" communicating with and understanding how to evaluate the job performance of their Mexican employees in Mexico and the increasing numbers of Hispanic employees in the U.S.-based operations. In the financial sector, as Mexico's banking opened up to foreign investment and as U.S. companies sought to increase their market share of the lucrative remittance industry among U.S.-based Latinos and Latin immigrants, several large banks, including Citibank and Bank of America, were frustrated by the greater success of Spanish banks, particularly Santander and Balboa Vizcaya, and Canadian banks, especially ScotiaBank and the Royal Bank of Canada, in nurturing their Mexican and U.S. Hispanic employees.

The difference, of course, was a matter of cultural intelligence. The Spanish, as a society, have centuries of experience interacting with Latins, being Hispanics themselves. The Canadians, although primarily the descendants of English settlers to North America, have significant experience dealing with a non-Anglo-Saxon population: the Quebecois. Canadians have found greater success with Hispanics than have Americans, and this cultural awareness was the single-most important reason for the superior results of Spanish and Canadian banks with Hispanics. "Mexicans," Anthony DePalma explains, "routinely tell survey takers that they like Canada's fairness and open society best—sentiments I heard repeated by the migrant farmworkers in Ontario who returned to Canada each year to work in the fields."[13] The same generous attitude toward Canadians is shared by middle- and upper-class Mexicans, many of whom prefer to send their children to Canadian prep schools, colleges, and universities. The Canadian government, in its policies, has striven to create *confianza* with Latin American countries. These strategies include things such as having a comprehensive guest worker program with Mexico (hundreds of thousands of Mexicans work in Canada under the auspices of the Canadian government and Mexican consulates, and there is no significant illegal immigration from Mexico to Canada); Canada, unlike the United States, places no restrictions on how foreign aid is used; and Canada refuses to use economic sanctions to retaliate against any Latin American country.[14] How Canadians have won Latin Americans over is a lesson non-Hispanic Americans cannot ignore.

The lesson for American management is that communication becomes more important as Hispanic, Latino, and Latin employees ascend in the American workplace. Five areas where communications are important are:

Provide company materials in both English and Spanish. This is important because reading comprehension skills in English and Spanish vary from employee to employee. Spanish language material applies for both company literature, and also those from government agencies, most of which already are published in Spanish.[15]

Offer managers and supervisors Spanish language classes. A basic refresher course of the equivalent of "High School Spanish 101" is the minimum standard for managers of nonsalaried Hispanic workers. This would allow for basic conversation; many community colleges offer "conversational" Spanish designed for professional and workplace settings.[16]

Stress the importance of confidentiality. When more than one language is spoken in the workplace, it is important that all proprietary and confidential information is discussed exclusively in English, because that is consistent with legal norms.

Managers should be sensitive to the Hispanic family model. Managers should be aware that Hispanics, Latinos, and Latins see family issues—such as personal leave, bereavement time, obligations to family members outside the nuclear unit and adult parents—in different terms than non-Hispanics.

Revitalize a diverse workforce. Hispanics prefer to work where management recognizes the importance of *confianza* and *simpatía*. Managers who take proactive steps to instill a sense of cultural respect build strong loyalty.

Armed with this cultural intelligence, it is now possible to see how, almost always, it is a lack of *simpatía* that leads to misunder-

standing certain cultural norms that contribute to inferior performance reviews of nonexempt Hispanic employees. Each
"issue" has its origin in how *simpatía* is understood in Hispanic
culture, especially for workers who are generally employed in
nonexempt positions.

Questions & Answers about Nonexempt Hispanic and Latino Employees

Why do Hispanics insist on speaking Spanish among
themselves?

In the same way that Latin immigrants will seek group cohesion by gathering together in public spaces, within organizations, non-Hispanic managers and supervisors express
frustration by the tendency of Hispanic employees to speak
Spanish among themselves. This is the equivalent of "linguistic loitering" in the workplace, because it is seen as creating a distance from other employees and it fans the
insecurities of other employees, who tend to think that Hispanics are saying things they don't want others to hear or
understand.

Why are Hispanics reluctant to look you directly in the eyes?

The Hispanic cultural values of showing respect for authority and valuing humility can be misinterpreted as evasiveness
or deceit by non-Hispanics. In the United States, Anglo American society imparts the lesson that it is a virtue to stand up
and speak up for oneself, and part of this is being unafraid
to look anyone directly in the eye. This ability, in fact, is
closely linked with truthfulness and forthrightness. In
American society body language in which an individual looks
down or away is seen as an indication that a person is trying to avoid a subject, or hide something. Not unlike other
cultures, particularly in Chinese and Japanese societies,

among Mexican Hispanics, not meeting a manager's gaze is a sign of respect; looking down emphasizes that the person is listening to what is being said, a mark of humility. This is especially the case among Mexican Hispanic women, where there is a deferential approach to dealing with men who are not family members. It would be wrong to conclude that Mexican Hispanic women can be more easily intimidated, but rather, a certain sense of discretion, decorum, and modesty discourages their making direct eye contact with males who are in a position of authority. In these differences, the tension between a collectivistic and an individualistic worldview are self-evident.

Why are Hispanics hesitant to call managers by their first names?

One of the unintended consequences of the Civil Rights and women's rights movements in the United States has been the tearing down of social barriers in the workplace. At times, this impulse for a more egalitarian approach to the work environment—where everyone is relegated to democratic cubicles and the corner offices are turned into conference rooms—is in keeping with the move from vertical hierarchies to horizontal ones. It is important to realize that organizations, by definition, need organization, and at times this is best fulfilled in a top-down hierarchy. Militaries, governments, and industrial factories and transportation companies all require clearly articulated chains of command and responsibilities. Among Hispanics, work is serious and the workplace is not seen as a place for socializing. The idea that a manager, supervisor, or another someone of higher rank and authority can be addressed by their first name is seen as disrespectful. Hispanics are made uncomfortable by a supervisor who wants to be their friend, or insists on being called by his or her first name. An additional component is that Hispanics, by virtue of being younger than other workers, are more likely to report to someone who is older than they are; addressing older persons by an honorific term is more comfortable.

Why do Hispanics say they understand directions when they don't?

There are two principal factors that contribute to the common complaint that Hispanic employees will say they understand directions when they clearly don't. The first is a language barrier; for many Hispanics, English is a second language, and many are not fluent in it. In these cases they may simply not understand the directions because of language incomprehension. To this linguistic obstacle, there are cultural ones as well. Many Hispanics, particularly Latin immigrants, are inclined to exhibit a "passive resolve," an embarrassment about not understanding directions, and thinking that they will be able to "figure things out" in the course of performing the actual task. The nagging self-doubt, which is inherent in the cultural mantra of *superarse,* further inhibits speaking up to get more explicit directions. This can prove frustrating, particularly to non-Hispanic managers and supervisors who have no experience with employees who have this worldview. One common complaint expressed by Anglo American (and Cuban American) executives who worked in Mexico after the implementation of NAFTA was their own "learning curve" on how to communicate effectively with Mexican workers. Now that those Mexican workers, and their U.S.-born Latino children, are in the American workforce, these issues are reverberating throughout the United States.

Why don't Hispanics speak up when there is a problem?

This complaint is linked to the language barrier. Latin employees are more inclined to display a "passive resolve," and put on a brave face when they encounter a problem, often internalizing its origin. Rather than thinking that the problem exists and should be resolved, they tend to believe that they are responsible for the problem, having somehow caused it, and will try to secretly "correct" the problem before their supervisor becomes aware of it, fearing that they will be blamed for the situation. In business as in life, however, things happen, or malfunction, or encounter unexpected situations; the nature of work is problem solving, not just executing tasks. An ill-advised sense of humility and communalism— Latin workers will confer with another Latin colleague in Spanish before reporting a problem to a supervisor—can create problems in the workplace, especially in the agricultural, food processing, and construction industries, where the nature of the work allows for fewer automated safety and quality checks.

Why are Hispanics often reluctant to wear safety equipment?

Although many have commented on the reluctance of Latin employees to wear safety equipment as a residual aspect of "machismo," the fact is that, until the 1990s, workplace safety requirements throughout Latin America did not meet international standards. Only after the countries of the region began to join the General Agreement on Tariffs and Trade, or GATT, did the process of standardization workplace safety rules become law. For many Latin immigrants, whether they are working in factories, construction sites, restaurants, or other industries where safety equipment is required, they are not used to safety equipment. It is as much

a generational difference—consider the two decades of public service announcements that were required before the
majority of American drivers began to habitually wear seat
belts when in a car—as one of old habits. The remedy is
compulsory training in the proper use of safety equipment,
and in the posting of bilingual signage reminding workers
that failure to wear safety equipment is a violation of company policy.

Why are Hispanics often uninterested in the firm's benefit plans?

For human resources professionals, the low participation
rates of Hispanics in benefits plans remains a source of frustration. By one measure, the Society for Human Resource
Management (SHRM), estimates that only 40% of Hispanic
employees participate fully in their firm's benefit plans. There
are two principal factors for this low participation rate. Foremost, particularly among Mexican Hispanics, the idea of
company-sponsored benefits is an unusual one. Their life
experience reflects Mexico's national-socialist development
model. The Mexican Institute of Social Security, or Instituto
Mexicano del Seguro Social, known as IMSS, is a comprehensive health care program that covers all bona fide workers. Latin immigrants from Mexico and even many Latinos
believe that Social Security is a health plan, and not, as it
is, a retirement and disability program.[17] "Social Security"
and "Seguro Social" may sound analogous, but they are not,
which creates obstacles for many employees. A further complication is cultural: In Mexico's development model, the
state guarantees benefits to employees in order to encourage job creation. In the United States, about a third of an
employee's total compensation is derived from benefits, such
as vacation pay, unemployment insurance, medical benefits,

and so on. In Mexico, the figures are reversed: about a third of an employee's compensation is in the form of wages, and the balance is derived from government-sponsored entitlement programs.[18] Latin and Latino employees mistakenly believe that the Social Security taxes taken from their paychecks are used for similar programs. A solution is providing more employee education and information in Spanish about benefits, with the aim of encouraging Hispanic and Latino employees to participate in benefit programs more fully.

What is clear, then, is that Hispanic, Latino, and Latin employees come from a different worldview, one where the relationship between employer and employee, subordinate and supervisor, department and the larger organization is more formal. Relationships are more deferential, and vertical hierarchies are preferred over horizontal, egalitarian structures.

This makes assessing the work performance more difficult, simply because what can be perceived as "dependability" or "discipline" by non-Hispanic managers, supervisors, or administrators, could be good manners or a deferential approach to the workplace. It is the ascendance of Hispanics in the workplace that has, over the course of the past decade or so, contributed to organizations evaluating the efficacy of the kinds of performance reviews that have dominated the workplace since the 1960s.

If an organization has not transitioned to a strategic reevaluation of the efficacy of performance reviews, it is recommended that traditional performance appraisals be modified to reflect anthropological criteria:

The implementation of a "Performance Management System" needs to reflect the issues that surround evaluating Hispanic, Latino, and Latin workers. Management should understand that Hispanics, Latinos, and Latins, culturally, invest tremendous passion in their jobs, on occasion taking constructive criticism as a personal affront. Performance can be affected by tendencies to be meticulous and "perfect," which can conflict with time management issues centered on delivering results on a quarterly basis. Management can overcome these issues by giving sufficient notice of the expectations of the Performance Management System, creating a task force to debrief employees, using focus groups and articulating the purposes, goals, and time frames involved. Managers, supervisors, and other administrators are more successful if they tailor communication for different audiences: managers, employees, and management. Management, through pilot programs and targeted training, can overcome the "Culture" vs. "Workplace" expectations, creating a level playing field for both evaluators and employees being evaluated.

Management should understand the "nuances" of conducting performance appraisals of Hispanic, Latino, and Latin employees. Managers, supervisors, and other administrators need to understand that there are cultural differences in philosophical approaches to life and work, specifically the "individualistic" American approach versus the "collectivist" tendency in Hispanic society. Management should factor in how this results in Hispanic, Latino, and Latin employees' reluctance to boast about their individual achievement, deferring instead to their "team" or "department." Management should compensate for how anxiety about fluency in English, or their accent, affects how a Hispanic, Latino, and Latin employee performs in an oral evaluation. Management can compensate for these issues by incorporating the concepts in the "Third Culture," a strategy to correct for the tendency in Hispanic culture to be modest and shy about the professional and career achievements of Hispanic, Latino, and Latin employees.

When conducting performance appraisals, human resources managers (HRMs) should incorporate the principles of the "New Approach," which emphasizes the pre-interview, interview, and post-interview preparedness that facilitates a more thorough and accurate evaluation. Managers, supervisors, and other administrators should articulate expectations and goals of the performance appraisals well before the actual evaluation takes place. Managers, supervisors, and other administrators should help evaluators identify potential areas of bias or cultural misunderstanding that can inform the evaluation process. Managers, supervisors, and other administrators should document the primary objectives of the evaluation, and assist evaluators in preparing questions they should ask themselves before conducting the appraisal.

In Review

- Traditional performance review appraisals are less effective for assessing Hispanic, Latino, and Latin employees.

- Cultural predispositions arising from a collectivistic worldview require managers, supervisors, and other administrators to implement review processes that are sensitive to the cultural predispositions of Hispanic society.

- The most significant cultural obstacle Hispanics, Latinos, and Latins encounter is in speaking in declarative statements, where they adopt an individualistic approach to thinking about their personal performance, how they fulfill their duties, and their distinct contributions to the organization.

Hispanics, Managers, and Labor Relations

One consequence of the *Hispanic diaspora* experience is the sociological impact of being part of the "out-group" in the American workplace. H. Tajfel and J. C. Turner, writing in "The Social Identity Theory of Intergroup Behaviour," expand on their "Social Identity Theory" first advanced in 1979 in discussing intergroup relations. Tajfel and Turner argue that group membership depends on self-categorization, and is determined by whether a person sees himself or herself as part of the "in-group" or part of the "out-group." "The status relations between dominant and subordinate groups determine the latter's identity problems," Tajfel and Turner explain.[1] In this discussion, the question can be seen as a process of "acculturation": do Hispanic, Latino, or Latin employees see themselves as minorities, members of the "out-group," not part of the mainstream of American life?

Consider a Latina employee working in a department dominated by Caucasian and African American males. She is part of the "out-group" by virtue of being Hispanic. She is also an outsider by virtue of being female. She can choose to reach out to other women, regardless of race or ethnicity, and form a bond: women, regardless of race or ethnicity, have long complained that an obstacle they face arises from the opportunities afforded men for social and business networking from which they are excluded by virtue of their gender: playing golf and being able to pursue other sports that entail athletic club facilities are common examples cited. The Latina employee can, instead, attempt to become part of the "in-group" by assimilating into the mainstream of American life: becoming "non-Hispanic" in lifestyle and worldview. She can opt to do neither, and choose to remain isolated.

There are considerations in either approach that have sociocultural impact. That there are "in-groups" and "out-groups" implies a hierarchy: one group is viewed as more desirable, powerful, and positive than the other. For the Hispanic diaspora in the American workplace, the comparisons with the dominant Anglo-Protestant American culture around them, there is the perception that the dominant, primarily Caucasian, group around them, the "in-group," is seen in a more positive way. One strategy for coping with the perceived lack of status, power, and their subordinate status is for Hispanic, Latino, and Latin employees to seek strength in the familiar—and in numbers. How the ascendance of Hispanics is fueling a revival of organized labor in the United States and changing the nature of management-labor relations is an emerging management issue. How labor unions are benefiting from the emergence of a Hispanic workforce and what this means for the practice of management is now discussed.

Managers should be aware that if *confianza* is absent, feedback, active listening, and self-disclosure will not evolve fully, and Hispanic employees will not be as forthcoming as is necessary for success in the workplace. These cultural differences with mainstream American culture can be more effectively bridged through a proactive way that emphasizes the "confidence building" that is the essence of *confianza*. Managers are more successful in nurturing the Hispanics they supervise by cultivating habits that signal management-labor relations that respect *confianza*. These strategies include an emphasis on basic skills, minimizing reports in favor of "formalized" discussions, emphasizing the fluidity of hierarchies, and building the common "vocabulary" of the organization.

Emphasizing basic skills entails providing opportunities to practice workplace skills, such as active listening, conflict resolution, problem solving in a teamwork setting, and hypothetical decision-making exercises. Minimizing written reports is a direct response to the cultural norms where teaching and instruction succeed in a "hands-on" setting rather than in "classroom" situations. Concepts surrounding interpersonal communication skills, problem solving in a teamwork setting, and decision-making are more successful as exercises rather than formal workshops. Although employees should be provided with manuals, workbooks, and other appropriate materials, these are best used to reinforce concepts, review case studies, and learn instructions. "Lessons," however, are best imparted when presented orally, demonstrated in a workshop setting, and practiced. Formalized discussion can best replace the disparate cultural norms between Hispanics and non-Hispanics in the American workplace. Whereas non-Hispanics are more comfortable with "frankness" and "honest" approaches to interpersonal relationships, many Hispanics, Latinos, and Latins interpret such approaches as "disrespectful" and "confrontational."

Manuals for Hispanic, Latino, and Latin Employees

Employee manuals should reflect that, as the nation moves toward becoming a bilingual consumer economy, Spanish in the workplace is inevitable:

> Management needs to establish and document policies that Spanish in the workplace should conform to the rules that apply to English in the workplace.

> Managers, supervisors, and other administrators need to understand that written and spoken Spanish in the workplace can contribute to and constitute a hostile work environment.

> "Codes of Conducts" can be used effectively to ensure that Spanish will not be used as a language that creates a hostile work environment.

Although non-Hispanic supervisors are well advised to workplace situations that involve personnel training, simulations, group discussions, or role-playing, it is necessary to 1) orally acknowledge the cultural differences between Hispanics and non-Hispanics, and 2) define and state clearly the purpose of the meeting, workshop, or training exercise to affirm the objectives, and set the boundaries, noting that cultural differences are being taken into account. To this end, a common "vocabulary" builds *confianza* among employees.

Cultural and linguistic differences often give rise to workplace tensions and misunderstanding, particularly in cases where managers rely on interpreters to "filter" down English text to employees whose command of the English language differs from little to proficient to fluent. Orders, memoranda, and requests should be presented in both English and Spanish, which alleviates the "translation" role of bilingual supervisors or co-workers.

In this process of conveying *confianza,* a proactive role by management, including human resources personnel, is critical. "[Human resource management] professionals should grasp and master the concept of value," Dave Ulrich and Wayne Brockbank argue in the *Harvard Business Review.* "At a basic level, values reflect the standards within a firm. . . . Value also means that someone receives something of worth from a transaction."[2] For managers, nothing conveys the concept that they are valued than for Hispanic employees to feel their direct manager has *simpatía* for them. Managers in nonunion companies who express *confianza* in their Hispanic employees encounter fewer labor relations problems. Strategies that create a nurturing, harmonious work environment are culturally important for Hispanic employees—for example, give unexpected praise; encourage employee participation in decision-making; pronounce employees' names correctly; show understanding of the relationship of employee to family; show willingness to help the Hispanic employee in day-to-day matters off the job. A compliment as simple as, "I've noticed you've been doing excellent work, Juan. Thank you and keep it up," is a welcome affirmation of Hispanic culture in an American workplace.

This may appear to be an expensive proposition, but most of the material that should be included in a basic employee manual consists of information that is already available in Spanish. The Equal Employment Opportunity (EEO) office, the Social Security Administration (SSA), workers' compensation departments at the state level, Labor Department regulations, and most trade organizations and related industry groups have their material available in Spanish. The material that is specific to an individual organization, of course, is unique, but it comprises only a small percentage of the material that should be provided in Spanish.[3] Another consideration, which reflects the reality of the emerging workplace, is that many low-level Latin and Latino employees do not read or write Spanish fluently. They are, in essence, functionally illiterate. In these cases, one strategy is to have a one-day workshop when a bilingual person is contracted, usually from a translation/interpretation company, to go over all the material in an onsite presentation, explaining the basic material orally. In addition to this being a practical solution to the problem of Spanish-language reading comprehension, it documents a proactive approach by management, and conveys tremendous *simpatía* to workers.

With this in mind, managers should be aware of two emerging trends in which the Hispanic diaspora is playing a significant—and unexpected—role. Foremost, unions are using the swelling ranks of Hispanics, Latinos, and Latins to increase their memberships and organize industries. U.S. unions hope to leverage the emerging Hispanic workforce to organize industries that have thus far eluded unionization, such as hotel workers, restaurant employees, and retail employees. Second, in many cases, unions are using the emerging tension between U.S.-born Hispanics who are not fluent in Spanish, and foreign-born Hispanics who speak Spanish better than they do English as an emerging management issue, entering the immigration versus native-born fray, to the disadvantage of U.S.-born Latino employees.

Labor Relations among Hispanics

After Mexico joined GATT, there was a rush of American and Canadian companies setting up, or expanding, their operations in Mexico. The wave of in-bond factories, known as *maquiladoras,* along the U.S.-Mexico border created new job opportunities, and an ever-expanding demand for labor to staff the light industrial manufacturing and assembly facilities. These opportunities resulted in a significant internal migration within Mexico: unemployed workers flocked to the "industrial parks" around Tijuana, Mexicali, Ciudad Juárez, and Monterrey among other cities. Corporate America similarly searched through its managerial talent to identify "Hispanic" supervisors and executives who could oversee the expansion of these operations. A disproportionate number of these managers, and the consultants hired when no internal talent was identified, were Cuban. In no time Cuban, or Cuban American, managers and supervisors found themselves on Miami-Mexico City flights, continuing on to Tijuana, Guadalajara, Monterrey, or other cities. Non-Hispanic management thought the matter had been resolved, unaware of the cultural clashes that would emerge between the temperament of the Cubans and the Mexicans.

To understand the heart of the conflict, it is necessary to revisit the fundamental difference between Caribbean Hispanics and Mexican Hispanics: Caribbean Hispanics are peoples from a white (European) and black (sub-Saharan African) heritage. Their worldview is very much analogous to the experience of the United States. Mexican Hispanics, on the other hand, are primarily peoples who are from a white (European) and Native American (indigenous, or First Peoples) lineage. The United States has systematically banished and removed Native Americans from the mainstream of society, and Americans have virtually no experience with, or empathy for, the worldview of the continent's indigenous peoples. Cubans are no different: the *Dia de los Muertos* celebrations of Oaxaca, where sugar candy in the form of skulls or dancing skeletons that adorn altars are as "exotic" to a Cuban as they are to mainstream Americans.

Although both were "Hispanic" in the linguistic and cultural sense, the Cuban view of the world, the business world precisely, was in sharp contrast to the Mexican perspective. There were, of course, immediate differences and conflicts. Cuban managers were almost always white, and the Mexicans they supervised were brown, *mestizo*. Cubans spoke in a rapid-fire staccato of Spanish, prone to be direct in their phrasing, and almost always using the indicative tense. Mexicans, in contrast, spoke at a slower pace, almost always phrased their words in the subjective tense, and in deferential tones. The Cubans thought the Mexicans were slow, and the Mexicans thought the Cubans were brash. From the outside, there were conflicts when a group of "abrasive" white managers were supervising a group of "people of color" they considered to be "slow." In no time, reports began to arrive at corporate offices throughout the United States that there were "conflicts" and "problems" between their Cuban managers and the bulk of the Mexican workers.

It was during this time that I worked with clients who encountered significant conflicts between their Mexican employees and the Cuban managers and executives. For non-Hispanics the problems were exasperating, especially because, in meetings between high-ranking Mexican and Cuban executives, everything operated smoothly. What was not apparent, however, was that in Mexico, as is the case throughout much of the world, corporate suites are occupied by white (European) men; Mexican executives and their Cuban counterparts are almost always descendants of Europeans. The conflicts occurred when Cubans left the comforts of executive suites in Mexico City, Guadalajara, or Monterrey, and found themselves with the rank-and-file factory workers at the *maquiladoras*, or when dealing with Mexican immigrants on the U.S. side of the border. It was then that the Caribbean Hispanic worldview conflicted with the Native American sensibilities of the Mexican Hispanic.

In the course of my own experience over more than two decades working in the Unites States and Mexico, I was struck by the consistent ways in which Cubans and Cuban American managers consistently saw themselves as both Hispanic *and* part of the "in-group" of American society. There was a sense of entitlement, by virtue of being granted automatic U.S. residency upon reaching U.S. shores; that privilege is not enjoyed by any other group within the Hispanic diaspora, and the sentiments expressed were ones of superiority: there was a certain disdain for the "inferiority" of the greater Anglo-Protestant American society at large. In fact, what proved surprising, as problems were resolved case-by-case, however, were the parallels to historic observations about Latin American societies. Cuban managers complained that the Mexicans lacked "common sense," or "refused to reason." Other Cubans observed that there was a "lack of ambition" or "little aspiration" among Mexican workers. Some complained that there was a "vacuous" sense to their "approach to life." It was as if the Cubans were channeling the Spanish missionaries who described the indigenous peoples as "gente sin razón," people without reason; or members of Maximilian's court who complained about the "nothingness" of the Mexican people. There was also the confounding reality that the Cubans grew impatient.

Throughout the 1980s and into the 1990s, Cubans working in Mexico, or with Mexicans in the United States, came to one of two conclusions. One group concluded that the Mexicans were, "*pobrecitos, tan buenos, pero son tan brutos,*" meaning, "poor little ones, so good, but such blockheads." This was more generous than those who concluded with this severe assessment: "*estos indios estúpidos, qué comemiardas,*" or, "these stupid Indians, what retards." The Mexicans, in their more circumspect way, also expressed their frustration with the Cubans. The adjectives used most often to describe the Cubans were "brash," "loud," "obnoxious," and "arrogant." Some Mexicans described them as "condescending" as if they were "Anglo-Saxons," by which they meant that the Cubans reminded them of the "ugly American" stereotype.

These cultural conflicts almost always proved too much to overcome, and most Cubans requested transfers, quit their companies, or simply grew tired of their assignments and balked at continued stints within a few years. There was, of course, a fatigue in boarding the first flight from Miami to Mexico on Mondays, living out of a suitcase four nights, and then boarding the last flight Thursday night back to Miami; or in relocating to the border and driving back and forth between San Diego and Tijuana, or El Paso and Ciudad Juárez. For organizations, the continuing personnel changes proved frustrating; there were not enough Mexican Hispanic managers for all the positions available, and Cubans were simply reluctant to relocate from Miami to Mexico or the U.S.-Mexico border, which they considered "hardship" assignments.

More than a decade later, attitudes have hardened. In the United States, Cubans, who consider themselves "Hispanic," attend meetings and conferences around the country with representatives from "Latino" organizations such as the National Council of La Raza or the Mexican-American Legal and Education Fund and nod their heads politely, then retire to their hotel rooms to take aspirin, massage their temples, and later in the evening join each other for after-dinner drinks, when they roll their eyes and laugh at the day's "Latino non-sense" proceedings. Then they would talk about how they couldn't wait to get back to Miami, leaving the Mexican Americans with their grievances, self-pity, and their anguish and their "Latinolandia" politics of disenfranchisement behind. Finally they would retire to their hotel rooms, catch up on the "real" America—as reported by the Cuban news anchors on CNN, Rick Sánchez and Soledad O'Brien—before confirming their flights bound for Miami, first thing in the morning.[4]

The existence—and how prevalent—of intra-Hispanic prejudices is a reality of life, and so is the hostility of Spanish-speaking Hispanics toward U.S. Latinos who are not conversant in Spanish. Like an onion, there are layers and layers of nuances, cultural and national biases among Latin Americans, intragroup rivalries among Hispanics as they jockey for status and privilege. Within the mosaic of peoples that fall under the umbrella of Hispanics, Latinos, and Latins in the United States, time and again, it is the Cubans who emerge on top. Despite this success, for the Cubans (as for many Puerto Ricans), there is no anguish that needs the "Latino" label; they believe themselves to be the avant-garde to what will be the Hispanic Century of the United States. There is, after all, an inherent sense of entitlement in being a U.S. citizen, as the Puerto Ricans are, or in being handed a monthly Social Security check for life once your political asylum papers are filed, as is the case with the Cubans. These are cultural and philosophical differences that persist, and these are reasons for the conflicts that emerge when Cubans are asked to supervise Mexicans, which is the case almost every time Caribbean Hispanics manage Mexican Hispanics. (Mexican managers of Cubans are almost unheard of, which speaks volumes about the discrepancies between the educational attainment levels between Latinos and Hispanics.[5]) It continues to prove challenging to reconcile these cultural differences, and establish a successful rapport within these organizations, as they attempted to take advantage of emerging opportunities between Mexico and the United States, and within the growing Hispanic and Latino markets domestically, with the inherent conflicts that characterize the Mexican Hispanic and Caribbean Hispanic worldviews.

Hispanic Acculturation: Perceptions of "In-Group" Culture by the "Out-Group"

Managers, supervisors, and other administrators have been slow to understand, or accept, the cultural and socioeconomic differences within the Hispanic community, and how there are strong differences that create both conflicts and opportunities. The tensions between Cubans and Mexicans, for non-Hispanic managers, are counterintuitive, and troubling. But for marketing executives, it is a fact of life that spills into cultural preferences that affect consumer behavior. Consider something as simple as coffee. Marilyn Halter describes how social anthropologists who entered the fields of marketing and merchandising have helped develop different campaigns for how coffee is best marketed to Cubans and Mexicans in the United States:

> The more sophisticated target marketers understand the limitation of too wide a scope for their multicultural constituencies. . . . For instance, although both Cubans and Mexicans are classified as Hispanics by virtue of their common language, in reality their sociocultural histories and patterns of settlement in the United States are quite divergent and demand differentiated marketing approaches.
>
> When marketing specialists at the Bustelo Coffee Company determined that Mexicans and Central Americans, compared with all other Hispanics, preferred instant coffee to espresso, they developed television commercials depicting their instant varieties to broadcast in Chicago and San Francisco's Bay Area, urban centers with substantial Mexican American communities. Bustelo's market research is so refined that the company has even tracked how tastes in coffee drinking change when people relocate. For example, Mexicans who move to Miami

or to New York tend to pick up on the espresso and specialty coffee trends, and subsequently their coffee consumption of instant coffee declines.[6]

From an anthropological perspective, the observation can be made that instant coffee is what less privileged consumers can afford, and as a person's purchasing power increases, their preferences change to espressos and other specialty coffees. A sociologist would also observe that there are distinct demonstration effects: Mexicans who move to Miami or New York suddenly see other "mainstream" Hispanics drinking coffees usually associated with Cuba or Puerto Rico, and adopt those beverage patterns.

The lesson, of course, is that management has to understand the nuances that inform cultural ideas that shape how Mexican Hispanics and Caribbean Hispanics approach management and the subject of labor relations differently. While, as marketers have learned, one group prefers instant coffee, another is in the habit of drinking espressos. Let us consider the following two studies. First, some background is in order for the "out-group" Mexican Hispanic employees, where socioeconomic conflicts often lead to the involvement of unions that result in political conflicts with management. The other case involved the more "amenable" way conflicts with Caribbean Hispanics have historically been handled. The implications for the workplace are obvious: Caribbean Hispanics are more "in-group" than Mexican Hispanics, and therefore, as Mexican Hispanics begin to move away from being an "out-group," they first emulate Caribbean Hispanics, before they begin to adopt the habits of Anglo-Protestant American society.

For Mexican Hispanics, their aspirational role models are Caribbean Hispanics, not mainstream American society. This fundamental misunderstanding results in a common mistake management makes about Hispanic employees in general, which is that the reluctance to speak up is seen as indifference, or even agreement. These are cultural differences, not unlike the Japanese custom of saying "yes," to statements, not because they are *in agreement* with what is being said, but simply to convey that they are *actively listening* to what one is saying. Listening is not the same thing as being in agreement. Among Hispanics, the insecurities that are an integral part of *superarse* manifest themselves in a deferential manner with their immediate supervisors. Silence is not agreement, and unless one understands the nuances that signal disagreement, tensions, grievances, and seething anger builds.

Now consider these "in-group" and "out-group" case studies that offer insights regarding the divergent ways the Hispanic diaspora expresses itself in labor disputes. First, this is how historian Mark Reisler describes the farm labor conflict that exploded in the Imperial Valley (California) Workers' Union Strike in 1928, which remains the classic case study of labor conflict with Mexican Hispanic employees:

> The union addressed its grievances to the chambers of commerce in El Centro and Brawley and requested their aid in negotiating with the growers. Dominated by growers, the chambers of commerce believed the union was weak and ignored the request. A strike ensued. . . . Employer reaction was predictable, as reported by Louis Bloch who investigated the strike for the California Department of Industrial Relations: "The organization of a union of Mexican[-American] laborers seems to have evoked in the growers an ardent wish for its earliest demise."
>
> The growers did not sit idly by "wishing" for the union's demise. Rather, they prepared to escort it to the grave. . . . The county sheriff deputized over forty farm foremen and superintendents and began to arrest strikers by the dozens, charging them with vagrancy and disturbing the peace. Local courts set bail at the prohibitive sums of from $250 to $1000. Mexican pool halls, which served as informal places of assembly, and the union office were closed down by the sheriff, and workers were threatened with mass deportations if they participated in the strike movement. Sheriff Charles Gillette's "ardent enthusiasm for law enforcement" overwhelmed the union, and the strike was broken in a matter of days . . .

The behavior of growers and local law enforcement authorities in the cantaloupe strike set a pattern for future labor confrontations. Company officials, Sheriff Gillette, and the local press all charged that the strike was fomented by outside "Red" agitators from Mexico, and they predicted it would lead to a communist uprising. They presented no evidence whatsoever to corroborate this contention. The union's tactic of using the chamber of commerce as an intermediary, plus its mutual-aid society origins, make such a charge most dubious. The Imperial Valley Workers Union was, on the contrary, an indigenous and independent movement of Mexican immigrant laborers . . .

"The atmosphere of the valley," reported the *San Francisco Examiner,* on October 9, 1933, "is that of a smoldering volcano." Growers and county officials reacted swiftly against the strike, which jeopardized most of California's cotton crop. Farmers evicted laborers from housing on their land, and police prevented peaceful picketing while arresting dozens. The strikers soon began to suffer food shortages and health problems. Local welfare authorities refused to extend them aid. Hospitals denied admittance to strikers' wives who were about to deliver babies. Nine infants at the Corcoran camp died of malnutrition. As mass starvation approached, Governor James Rolph, acting on federal advice, ordered the California Emergency Relief Administration to provide the strikers with relief. This was the first time laborers of any kind ever received food from a federal agency during a strike. The relief, however, came with strings attached. A fact-finding committee established by the governor and California NRA Administrator George Creel, who also served as mediator, recommended a compromise wage settlement of $.75 per hundredweight. To encourage union acceptance of the compromise, all relief was halted. After some hesitation, the union agreed, and workers returned to the fields . . . [7]

In this instance, there is a cultural phenomenon that differentiates the Mexican Hispanic and the Caribbean Hispanic in terms of conflict resolution.

Second, this is how Caribbean Hispanic employees, closer to being part of the greater, mainstream American "in-group," handle a dispute, mindful that the cultural awareness of non-Hispanic managers is crucial to a superior organizational outcome:

> A new manager from the Midwest was hired for a troubled New York cut-and-sew contractor. The firm had a large contingent of workers from the Caribbean (primarily Puerto Rico and Haiti) and a poor record on productivity and quality. Full of vim, vigor, and a burning desire to prove himself, this new manager decided to improve the situation by getting "closer" to the mostly Spanish-speaking workforce. Hispanic employees made up 87% of the contractor's team.
>
> He doffed coat and tie, and dressed in jeans and sports shirt. Asking his Hispanic employees to call him by his first name, he toured the plant floor with a translator, looking for ways to "help" workers while correcting their errors and speeding production. He felt he was "establishing good relations" by simultaneously pushing hard for better quality and productivity while reducing the visible economic and status gap between him and his workers. Despite his "corrective" tactics and casual approach in dress and conduct, plant performance continued downhill.
>
> Why? Because he did not understand the mind-set of the Hispanic workers. Like many Americans, he was unaware that managing employees with different Hispanic backgrounds, cultures, and psychology is different from managing an Anglo workforce.
>
> Hispanic employees considered this new plant manager uncultured, boorish. He did not know that Hispanics generally expect the "boss" stereotype to be reflected in appearance, that is, the higher the status or importance of the job, the more formal the attire.

> The poor performance was not caused because the casually
> dressed manager insisted on improving quality and productivity,
> but because his manner of address was not formal enough for
> his heavily Puerto Rican workforce when the inevitable
> production problems occurred. The Puerto Ricans wanted him
> to be proper, aloof, reserved, and very formal. Quality of the
> plant's shipments continued to be poor, and customer
> complaints about late delivery burgeoned. We will return to
> this apparel business' quandary and some solutions for it
> throughout this article.[8]

In the same way that it is important to explain to Latin employees who are immigrants that "Social Security" is a retirement program in the United States and not equivalent to Mexico's "Seguro Social," a national health system, it is also important to convey the notion that labor unions in the United States, unlike Mexican labor unions, are not affiliated with the government.

To these cultural differences, there is another important consideration, and it derives from the worldview of the indigenous peoples that informs the Mexican Hispanic worldview: passivity bordering on fatalism.

The "Fatalism" and "Passivity" of the Mexican Hispanic

What does this mean? Recall the frustrations that Europeans have long expressed in trying to understand the philosophical worldview of the indigenous peoples they encountered. The Spanish missionaries, exasperated, came to the conclusion that there are simply two kinds of people in the world: people of reason, and people without reason. Centuries later, the French-imposed Emperor Maximilian regretted the "nothingness" of the Mexicans, and how "passive" they were.

In our time this reverberates by what we, in the contemporary world, call lack of follow-through.

CASE STUDY

The "Passive" Character of Mexicans and Mexican Hispanics

Europeans in Mexico have long expressed reservations about the stoicism and passivity of the First Peoples who predated the arrival of Columbus. Throughout the nineteenth and twentieth centuries, Mexican intellectuals sought to understand the worldview of the Native American peoples, and how at odds this way of looking at things was compared with traditions familiar in the Judeo-Christian world. In recent years, two examples—one in Mexico and the other in the United States—offer insights into this continuing challenge for managers and supervisors working with Mexican immigrants to the United States and Mexican Hispanics.

In 2006 massive demonstrations were held throughout the United States championing for immigration reform. "A crowd estimated by police at more than 500,000 boisterously marched in Los Angeles on Saturday to protest federal legislation that would crack down on undocumented immigrants, penalize those who help them and build a security wall along the U.S.' [sic] southern border," Teresa Watanabe and Hector Becerra reported in the *Los Angeles Times*. "At a time when Congress prepares to crack down further on illegal immigration and self-appointed militias patrol the U.S. border to stem the flow, Saturday's rally represented a massive response, part of what immigration advocates are calling an unprecedented effort to mobilize immigrants and their supporters nationwide."[9]

Immigration reform advocates predicted the beginning of a national movement when Hispanics, Latinos, and Latins across the country took to the streets in rallies, marches, and demonstrations. "There has never been this kind of mobilization in the immigrant community ever," Joshua Hoyt, executive director of the Illinois Coalition for Immigrant and Refugee Rights, told the *Los Angeles Times*. "They have kicked the sleeping giant. It's the beginning of a massive immigrant civil rights struggle."

Not unlike the early morning fog that vaporizes without a trace, where, in the three years since those massive rallies across the country erupted, has all that energy and determination gone?

That same year, in Mexico, the most contentious presidential election in that nation's history was held in July. Felipe Calderón, candidate from the right-of-center PAN, narrowly defeated Andrés López Obrador, candidate from the left-of-center PRD. The election was so close that many of López Obrador's supporters denounced what they claimed was election fraud. For his part, López Obrador refused to concede defeat, and staged rallies—some drawing more than half a million people—declaring to set up protests, stage sit-ins, and render Mexico "ungovernable" unless his victory was recognized. In one rally, on July 30, 2006, more than half a million supporters filled the plaza and streets surrounding the Presidential Palace in Mexico City. "I propose we stay here permanently until the court resolves this," he declared to his supporters. "I declare that we stay here day and night."[10]

Although there were, as there are in elections the world over, irregularities here and there, the recount sampling confirmed that Felipe Calderón had received about 240,000 more votes than Andrés López Obrador, Mexico's Supreme Court ruled. "We do not recognize Felipe Calderón as president, nor any officials he appoints, nor any acts carried out by his de-facto government," López Obrador told reporters.[11] He went further, vowing to create a "parallel" government that would take over the nation. "Andrés Manuel López Obrador, convinced he won't be awarded the presidency, has vowed to create a parallel leftist government and is urging Mexicans not to recognize the apparent victory of the ruling party's Felipe Calderón," Mark Stevenson reported in the *Washington Post*. "Some predict his parallel initiative— which López Obrador's supporters call the 'legitimate government'—could turn those protest camps into the core of a violent revolt, especially if the government tries to shut it down."[12]

Felipe Calderón took office, and Andrés López Obrador was relegated to staging rallies around the country, which were hardly more than an inconvenience to the Mexican government. In the United States, immigration reform slipped from the spotlight and all the predictions about the unstoppable political clout of Latinos to force Washington to move forward on this issue came to nothing.

In both cases, from all appearances, there were the ingredients for sustained political movements. American civil rights activists were incredulous to the turnout in marches across the country, and predicted a sustained—and successful—"Latino" civil rights movement, modeled on the African American civil rights movement, but centered on immigration reform as a question of human rights. Mexico watchers looked on with apprehension, at the prospect of massive riots and violence throughout Mexico as two men claimed to be the "legitimate" presidents; State Department personnel prepared to issue "travel advisories" at the first sign of civil unrest as Mexico's inauguration day approached.

What commentators failed to consider was the worldview of the indigenous peoples: Jean-Paul Sartre declared the Mexicans to be the first existentialists. Mexicans and Mexican Hispanics are slow to anger, seek others who have their *confianza,* organize along the principles of communalism to pursue goals with which they have *simpatía,* and then vent their frustrations in one single act of community expression. That energy invested in these demonstrations has their cultural context, and the demonstration *itself* is the goal, an idea that is counterintuitive to mainstream Americans. The purpose is a *public display* of intent and expression of common purpose, expressing a single opinion in a communalistic fashion. That is the objective, *in its entirety.* There is no follow-through, there is no political movement, and there is no subsequent repercussion apart from the collective display of unity.

In consequence, there is no immigration reform in the United States, and no civil war in Mexico.

From a Western perspective, there is an inexplicable element to this way of thinking that is almost Shakespearean in its tragedy.

It is, in fact, something out of *Macbeth*: "Life's but a walking shadow, a poor player, that struts and frets his hour upon the stage, and then is heard no more; it is a tale told by an idiot, full of sound and fury, signifying nothing."[13]

What are the management lessons from this case study when it comes to labor relations with Hispanics, Latinos, and Latins to be taken from these differences?

There are several, and they speak to a two-part approach to labor relations. In the previous chapter we saw how cultural differences among Hispanics are accelerating the process by which performance reviews are conducted. The observation that, when it comes to the communal tendency of the Mexican Hispanic, there are cultural obstacles to what, in mainstream American society, is seen as "natural" follow-through, successful managers and supervisors need to develop *interpersonal intelligence:* how to harness the cultural sensibilities of the Hispanic, Latino, and Latin workforce in a way that contributes to achieving goals. In Spanish the word is *colaborar,* to collaborate. But whereas in English, to collaborate is descriptive of a certain set of actions, among Hispanics there are cultural connotations: *colaborar* means to collaborate as a *team player. Colaborar* is what Hispanics do to show allegiance and emotional investment. A Hispanic mother asks a co-worker to *colaborar* not just to buy a box of Girl Scout cookies, but as a way for that co-worker to show affection for her friend, a maternal affection for her friend's daughter's troop, and as an act of solidarity with the ideals and values exemplified by the Girl Scouts of America.

That is a great deal to ask of a three-syllable word, but there is a great deal of "social capital" in that one word: *colaborar.*

For the Hispanic, Latino—and certainly Latin—nonsalaried employee, managers and supervisors need to approach labor relations armed with interpersonal intelligence. This strategy has been used, primarily in California and Texas, as a way of addressing concerns among rank-and-file employees who harbor grievances and express job dissatisfaction. For many organizations, proactive measures to ameliorate employee discontent are seen as a strategy to keep at bay efforts to organize workers into unions. On one level, attempts to address employee concerns, foster a nurturing workplace environment, and prevent labor issues from becoming alienating and embittering are sound management policies. If you review Spanish-language reports, manuals, and labor materials, it is surprising to see how often the word *colaborar* is used, underscoring the pervasive nature of that concept throughout Latin America.

That said, it cannot be stressed enough that the history of unions and unionism in Mexico is far different from unions in the United States. In Mexico, unions were, until 2000, affiliated with the government, and they functioned under government auspices. Mexican Hispanics see unions as government-aligned entities that mediate between employers and government authorities. This is fundamentally different from the United States experience, where unions are independent of the federal government. Not unlike the natural misunderstandings when Americans say "Social Security" and Mexicans say "Seguro Social," Mexican Hispanics do not see unions and management to be adversaries, or antagonists, but rather, they see them as natural partners working to ensure that labor laws are followed.

This is a cultural and socioeconomic conflict that is fraught with suspicions and misunderstandings: Mexican Hispanics see efforts to keep unions away as an act that undermines *confianza* and shows a fundamental lack of *simpatía* from their managers and supervisors. This is a different way of saying that Latino and Latin employees are predisposed to support union membership. This is also one reason Hispanics have encountered significant labor problems at Wal-Mart, the nation's largest employer, and one of the most antiunion companies in the United States. Without entering into the merits of unions or of Wal-Mart's position, it is important to understand the cultural and historic ideas and ideals that inform the perceptions of Hispanic, Latino, and Latin employees. What can be pointed out with certainty, however, is that by approaching an American workforce with a Hispanic "collectivistic approach," it is possible to approximate a "communalism" that is consistent with a successful business model: Costco pays an average of $17 an hour, covers 90% of health insurance costs for all its employees, and enjoys greater employee and customer satisfaction than its largest competitors— Sam's Club and Wal-Mart. "We're trying to build a company that's going to be here 50 and 60 years from now," Costco CEO Jim Sinegal argues, sounding more like a collectivist than an individualist. "We owe that to our employees, that they can count on us for security. We have 140,000 employees and their families; that's a significant number of people who count on us."[14]

What is also clear is that many of the things that employees hope to find in unions are consistent with the cultural comfort of working in an environment where there is a vertical hierarchy, and where managers and supervisors understand the notions of *confianza* and *simpatía*. How Wal-Mart has missed these concepts is instructive, and it represents a cautionary tale for others. "New employees [at Wal-Mart] are shown videotapes explaining that instead of unionizing, they benefit from the open door policy, allowing them to take their complaints beyond the supervisors to higher management. When the United Food and Commercial Workers tried to organize workers across the country, labor experts were brought in for 'coaching sessions' with personnel who support unionization," PBS reported in *Store Wars: When Wal-Mart Comes to Town*. "Employees complained that these were intimidation sessions. Many such complaints are currently on file with the National Labor Relations Board."[15]

The sense of grievance among Mexican Hispanics is further intensified by the cultural misunderstanding that the notion of "union" conveys to non-Hispanics in the United States. When managers or supervisors express hostility toward unions and union membership, this constitutes a profound and lasting affront to Hispanics in general. The contempt speaks more to the cultural values— communalism, *confianza,* traditional values in the concept of *colaborar*—that are internalized. The message conveyed is that management doesn't value Hispanic culture, society, or tradition, and therefore managers and supervisors see little that the Hispanic employee can bring to the table, especially if a union representative comes along for a free meal. These, of course, are false impressions, but that's how the human mind works: no matter how often and how many different ways to say it, for instance, siblings are often jealous of each other, even when parents strive to be consistently fair.

At the essence of human psychology, we *internalize* all manner of *rejection* in predictable patterns; this why psychology is a discipline. In the emerging American workplace, it is a matter of interpersonal intelligence. A fundamental key to making things "work" is to understand how to use properly the concept of *colaborar*, not to subvert cultural values. This is what is lost in translation, and executives at Wal-Mart, not unlike at most American companies and organizations, speak past their Hispanic, Latino, and Latin employees, resulting in miscommunication that alienates and creates tension in the workplace. One fact that is often overlooked, for instance, is the ability of human beings to form strong emotional bonds to both their organization, and how they prefer to nurture teamwork.

Consider the compelling drama that unfolded when Pan Am World Airways went out of business. Three unions generally represent airline workers, one for pilots, another for in-flight crews, and another for ground personnel. The strong bonds that employees have for their respective unions in no way diminished the love they had for Pan Am. In Miami, long after Pan Am had ceased to exist, it was not uncommon to see people driving around with bumper stickers that read, "Gone but not forgotten." In New York, when Met Life bought the Pan Am building and announced it would rename —and rebrand—the building, the day the Pan Am logo was taken down, former Hispanic and Latin employees held a "wake." "It was like a second death," one pilot told reporters at that time.

This is the kind of loyalty and pride that encapsulates what Hispanic society denotes through *colaborar*. Critics charge management of attempting to coop this cultural value as a way of diminishing support among nonsalaried employees for unions, union organizing, and union membership, to the detriment of the well-being of

Hispanics, Latinos, and Latins. An emerging body of research, in fact, documents that union membership increases the well-being of Hispanic, Latino, and Latin nonsalaried employees. "The benefits of unionization were also high for Latino workers in typically low-wage occupations. Latino workers in unions in otherwise low-wage occupations earned, on average, 16.6 percent more than their non-union counterparts. Unionized Latino workers in low-wage occupations were also 41 percentage points more likely than comparable non-union workers to have employer-provided health insurance, and 18 percentage points more likely to have a pension plan," John Schmitt, of the Center for Economic and Policy Research, reported in September 2008. "The findings demonstrate that Latino [sic] workers who are able to bargain collectively earn more and are more likely to have benefits associated with good jobs. The data, therefore, suggest that better protection of workers' right to unionize would have a substantial positive impact on the pay and benefits of Latino [sic] workers."[16]

Civil and labor rights activists point to these statistics as evidence for greater Hispanic membership in unions. "While expanding union-worker membership is important, we must stand firmly on the side of those in the fight for social and economic justice, concretely this means supporting the rights of undocumented immigrant workers, African American workers, Latinos [sic], women, and the poor," Karega Hart, a black activist, wrote in "The Black Commentator."[17]

Faced with the prospect of acrimonious labor relations, management throughout corporate America remains ambivalent about their relationship to nonsalaried Hispanic, Latino, and Latin employees. The "emotional" baggage that non-Hispanics associate with unions colors their ability to embrace a fresh approach, one that transcends American labor history. The more successful organizations, however, are the ones that incorporate the values Hispanics embrace through proactive management. There are many advocates of union organizing who are critical of any management effort to appeal directly to Hispanic, Latino, and Latin nonsalaried employees through proactive policies.

Hispanics, Organized Labor, and Labor Relations

For organized labor, the ascendance of Hispanics, Latinos, and Latins in the workplace presents an opportunity to increase membership, and regain political clout, which naturally occurs during economic downturns. That Mexican Hispanics are an "at-risk" population, there are powerful socioeconomic forces that embolden the expectations of labor leaders. For many organizations, deeply ingrained in the business culture is an antagonism toward union membership and union leadership. As has been shown, in the nationalist-socialist development models pursued throughout Latin America in the previous century, oftentimes organized labor operated as an extension of the national government, an instrument through which social programs and goals were met. This meant, of course, that unions were seldom "independent," but rather, were always dependent on the government in power.

In the Hispanic diaspora, that framework, in which unions are one mechanism by which members of the "out-group" seek to adopt the characteristics of the "in-group" is one strategy for moving from acculturation to assimilation, a means by which Hispanics hope to integrate themselves more fully into the mainstream of American life. For management, it is instructive to understand the underlying forces inherent in the Hispanic diaspora that are driving changes in management-labor relations.

Among these are: Organized labor in the United States is benefiting from the tendency of the Hispanic diaspora, the "out-group" in the American workplace, to adopt the characteristics of the mainstream, Anglo-Protestant American "in-group" around them. Hispanic cultural values are collectivistic in nature and favor an approach to problem solving that is communal in nature. Latin American societies have a strong tradition of officially sanctioning unions. Hispanic workers prefer to use labor unions to speak on their behalf to management, often to compensate for the lack of fluency in English. Hispanic workers see labor unions as organizations not to confront management, but to articulate their concerns and interests, mechanisms for ensuring that their "dignity" is recognized, that they are as individuals "respected" by their managers and supervisors, one way of compensating for the disparate power, status, and economic levels between "out-group" and "in-group" members.

Hispanic, Latino, and Latin membership support for unions is generating a backlash against Hispanics' ascendance in the United States, one that intrudes onto the American workplace. This situation is exacerbated by the emergence of "brown" in the nation's discussion of race. As race relations in the United States move from "black-white" to "black-brown-white," the phenomenon of "black on brown" tension is emerging as a social problem for the nation. Management should recognize this as an issue in the same way that it once recognized both racial discrimination and sexism as impediments to a healthy work environment. Organizations should adopt policies that affirm and validate the concern Hispanic, Latino, and Latin employees have for the subtle resistance they encounter as a direct consequence of their ascendance transforming the nation's demographics.

These concerns come at a time when, through the natural expansions and contractions of the business cycle, the American labor market is moving toward a more inclusive approach, where the concerns of labor are of foremost priority for policymakers. This approach is consistent with both the priorities of the "New Deal" and the "Great Society" that, together, since the 1960s, resulted in paternalistic legislation. This socioeconomic approach, which was favored prior to the advent of globalization in the 1980s, encouraged proactive laws that have strengthened social-welfare states. This is consistent with contemporary American economic thinking. As Cornell economist Robert Frank explains:

> Paternalistic laws are often attacked on the grounds that they unjustly abridge individual freedom. . . . True individual sovereignty implies that people have not only the right not to be restricted by others—as the libertarian position stresses—but also the right not to be subjected to behavior they consider harmful. If the concept of individual sovereignty is to have any intelligible meaning at all, there can be no distinction

> *in principle* between the legitimacy of these two subsidiary
> rights: The right not to be offended is just as worthy of our
> respect as the right not to be restricted. Yet these rights
> cannot be exercised simultaneously. . . . The libertarian who
> insists that the right not to be restricted cannot, as a matter of
> principle, ever be negotiated away, shows contempt for the
> rights of people to resolve such issues for themselves.[18]

Galbraith described the benefits of this process as it occurred in the United States, decades before reporters commented upon the ability of local governments to provide basic services, this way:

> The poor in the United States, while none could doubt their
> degradation and misery, were once largely invisible—poor
> blacks were hidden away on the farms and plantations of the
> rural South with primitive food, clothing, and shelter, little in
> the way of education, and no civil rights. Many poor whites
> were unseen on the hills and in the hollows of Appalachia.
> Poverty was not a problem when distant, out of sight. Only as
> economic, political, and social change brought the needy to the
> cities did welfare become a public concern, the poor now
> living next to an unnerved urban population, the former's
> material want standing in deep contrast with the material
> comforts of the relatively affluent city dweller.[19]

In the changed American workplace, where Hispanic sensibilities are shaping how the workplace operates, tapping into the concept of *colaborar* requires specific policies and approaches to labor relations that meet the criteria inherent in Hispanic society, some of which are discussed in the following text.

Listen carefully, encouraging employees to speak slowly and calmly: One of the cultural consequences of *superarse* is an inherent lack of confidence and assertiveness in expressing one's point of view. For many nonsalaried Mexican Hispanics there is the tendency to avoid direct eye contact, particularly with supervisors. Observe body language and send signals of reassurance, which include leaning toward the employee and never crossing your arms when listening.

Communicate clearly, concisely, and in accessible language: state job instructions clearly, and be careful about being too impatient with language; the average Latin employee has a sixth grade education and reading comprehension skills are not at a high school level.

Encourage employees to speak up about their wants and needs: take an added interest in your employees' adjustments to life here: Do they know how to access medical facilities, insurance, and public safety? Are their families getting involved in community programs? These approaches foster *confianza* and convey a manager's or supervisor's *simpatía* to their staff and direct-reports.

Encourage and motivate through praise: don't be reluctant to give out pats on the back and praise good work, but praise a team publicly and an individual privately. Any physical contact, such as a pat on the back or a squeeze on the shoulder, should be done in public view, and accompanied by work-related praise. Male managers and supervisors, as always, should be particularly mindful of appearances when dealing with female employees: the line between camaraderie and *confianza* can be crossed in a careless gesture or thoughtless comment.

Develop weekly or monthly meetings in which employees are encouraged to speak up: one way of building *confianza* is to inculcate a certain level of trust, where employees believe their opinions matter, and that they are encouraged to think of proactive, constructive ideas and criticisms to improve their work environment and their productivity. This is a process of empowerment, one in which employees increase their sense of self-worth, value to the organization, and confidence.

Engage in proactive problem resolution: one of the principal elements of *colaborar* is that it encourages creative problem-resolution, which reinforces *simpatía* among employees. If appropriate allow a unit or department to select a "go-to" person to be a sounding board for employees' concerns. This is particularly important when it comes to non-Hispanics who, as they witness the changing demographics around them, become apprehensive and insecure; tensions between Hispanics and black employees are of great concern.

Coordinate efforts to build employee-generated consensus: encourage employees to take a greater role in decisions and management tasks, and provide them with management skill training, consistent with the ideals of communalism. Inherent in the Mexican Hispanic's worldview is the tendency to generate a consensus, one reason labor unions have met with tremendous success in enlisting Latinos and Latins as members.

These policies are reinforced when certain actions are taken that convey to employees that managers are sensitive to their worth as individuals and the obstacles they confront acculturating to the greater non-Hispanic society in which they live. Recommended steps for cultivating employee loyalty through *simpatía* include:

- Learn to pronounce names properly. This shows respect on a personal level and conveys that managers recognize the importance of each employee as an individual.

- Express your understanding of the importance of visiting family on the holidays and provide adequate time off for your workers. This may conflict with company policies, which is one reason that human resources are struggling to accommodate Hispanic cultural values, not unlike the religious requirements of Jewish employees (and to a lesser extent Muslim employees) have been incorporated by most organizations.

- Many Hispanic, Latino, and Latin employees have extra difficulty securing transportation to and from work. Helping in this area encourages your employees to see themselves as an integral part of the organization, and to have greater self-confidence.

- Managers and supervisors at some organizations help their employees by offering phone cards and money transfers to their home countries. Many human resources departments work with Latin (and Latino) employees to support various community projects in their hometowns through Hometown Associations, known as HTAs.

In some ways, we have come full circle, because the collectivistic values of the Hispanic diaspora encourage the resurgence of American unions, while providing management with strategies to incorporate what Hispanic, Latino—and certainly Latin—employees look for through collective bargaining and union representation as they acculturate from the "otherness" of being an "out-group" toward the mainstream status associated with being part of the "in-group." Here, too, is where there is a convergence in the American workplace and the greater Hispanic worldview. In fact, if the core values are adequately addressed through management that is responsive to the social needs and private wants of their employees, how is this objectionable? What is important for managers and supervisors throughout the United States to understand, moreover, is the more successful approach that needs to be taken to achieve a superior societal outcome. It is possible to harness the power of *colaborar* and to use this cultural value as a way of strengthening the concepts of *confianza* and *simpatía*.

In the absence of strong governments in Hispanic countries that have been unable to deliver crucial services to all their citizens, other social forces evolved, with the communalism inherent in the concept of *colaborar* being a central component of the Hispanic diaspora's "social capital."

In Review

- The "out-group" status of the Hispanic diaspora in the United States affects labor relations with "in-group" Anglo-Protestant American management.
- Globalization revealed cultural differences among members of the Hispanic diaspora.
    - Mexican Hispanics resist Cuban American managers.
    - Cuban, and to a lesser extent Puerto Rican, Hispanics encounter the same difficulties understanding the collectivistic worldview Mexican Hispanics inherited from the continent's First Peoples.

- Acculturation levels differentiate Mexican Hispanics from Caribbean Hispanics, making the former more inclined to prefer to engage in dialogue with management through union representatives.

- Mexican Hispanics display a greater "passivity," which favors union membership for collective bargaining.

- Management can use *confianza* as a strategic approach to duplicate the traditional role of unions in building a rapport with Hispanic, Latino, and Latin employees, provided these strategies enhance employees' "social capital."

Part III

The Hispanic Employee and the Organization's Future

The single-most important issue for Hispanic, Latino, and Latin nonex-empt employees ("blue-collar" Hispanic, Latino, and Latin workers) is how they are perceived by their non-Hispanic colleagues in the work-place. Hispanic employees, more than non-Hispanics, express frus-tration at the career advancement roadblocks they encounter in the workplace. The traditional ways to signal to managers that an employee is ready for greater responsibility—documenting achievements and responsibilities in the current position, scheduling a meeting to dis-cuss their roles and career objectives, requesting to move to the "next" level within an organization—often fail to work for Hispanics as a demographic group.

The role of *superarse,* the cultural equivalent of "getting ahead" in American culture, is one that is ingrained in Hispanic cultures, particularly among Latins, who, by the simple virtue of having immi-grated to the United States—and becoming part of the Hispanic dias-pora—have taken a bold step in "getting ahead." Managers can be more successful in cultivating Latin employees by recognizing that whatever task they are doing for the organization, this is simply another "step" on the road to becoming a better person and build-ing a better future for themselves and their families. To this end, artic-ulating goals, instructions, and objectives with clarity of purpose is crucial.

Cultural and linguistic differences make it crucial that unam-biguous and clear instructions are disseminated, and that classroom training opportunities are afforded. How workshops, training, and workplace procedures can contribute to an individual's ability to *superarse* and how these steps are part of the organization's success—how each employee contributes to the organization's ability to fulfill its "mission statement" in the "big picture"—telegraphs the unity of purpose to which everyone contributes.

How can managers balance the expectations of Hispanic, Latino, and Latin employees with the realities of pragmatic management?

How to Keep Hispanic Nonexempt Employees Challenged and Satisfied in the Workplace

To a large degree, Hispanic, Latino, and Latin employees are held back by their own fears, and of these, language looms large. As heirs of cultures that favor communalistic approaches to societal development, there are strong inhibitions in embracing the individualism of American society. Although there are higher rates of small business ownership among Hispanics than non-Hispanics, these initiatives reflect a "family" business (communal initiative), not an "entrepreneurial" one (individual initiative). In larger organizations, Hispanic employees who identify themselves as "Latino" face emerging challenges associated with their lack of fluency in Spanish. The question of language is closely associated with the success or failure of acculturating and assimilating into the mainstream of American life, in which education is a major component. For human resources professionals, a parallel concern centers on the health risks Hispanics, Latinos, and Latins face, and how they are an "at risk" population in the workplace. Strategies for addressing these issues are discussed subsequently.

The Linguistic Glass Ceiling

From the 1910s through the early 1950s it was common for Hispanic students, primarily those of Mexican ancestry in Texas, California, and the Southwest, and Puerto Ricans in the Northeast, to be punished for speaking Spanish in school.[1] This was consistent with the ideas of the time, when "immersion" was seen as the most effective way of helping students learn English, acculturate to mainstream American life, and become integrated into American society. Not unlike generations before them, starting with the waves that arrived through Ellis Island in New York during the nineteenth century as part of the Industrial Revolution, contemporaneous theorists advanced the ideas that the United States was, and would remain, a monolingual society. Generations of Hispanics, Latinos, and Latins accepted this. "We understand the importance of hard work, learning English, and getting an education, and we want to work together to help everyone share in the American Dream," Raúl Yzaguirre of the National Council of La Raza (NCLR) commented as recently as 2004.[2]

Since the 1970s, however, an unexpected thing happened on the way to English as a Second Language (ESL) class: the United States embarked on the road to becoming a bilingual consumer economy. In this century, many Latinos and monolingual Hispanics are not fluent in Spanish, and this lack of fluency—as the United States continues to evolve as a bilingual consumer economy—impedes their career advancement.

These linguistic obstacles in corporate communications—the unanswerable problem of the Spanish language in the workplace—is made even more vexing by the problem of Latino children who need to learn their own native language, Spanish. "Spanish 101 for Latinos" is a serious matter, a continuing issue central to the career advancement of U.S.-born Latino employees. "To fully understand the goals and challenges of teaching Spanish to Spanish speakers," the Southwest Comprehensive Center, under contract to the Department of Education, declared, "it is important to understand the diverse backgrounds of students who participate in Spanish courses and their motivations for studying a language they already know."[3] A possible solution: accept the emergence of a bilingual consumer economy? How can a firm most efficiently manage the Hispanic salaried employee to achieve its goal of a sustainable competitive advantage? To a large extent the answers are found in the cultural traits Hispanics share. Managers who earn the *confianza* of the Hispanic, Latino, and Latin employee will elicit greater loyalty, particularly important during turbulent economic times.

One strategy successfully used throughout the United States and Latin America among promising employees is to offer the opportunity for them to *superarse* through continuing education benefits (such as tuition rebates), or establishing company-sponsored English as a Second-Language classes (for Hispanics and Latins, primarily), accent elimination classes (for Latins), and Spanish 101 for Latinos (SfL) for U.S.-born Latinos. The question of language becomes crucial, a conflicted barrier that divides Hispanics. The subject of a "linguistic glass ceiling" was mentioned in Chapter 5. A closer examination of this issue reveals there are two sides to the matter.

For Latin immigrants, who are fluent in English and who were recruited from their home countries for specific management and executive positions, there are insecurities about pronunciation of American English. Time and again, working with Hispanic executives at Fortune 500 companies, the concern, quietly voiced, is their desire to speak with standard American English pronunciation, a "Walter Cronkite" or "Tom Brokaw" Midwestern American sound. Accent elimination courses are a benefit that is often provided to them, one way of enticing them to perform their duties with more confidence. This concern, of course, is not relegated to Latin immigrants alone, but to most managers recruited overseas for whom English is a second (or third) language. Human resource professionals are well versed in the obstacles this category of employee poses, and how to provide these benefits.

It becomes a more complicated matter when the subject becomes the fluency in Spanish of U.S.-born Hispanics, primarily Latinos. The assumption non-Hispanics make is that Latino employees are fluent in Spanish. This is seldom the case; most are proficient in Spanish, but few are fluent. An even smaller percentage is well versed in business Spanish. In the late 1990s, I assisted companies in California, Illinois, New York, and Texas to expand efforts to reach Hispanic consumers in the United States and increase their cross-border business. One daunting obstacle was the inability of "Latinos"—almost always Mexican Hispanics or Puerto Ricans—to be able to converse in business Spanish. It remains disheartening to ask a Latino how one says, "To whom it may concern" in Spanish and see a blank stare.

This linguistic glass ceiling has long been an issue among Hispanic intellectuals in the United States. "[E]ducators testified [in 1966] before the U.S. Commission on Civil Rights that Mexican-American children were being punished for speaking Spanish on school grounds in other parts of the country," Rubén Salazar, an award-winning Hispanic journalist wrote in a classic Op-Ed piece, "Mexican-American's Dilemma: He's Unfit in Either Language," published February 27, 1970, in the *Los Angeles Times*. "Belated bilingual education programs for Mexican-Americans are geared toward using the Spanish language as a tool only until the Chicano kid has learned enough English to overcome the 'problem' of speaking Spanish. These are not truly bilingual programs, which should be the teaching of both languages on an equal basis."

Almost four decades later, the problem Salazar identified is still true. "At the various jobs I've worked, I have often seen workers discriminated against because of language, but usually it is because they don't speak English," David Madrid says. "Here, I feel discriminated against by my peers because I don't speak Spanish. I've always been aware of the social segregation between Chicanos and Mexican immigrants, at school and on the street. At this job, I feel unwelcome, and even face animosity, because I am Chicano and can't speak Spanish."[4] Recall James Hamilton-Paterson's observation, which here fits attitudes of many Latinos whose high school dropout rates show that they remain "unconvinced by the idea of education."

It can be discouraging, particularly when U.S.-born Latinos express frustration, and anger, at being passed over for promotions by foreign-born Hispanics and Latin American immigrants who are fluent in both English and Spanish. The resentment that many Latinos experience constitutes an impediment to their career development and success in the business world. It is a phenomenon of increasing economic importance, especially during times of economic transition, when fully bilingual and bicultural Hispanic job candidates outshine monolingual and assimilated Latino ones. This is not lost on college administrators, who, in the same way that they find that they have to use affirmative action to keep qualified Asian students from being accepted into certain schools, they now have to contend with the predominance of Caribbean Hispanics, whose success displaces Mexican Hispanics.

For Mexican immigrants, and many Mexican Hispanics, a further complication is that there are differences between wages and salaries in the United States and many Latin American societies. Consider that, for instance, in Mexico, the federal government establishes guidelines on salaries that are based on the minimum wage. The salary for a medical assistant, as an example, may have a federal guideline of, say, between eight and ten minimum wages. So if the minimum wage is X, then a medical assistant should be expected to make between eight and ten times that figure. That is the norm for just about every professional. In the United States, salaries are not multiples of the minimum wage, and this creates a conflict in helping Latin and Latino employees understand what is "fair."

The Challenge of Acculturation and Continuing Education

For Latin immigrants and less-privileged Latinos, one obstacle encountered, by virtue of being in the Hispanic diaspora, is the social isolation that is associated with being a minority. The desire to *superarse* is one manifestation of the desire to move from being shackled to the limitations of being part of an "out-group" and to expand their opportunities by becoming part of the "in-group" to the best of their abilities. If the Hispanic, Latino, and Latin workforce is divided into various levels of acculturation, where "fully acculturated" is the same as assimilation; "partially acculturated" denotes a person who is bicultural, proficient in non-Hispanic American society; and "unacculturated" identifies an individual who is isolated, meaning he or she is "Hispanic dominant," the results are instructive:

- 21% are "Fully Acculturated"
- 23% are "Partially Acculturated"
- 56% are "Unacculturated"[5]

Three out of four Hispanic, Latino, or Latin employees are not "proficient" in understanding, or capable of participating fully, in the mainstream American society.

Social critics, including Harvard's Samuel Huntington, use these results to argue for mandatory immersion, including making English the official language of the United States. This view is substantiated by studies of the military, where a strong, hierarchical line of command structure and a culture of strict discipline prevail; Latinos and Latins have been shown to acculturate more efficiently in this environment. In fact, when the military draft was in place, the highest rates of acculturation were reported. "[T]he end of the draft may have eliminated a useful forum for intercultural and intracultural learning for both [Hispanic and non-Hispanic enlisted personnel], although the volunteer military does have an impact on Latino acculturation," David Leal reported in the journal *Armed Forces & Society.*[6]

This is consistent with organizations that have proactive programs to help Hispanic, Latino, and Latin employees acculturate. In addition to offering, or facilitating, English as a Second Language (ESL) classes, there are other immersion workshops and continuing education opportunities that play a pivotal role. Elected public officials hold seminars to work together and develop strategies that help organizations throughout the nation implement programs that empower Latino and Latin employees through educational opportunities. "As the second largest population group in the United States, the educational attainment of Latino youth is intrinsically connected to the nation's future success," Samuel Robles of the National Association of Latino Elected and Appointed Officials (NALEO) says. "Demographers have long projected the social and economic trajectory of the country's shifting population trends. Census population estimates indicate that the Latino population will continue a rapid rate of growth. The steady increase of this very youthful population makes it imperative that Latino youth benefit from full access to educational experiences of the highest quality."[7]

This remains an elusive goal, particularly during economic downturns when budget constraints in the public and private sectors alike are severe. Given the constraints imposed by prevailing economic

circumstances, management has to work within the realistic parameters when it comes to offering, subsidizing, or reimbursing for educational opportunities. Oftentimes, in-house workshops and
seminars, many of which can be conducted with the participation
of organized labor at organizations that are unionized, increase the
acculturation levels of employees. Here is one area where the collectivistic cultural traditions foster the necessary *confianza* among
Latino and Latin employees for greater participation—and success—
of these initiatives. That said, the limited success of public education to prepare Hispanics for a more thorough integration and
participation in the mainstream of American life continues to challenge employers. At a time when the demands of globalized economies
are greater than ever before, the American workforce is undergoing
fundamental changes that are institutional in nature, and the need
for an educated, acculturated workforce continues to grow.

An "At-Risk" Employee

Implicit in framing Hispanics as a demographic whose "otherness"
designates them as an "out-group" is the notion of stress: members
of the Hispanic diaspora, like members of all other diasporas and
minorities, live with stress and anxiety that are sociocultural in origin, and on many levels, *subliminal.* That the origin of this stress is
metaphysical does not mean that there are no *physical* manifestations over an extended period of time. In fact, one of the most critical public health issues confronting the United States is the realization
that Hispanics, Latinos, and Latins are an "at risk" population for
chronic medical conditions.

At the beginning of this book, the observation was made that
anthropologists classify human societies based on the principal carbohydrate in their diets: wheat, rice, or corn. There may be adap-
tive responses to foods, and when other factors are taken into
account, as Hispanics adopt diets that are more consistent with
dietary norms in the United States—more wheat- than corn-based—
there is an increase in health problems associated with these dietary
changes. As a general rule, blue-collar Hispanics, Latinos, and Latins
suffer higher incidence of poverty than white-collar Hispanics,

Latinos, and Latins. To this, factor in the fact that Mexican Hispanics, who are *mestizos*, are more likely to be blue-collar workers than Caribbean Hispanics, who are black or white. Finally, take into account the stresses associated with the "lookism" associated with the more apparent "otherness" of brown Hispanics, Latinos, and Latins versus white or black Hispanics, Latinos, and Latins, and there are measurable differences that affect the specific demographic groups within the Hispanic diaspora in the United States.

One of the more unexpected observations, documented by the National Institutes of Health, the Centers for Disease Control and Prevention, and the Mexican Migration Project, among other organizations, is that the longer a Latin immigrant remains in the United States, the worse his or her health becomes.[8] It is as if living in their home countries, where people tend to eat lower on the food chain, becomes a health obstacle the longer they remain in the United States, where their dietary habits consist of highly refined, packaged, and pre-packaged foods. At times, there are stark paradoxes. Hispanics who describe themselves as "Hispanic women," aged 25–40, for instance, once they earn a graduate degree, earn $7,867 more annually than their non-Hispanic counterparts.[9] Hispanics who describe themselves as "Latina women," aged 15–24, on the other hand, have the highest suicide rates of any group. "Latina teenagers in the United States are attempting suicide more than any other group in the nation. In 2005, 14.9 percent of Hispanic female youths attempted suicide, according to the Centers for Disease Control and Prevention, compared with 9.8 percent of black female youths and 9.3 percent of white female youths," Christina Hernández reported in the Columbia News Service in the summer of 2007.[10] This is an alarming difference in fate. It is, however, the end result that is, to a substantial degree, a product of different educational attainment levels, how each group of women sees itself, and its place in the American society. Indeed, it is amazing to see what a little *more* education and *a little* less anguish will do for one's prospects in life.

The Hispanic diaspora is also at greater risk for certain conditions than non-Hispanics, and these increased risks, over the course of their working lives, are of concern to managers, supervisors, and other administrators. "The effect of acculturation on Latino health is complex and not well understood," Marielena Lara and colleagues wrote in "Acculturation and Latino Health in the United States," published by the Rand Corporation.[11] "In certain areas—substance abuse, dietary practices, and birth outcomes—there is evidence that acculturation has a negative effect and that it is associated with worse health outcomes, behaviors, or perceptions." For the purposes of this discussion, management should remain cognizant that blue-collar Hispanic, Latino, and Latin workers are more at risk for certain medical problems than non-Hispanic employees, specifically the following:

Diabetes: "For Latinos, acculturation was related to increased education, and more acculturated Latinos were less likely to have experiential models of the disease [diabetes]," Catherine Chesla and colleagues wrote in "Differences in Personal Models among Latinos and European Americans."[12] This means that Hispanics, Latinos, and Latins with lower educational attainment—and the accompanying incomes—are at greater risk for diabetes. The estimated cost to American business is a staggering $174 billion a year in health care costs, and the problem is so acute there is an organization dedicated to helping organizations develop strategies to deal with diabetes in the workplace: diabetesatwork.org. The costs for non-Hispanic employees are higher, reflecting both a higher incidence of diabetes, and the fact that Latinos, more so than Hispanics or Latins, acquire diabetes at an earlier age in their work lives.

Obesity: The American population is experiencing an epidemic of obesity, and related health issues associated with being overweight. Hispanics, Latinos, and Latins, on the other hand, are among the segments of the population that are at higher risk for obesity. It is believed that the stress related to acculturation contributes to the coping mechanisms within the Hispanic diaspora that contribute to higher rates of obesity. "Among Latinos, acculturation has been associated with obesity risk, suboptimal dietary choices including lack of breast-feeding, low intake of fruits and vegetables, a higher consumption of fats and artificial drinks containing high levels of refined sugar, smoking, and alcohol consumption," Rafael Pérez-Escamilla and Predrag Putnik reported in the Journal of Nutrition.[13] These findings are confirmed by other studies.[14] This chronic condition affects the overall health costs of every organization, and as Hispanics, Latinos, and Latins increase their presence in the American workforce, preventing obesity among employees becomes a more urgent management task.

Alzheimer's: Although a genetic predisposition is not suspected, for the Hispanic diaspora, there is a higher incidence of Alzheimer's. Several "factors, many linked to low income or cultural dislocation, may put Hispanics at greater risk for dementia, including higher rates of diabetes, obesity, cardiovascular disease, stroke and possibly hypertension," Pam Belluck reported. "Less education may make Hispanic immigrants more vulnerable to those medical conditions and to dementia because scientists say education may increase the brain's plasticity or ability to compensate for symptoms. And some researchers cite as risk factors stress from financial hardship or cultural adjustment."[15] In this report, public health officials are studying factors that may be responsible for the higher incidence among Hispanics: "We are concerned that the Latino population may have the highest amount of risk factors and prevalence, in comparison to the other cultures," María Carrillo, director of medical and scientific relations at the Alzheimer's Association, explains. Is there subconscious stress of living in the Hispanic diaspora that increases the risk factors associated with degenerative cognitive conditions?[16]

A Management Solution: Nurture *Confianza*

These "at-risk" conditions reflect, to a large degree, problems associated with acculturation levels, of course. But they also reflect an absence of *simpatía,* where Hispanic employees, by virtue of being members of an "out-group," lacking confidence in their language

skills, or not understanding fully how the American workplace operates, become disenfranchised and frustrate their supervisors. The
tendency to refer to how things are done in the "old country," and
the desire to recreate the collectivism and group cohesion with which
they are familiar creates problems in the workplace. The traditional
explanation for these obstacles has been that Hispanic employees
display various degrees of acculturation into the mainstream of
American life, and that the overwhelming majority are not fully
assimilated.

Concerns over the causal links between "out-group" status,
"acculturation," and being "at risk," are correct; but these are
exacerbated by managers reaching out to address the perceived
lack of "trust" that Hispanic employees feel. One reason Hispanics
depend on traditional approaches to "group cohesion" strategies
is that they feel alienated from their employers. That they are not
fully assimilated into the mainstream of American life contributes
to the sense of alienation and the resulting marginalization. The
solution, then, is for a proactive program to instill *confianza,*
which is best done between management and human resources.
The larger issue, of course, is one of understanding what motivates Hispanic employees. As is the case with people who are entering a new environment, Latin employees seek to build the
emotional bonds and trust level that is analogous to what constitutes *confianza.*

Recognizing that levels of acculturation are as different as the
individual employee, management should be mindful of not coming across as condescending, but rather, as concerned about the welfare of the employee and committed to helping the employee succeed
in the United States. The psychology of the Hispanic diaspora is
already one of alienation, and when language difficulties are added
to this equation, lack of trust mounts; particularly, as we have seen,
even "simple" assumptions—that Social Security in the United States
approximates Mexico's *Seguro Social,* for instance—are
incorrect.

This is what motivates Hispanic employees—particularly
Latins—and it is the sense that their employer is as committed to

them as they are expected to be to them. The emotional bonds that connect employee and employer are, in fact, one way of transcending the question of acculturation: integrity is a universally acknowledged trait in human societies. It is by addressing the concerns around the cultural value of *simpatía* that managers can cultivate *confianza*, and the bonds of loyalty that flow from tapping into the cascading levels of acculturation.

Strategies that are best implemented are ones that foster *confianza* and address the higher level of anxieties and stress blue-collar members of the Hispanic diaspora encounter in the American workplace. The following paragraphs describe some strategies employers can use.

The orientation of the Hispanic, Latino, and Latin employee is critical because it will determine the employee's success within the organization. Managers play a strategic role in preparing line managers to incorporate Hispanic, Latino, and Latin employees into their department. Management policies should include tools for assessing the needs for, and the identification of, mentors. Managers can avail themselves to mentors who can act as "counselors" or "guides" during the initial thirty- to ninety-day commencement in order to achieve a successful introduction.

Hispanic, Latino, and Latin employees value continuing education as part of their development as employees of the organization and their careers. Managers and supervisors need to recognize the three areas where Hispanics indicate the desire to "develop," specifically, in terms of language skills, acculturation into the mainstream of American life, and in their hesitation about geographic relocation. The organization's policies should recognize that Hispanic, Latino, and Latin employees can, and need to, play a central role in the recruitment of suitable candidates, both for hiring purposes as well as for nurturing bonds of loyalty.

A consequence of the emergence of the United States as a bilingual consumer economy is that Spanish is an inevitable part of corporate life. The organization's policies should encourage Spanish-speaking employees to become fluent in English, and should make accent reduction or elimination courses available. The organization's policies should recognize that many English-speaking employees should have a fundamental understanding of Spanish, not only to work with their Hispanic colleagues, but with the increasingly bilingual external constituencies. The organization's policies should recognize that "Spanglish" is to be frowned upon, because it is a form of slang that undermines efforts to communicate with external constituencies that demand to be addressed in standard written Spanish.

There continue to be myths about "diversity," which undermine effort to integrate the American workplace. The distinctions between "affirmative action" and "diversity" need to be understood by all employees throughout the organization. The differences between the public versus the private objectives of diversity training should be articulated clearly to all employees throughout the organization. The specific "at-risk" medical conditions that disproportionately affect Hispanic, Latino, and Latin employees need to be addressed in a proactive manner.

The key to keeping non-salaried Hispanic, Latino, and Latin employees challenged and satisfied in the workplace is through cultural intelligence, where an organization's policies speak to the cultural values—*simpatía* and *confianza*—in the process of nurturing the natural acculturation process that unfolds when members of an "out-group" seek to participate more fully in the mainstream culture of the dominant society in which they find themselves. For members of the "blue-collar" Hispanic diaspora, this entails specific objectives discussed in this chapter. Among these are language issues, which include proficiency in English for some and "Spanish for Latinos" for others; the processes by which acculturation occurs, which includes opportunities for continuing education; and management's recognition of the special risk groups for chronic medical problems in which Hispanics, Latinos, and Latins find themselves are the elements that convey an organization's commitment to help each employee find the best way to *superarse*.

In Review

- The desire of the Hispanic diaspora to *superarse* contributes to certain expectations of their employers.

- – The Hispanic linguistic glass ceiling in which U.S.-born Latinos are unable to converse in business Spanish
- – The obstacle Latin immigrants face in speaking English without an accent and with confidence
- – Bridging the linguistic divide between Hispanic, Latino, and Latin employees who may or may not master both English and Spanish

- Hispanic, Latino, and Latin employees face various levels of acculturation and assimilation, which may impede their career advancement.

- Hispanic, Latino, and Latin employees, by virtue of being members of an "out-group," face higher stress and anxiety levels than non-Hispanics, making them an "at-risk" population for chronic medical conditions.

Chapter 8

Nurturing the Hispanic Exempt Professional

The greatest obstacle for managers is to nurture, cultivate, and develop the next generation of mid- and upper-level managers who will run the American workplace. Hispanic, Latino, and Latin employees who are "exempt" from the Fair Labor Standards Act of 1938 are primarily "white collar." The classifications—Mexican Hispanics and Caribbean Hispanics—introduced at the beginning of this discussion now pose tremendous obstacles for organizations throughout the nation. If almost 80% of all Hispanics in the United States are Mexican Hispanics, it is of no small importance that almost 80% of all Hispanic, Latino, and Latin college graduates are Caribbean Hispanics. If most Caribbean Hispanics live east of the Mississippi, then there are both racial and geographic challenges: most Hispanic, Latino, and Latin college graduates—the pool from which white-collar employees are derived—are Caribbean Hispanics, who also happen to live along the Eastern seaboard. These are constant and significant staffing obstacles few organizations have been able to overcome.

There are several challenges. Foremost is the matter of race: white and black Hispanics are candidates for positions in which their direct reports are brown Hispanics. There is also the matter of geography: Caribbean Hispanics are reluctant to move west, and their presence in management outside the Eastern seaboard is scarce. These demographic facts explain the "unnatural" stratification of the Hispanic diaspora in the United States: Caribbean Hispanics, college educated, white collar, and solidly middle class, have, in communities throughout south Florida and certain industries in the greater New York metropolitan area, reached "tipping points," where they fuel their own communities as if they were in Hispanic-dominant societies.

Writing in 1980 of the Cuban and Cuban American domination of south Florida's business, cultural, and political life in *Miami,* Joan Didion reported, with alarm, how they were living the "American dream" in the United States and *in Spanish:*

> An entrepreneur who spoke no English could still, in Miami, buy, sell, negotiate, leverage assets, float bonds, and, if he were so inclined, attend galas twice a week, in black tie. . . . [And among] Anglos who did not perceive themselves as economically or socially threatened . . . there remained considerable uneasiness on the matter of language, perhaps because the inability or the disinclination to speak English tended to undermine their conviction that assimilation was an ideal universally shared by those who were to be assimilated.[1]

Miami stands in sharp contrast to efforts to cultivate Hispanic talent for managerial positions in other parts of the country, with Los Angeles being one striking example. "IBM is deeply committed to galvanizing the U.S. corporate sector and other stakeholders in addressing the serious shortage of professionals in STEM [Science, Technology, Engineering and Mathematics] careers, particularly in the Hispanic community," Nicholas M. Donofrio, Executive Vice President, Innovation and Technology at IBM, told a Corporate Social Responsibility reporter in May 2008. "This summit is a call to action to challenge business leaders to address an issue that could undermine the country's leadership in today's global economy."[2]

The goal of finding college-educated Mexican Hispanics in sufficient numbers remains elusive across the board and around the country. Since the late 1990s, when Hispanics began to move up through the ranks of organizations throughout the economy, it continues to be a difficult matter to identify Hispanic, Latino, and Latin salaried professionals in sufficient number for all the management positions available, even in periods of economic contraction. The obstacles already discussed in previous chapters—college-educated Caribbean Hispanics are reluctant to move west of the Mississippi, and Mexican Hispanics are not graduating in sufficient numbers to fill mid- and upper-management positions—are compounded by cultural preferences and sense of community of Hispanic, Latino, and Latin employees.

Successful strategies realize that there are strategic ways of supervising the Hispanic salaried professional (HSP) to enhance an organization's "human capital." The concerns of white-collar members of the Hispanic diaspora are different from those of blue-collar employees. As a group, HSP employees demonstrate confidence and, because they tend to perceive themselves as being fully bicultural, there is often a sense of cultural superiority when dealing with monolingual colleagues and co-workers, whether they are Hispanic or non-Hispanic. HSP employees often treat Hispanic, Latino, and Latin colleagues who are not fully acculturated into mainstream American society in an avuncular manner, though there is a minority that holds them with impatience and disregard. At the same time, HSP employees can be curt with non-Hispanics, displaying indifference to individuals they perceive as lacking in their "well-roundedness" or "life experience" by virtue of not being proficient in a different culture.

One of the more compelling analyses of the roles managers play in the success of an organization was conducted by James Baron, Michael Hannon, and M. Diane Burton who examined how the philosophical approaches of start-up founders in Silicon Valley affected the success of these enterprises.[3] Of the firms in which the founders espoused and embraced a commitment-based employment model, which was defined in part by an explicit commitment of management to the employee and which endeavored to complement the firm's and employees' cultural worldviews, these were the ones that had higher productivity and fewer management conflicts.[4] In essence, when management clearly articulated and defined the role of managers to include being proactive in nurturing the organization's "human capital"—its employees—there was direct impact on the firm's bottom line.[5] These approaches are consistent with the values of Hispanic society, the "we're all in this together" mentality that is in contrast to the more Anglo-Protestant American individualistic perspective where it's "every man (or woman) for himself (or herself)."

How do organizations successfully manage their Hispanic, Latino, and Latin "human capital" as they embrace a more collectivistic management approach? From a management perspective, although these concerns are not without merit, it is sufficient, in most cases, to be cognizant of the "privileged" position of HSP employees and be able to negotiate both Hispanic and non-Hispanic culture and social norms, fostering a sense of entitlement. That said, it is advisable for non-Hispanic managers to follow the "Seven Management Principles" that speak to the HSP. These are:

- Engage employees in company culture, to better integrate the HSP into the organization, affirming the organization's *simpatía* to the HSP;

- Establish informal networking, to allow the HSP employees throughout the firm to know each other and cultivate cohesion;

- Provide informal development opportunities, to allow the HSP to understand the totality of the organization's structure and operations, instilling *confianza;*

- Signal organizational commitment to advancement, an important element of the cultural imperative to *superarse;*

- Serve as a forum for encouraging open discussion, an essential element as the American workplace continues to become more Hispanic-dominant;

- Serve as a point of contact for recruiting efforts and to bounce ideas around, a crucial element in instilling the sense of *confianza* and camaraderie; and

- Generate feedback to upper management about the wants and needs of the HSP in the organization, to better fine-tune an organization's *simpatía.*

A classic textbook example of how these seven principles were implemented successfully is how American Airlines entered the south Florida market. When Pan Am and Eastern Airlines went bankrupt, their routes to Latin America were sold, respectively, to Delta and

American. Delta failed miserably in the Miami market, unable to nurture the predominantly Hispanic and Latin workforce in Miami-Dade County. After breathtaking turmoil in consolidating its operations, the non-Hispanic management, working out of Atlanta, began to miscalculate how to reach out to consumers in Latin American (because Latin American travelers prefers Miami as gateway to the United States, not Atlanta); and Delta mismanaged employee relations in south Florida. Delta, in defeat, retreated to its hub in Atlanta, canceling scores of international routes that originated in Miami, and lost millions of dollars. Its failure in Miami convulsed the carrier toward its eventual bankruptcy filing. American, on the other hand, has flourished, making Miami a hub that rivals its principal hub and world headquarters in Dallas/Ft. Worth. How American Airlines was able to take the same Hispanic, Latino, and Latin workforce and market to a customer base comprised of the same demographics, making their Miami operations into a powerhouse, generating millions in profits, bears careful study.[6]

American Airlines' success—and Delta's failure—speaks to all managers interested in nurturing their Hispanic, Latino, and Latin employees. These are the strategies that were implemented flawlessly by American Airlines when it took the former Latin American routes from Eastern Airlines and created a major international hub in Miami. It is a living corporate testament to the ability of Hispanic, Latino, and Latin managers to rise through the ranks of an organization. It is through the proper management of the HSP that organizations throughout the United States can achieve a sustainable competitive advantage.

The seven principles allow organizations to overcome the fact that Hispanics, Latinos, and Latins do not respond to traditional recruiting efforts. The nature of being an "out-group" leads many to believe that "proven" methods will not assist them in securing employment: traditional methods are perceived as being too individualistic and not collectivistic. Abe Tomas Hughes, chairman of the board of the Hispanic Alliance for Career Enhancement (HACE), argues that this is an example of how members of the Hispanic diaspora are not fully assimilated, and may not understand how these methods work.[7] Even among the most sophisticated white-collar Hispanic professionals, there are cultural nuances that inform how opportunities are evaluated within a cultural context. Hispanic employment Web sites, for instance, tend to advise on how best to brand an organization among white-collar Hispanic and Latin professionals with the following advice to non-Hispanic recruiters[8]:

- Hispanic and Latin professionals often do not respond to "cool" or trendy descriptions of work or work environments.

- Describing employment in terms such as "young," "dynamic," or "entrepreneurial," and statements such as "define your own job" do not resonate with white-collar Hispanic employees in that same manner as the phrases are intended to resonate within non-Hispanic American society.

- College-educated Hispanic and Latin candidates tend to seek out job opportunities that are clearly solid and have defined paths.

- Job titles hold a great deal of weight with Hispanics, Latinos, and Latins, especially when designed in a manner that provides a sense of movement toward higher positions.

With these recommendations made, management needs to recognize three specific areas where white-collar Hispanic, Latino, and Latin employees can best be nurtured:

Accent Elimination: White-collar Hispanic and Latin employees, particularly, are sensitive to speaking English with an accent. This is not surprising; throughout the United States there is discrimination, for instance, against speaking with a Southern accent, a testament to the lingering power of cultural preferences. Cognizant of the role language plays in discrimination, the Equal Employment Opportunity Commission warns employers: "Because linguistic characteristics are a component of national origin, employers should carefully scrutinize employment decisions that are based on accent to ensure that they do not violate Title VII."[9] There are clear exceptions, and circumstances under which employers can use their discretion to accommodate for the question of accents, but these are rare. In the United States, English spoken with a foreign accent is almost universally frowned upon and puts the speaker at a competitive disadvantage in the labor market.[10] English spoken with a Spanish accent subjects the speaker to prejudices. The accent bias against Hispanic, Latino, and Latin employees is similar to the prejudice that individuals who suffer speech impediments, such as stuttering, endure. One has only to recall, for instance, the running joke on "I Love Lucy" of Ricky Ricardo's accent to understand how, on a cultural level, American society finds Hispanics who speak English with a Spanish accent a laughing matter.[11] The cultural resistance to regional or foreign accents forms a subtext in which many white-collar Hispanic and Latin employees believe they are passed over for promotions, or their contributions are not fully recognized, because of how they speak. "There was an incredibly strong statistical correlation between judging someone cultured, intelligent, competent, etc., and placing them into prestigious jobs and their lack of a readily identified accent," Dianne Markley, director of marketing at the University of North Texas at Denton, reported of the findings of the "U.S. Regional Accent Discrimination in the Hiring Process: A Language Attitude Study."[12] These studies are validated with crushing personal experiences. "I also knew that it was far harder to bend one's tongue to accommodate the American ear than to assimilate," Andrew Lam, a Vietnamese American writes. "My uncle [who spoke with a heavy accent], for instance, was not rejected for lacking qualifications or intelligence. It was his unruly tongue that gave his foreignness away, pronouncing him interminably alien and, unfortunately, unemployable. . . . 'Speak like Connie Chung and you're okay. Talk like me and you end up running a grocery store.'"[13]

Mentoring: The Hispanic diaspora is often compelled to provide guidance for the younger generation, whether this is in the community or in the workplace. Among white-collar Hispanic and Latin employees, mentoring programs, in which they can be mentored or in which they mentor others, constitutes an appealing incentive. "I have lived in the monster and I know its entrails; my sling is David's,"

José Martí, the nineteenth-century Cuban poet and liberator wrote, of having lived in the United States as a member of the "out-group." How to implement a mentoring program for HSP employees to address the alienation they feel by virtue of being an "out-group" is discussed in detail in the next chapter.

Expansive Redefinition of Social Responsibility: The concerns of white-collar Hispanic, Latino, and Latin employees center on a less compartmentalized approach to "live/work." This is reinforced nicely by both the communal impulse of the Hispanic worldview, and our expanding understanding of corporate social responsibility. In the same way that mentoring is a proven strategy for nurturing an organization's "human capital," it is expected that employers play a role in the lives of the communities in which they have a presence. This is a natural outgrowth of Hispanic cultural preference for hierarchies, where employers enjoy high status in the community, by virtue of providing livelihoods to residents, and where there are social expectations that organizations use the economic privilege at their disposal to benefit the local community, or address social areas. One area that has found resonance among many white-collar Hispanic professionals centers on addressing the socioeconomic factors that contribute to the high school dropout rates among Latino and Latin youth. Hispanic, Latino, and Latin teenagers and young adults, aged between sixteen and twenty-four, are twice as likely as African Americans and four times more likely than non-Hispanic whites to drop out of high school.[14] If a pregnancy is involved, the figures skyrocket: more than two-thirds of Latina teenage mothers drop out of high school, compared to 58% of non-Hispanic teenage mothers in general.[15] Once they drop out, they seldom return to finish their educations: Latina teenage mothers are less likely to complete high school or enter college than those who delay childbearing until at least age twenty.[16] "When you pick apart the numbers, you see that the Hispanic dropout problem has several different components that call for different policy responses," Richard Fry, a senior research associate at the Pew Hispanic Center, reports. "Aside from the education issues, there is also a broader economic challenge evident in the work history of Latino youth who leave high school. The need to work is clearly one major reason Latinos drop out."[17] There are, of course, many areas in which organizations can become involved in the communities in which they conduct business; the more effective approaches are the ones that tap into desire to *colaborar* in order to solve social problems. The appeal of social responsibility by becoming involved in local schools is that, apart from the cultural predispositions of such an approach for HSP employees, it allows organizations to become involved in nurturing future employees; from high school to college graduation is only a matter of years, and being able to draw from qualified, local candidates is a high priority for most employers, the periodic changes in the business environment notwithstanding.[18]

In nurturing HSP employees, there are two special categories of white-collar Hispanic, Latino, and Latin employees that pose special challenges for managers, supervisors, and other administrators: Cubans and Puerto Ricans. These segments of the Caribbean Hispanic community, in the context of the Hispanic diaspora in general, and their influence on Mexican Hispanics in particular, offer insights that are integral to expanding non-Hispanic management to the cultural, social, and historical nuances that shape attitudes and opinions of all U.S. Hispanics, Latinos, and Latins. Without this background story, which is designed to increase non-Hispanic management's cultural intelligence, conflicts can emerge, particularly for organizations that have operations in various geographic locations throughout the United States. Consider the following sections on these two communities.

The Special Case of Cubans and Cuban Americans

It has been noted that four out of five U.S. Hispanics are of Mexican or Central American ancestry, and that of these, consistent with statistics compiled by the Bureau of Labor Statistics and the Census Bureau, the sweeping majority work in nonexempt jobs, as defined by the Fair Labor Standards Act of 1938. A further analysis reveals that the majority of Hispanics, Latinos, and Latins employed in exempt positions, more commonly referred to as "salaried," "non-hourly," "professional," or "management," are Caribbean Hispanics. This is further reinforced by statistics that document that almost four out of five U.S. Hispanics who continue their education beyond high school are likely to be Caribbean Hispanics.

These demographic and statistical facts result in a distorted labor market. What this means, of course, is that while almost 80% of all U.S. Hispanics are Mexican Hispanics, approximately 80% of all college-educated U.S. Hispanics are Caribbean Hispanics. When we examined the conflicts that emerged when Mexico first entered GATT and then NAFTA was implemented, in organizations throughout the United States that sought to expand operations or seek new opportunities in Mexico, a disproportionate number of managers and supervisors placed in charge were Cuban American or Cuban-born. For non-Hispanics, the obstacles that emerged were as surprising as they were unexpected. These same challenges confront managers and supervisors today, primarily because of the demographic realities: four out of every five applicants for an exempt position are Caribbean Hispanic, creating disequilibrium in the workplace between hourly employees (Mexican Hispanics) and salaried personnel (Caribbean Hispanics).

A further consideration—or complication, depending on your perspective—is that there are tensions among Caribbean Hispanics. By far, Cuban Americans and Cuban-born Caribbean Hispanics have the highest educational attainment level. Puerto Ricans, while ahead of Mexican Hispanics, lag behind their Cuban American and Cuban-born colleagues. Within organizations, this creates problems: organizations find that tensions arise between Puerto Ricans and Cuban Hispanics as the latter are promoted at a faster rate and to higher levels of responsibilities than the former. For organizations, this creates a problem; Cuban sensibilities inform how all Hispanic programs are developed throughout organizations in the United States, creating cultural and socioeconomic distortions. Consider a few examples that are instructive. When the Smithsonian Institution launched a Hispanic program, it availed itself to Miguel Bretos, who was born in Cuba.[19] When the Coca-Cola Company appointed its first Hispanic CEO, it was Roberto Goizueta, who was born in Cuba. When the George W. Bush administration wanted to have a diverse cabinet, it tapped Carlos M. Gutiérrez, who was born in Cuba, as Commerce Secretary. When PBS launched its Spanish-language sister channel, V-Me, Carmen DiRienzo, a Cuban American, was named president. And so it goes throughout American society. When the *New York Times* sought a "dynamic duo" of Latina reporters to bring a different sensibility to their newsroom, they settled on Mirta Ojito and Mireya Navarro, who—need I say it?—are not "Latina" but "Hispanic" because both are Miami Cubans. And so it goes, from sea to shining sea.

A stratification thus unfolds, one in which Mexican Hispanics are at the bottom of an organization, Puerto Ricans (and other Caribbean Hispanics and Mexican Hispanics) languish in "middle management," and Hispanics of Cuban ancestry dominate the ranks of the Hispanics in the highest echelons within organizations. To this phenomenon, a further complication: recruiting the highest-level executives directly from Latin America. Consider one stark example: when the *Los Angeles Times* wanted to have a "Latino" voice in its editorial department, it hired Andrés Martínez, who was born in Mexico City. There are more Mexicans in the City of Los Angeles than there are in the City of Guadalajara, and the *Los Angeles Times* was unable to find one qualified Mexican American Angeleno to speak for the concerns of Hispanics, Latinos, and Latins in southern California, so it had to recruit one from Mexico, and pay for his moving expenses and give him a map of the city so he could find his way around.

Cubans are the most successful of all Hispanic, Latino, or Latin demographic groups in the United States. Cubans speak in declarative sentences almost as often as do non-Hispanic whites.[20] In many ways, as a group, they are the most assimilated Hispanic demographic, one that, when measured in educational attainment levels and per capita incomes, rivals those of non-Hispanic whites. There are, however, distinct obstacles, and these arise from the fact that

Cubans, not unlike non-Hispanic whites in the United States, have little or no experience dealing with Native American worldview that informs that perspective of the Mexican Hispanic.

What does this say about the challenges of nurturing Hispanic, Latino, and Latin employees within an organization?

The Peculiar Challenge of the Puerto Rican Employee

The political status of Puerto Rico, an American colony where the Latin occupants are U.S. citizens, means that Puerto Ricans live in a world of ambivalence: non-Hispanic Americans do not automatically see them as nonimmigrant fellow citizens; other Latin Americans suspect their "authenticity" as Hispanics; and other Hispanics in the United States feel a lack of empathy from fellow Latinos who are exempt from the drama of immigration laws and the trauma of divided families these immigration policies create.

Among Puerto Ricans, this sense of ambivalence affects how they see themselves, the educational attainment decisions they make, and results in melancholy and conflict: confident of their status as U.S. citizens, but insecure about their "resonance" and authenticity as Hispanics. "Both in Latin American and the United States, Puerto Rico stands for something which cannot be assimilated," Jean Franco writes in the introduction to *Divided Borders: Essays of Puerto Rican Identity.* "It is island and continent, a colony and a nation, a community bound by a language that some Puerto Ricans do not speak."[21] For managers, supervisors, and other administrators, Puerto Rican employees pose their own set of peculiar obstacles as illustrated in the following text.

Puerto Ricans are divided by language. Puerto Ricans living on the mainland are often no longer fluent in Spanish. This limits their ability to move through the ranks of an organization, particularly as the U.S. economy is fast becoming a bilingual consumer economy. The linguistic divide also works in reverse: Puerto Ricans who live in Puerto Rico cannot be assumed to be fluent in English.

Puerto Ricans' educational attainment levels, although higher than those of Mexican Hispanics, fall short of those of Cubans and Cuban Americans. Puerto Ricans are disproportionately relegated to the ranks of lower and middle management, facing generational limitations to promotions that, as a group, are frustrating. The socioeconomic factors that contribute to the lower educational attainment level, whether it is poverty or lack of family encouragement, create disparities that have social repercussions. Within the Puerto Rican community, the question of race has emerged as a factor to "explain" socioeconomic failings. This social constraint can best be understood in the social context of the American experience, which is discussed subsequently.

It is seldom disputed that immigrants to the United States have been people seeking better opportunities for themselves and their families—whether they were the Puritans seeking the freedom to practice their faith, the Irish in the nineteenth century who fled the consequences of the potato famine, the scores of Europeans who sought to rebuild their lives after the world wars, or hundreds of other ethnic and national groups that have escaped impediments of one kind or another. Puerto Ricans are no exception, and there are social consequences to immigration, which began in earnest after the Spanish-American War, when Spain surrendered Puerto Rico to the United States. In 1902, the Treasury Department reclassified Puerto Ricans as "aliens," because their sustained emigration to New York was seen as a "burden" on that city's welfare. In *Gonzales v. Williams*, however, the Supreme Court ruled that Puerto Ricans were not "aliens" and therefore could not be denied entry onto the mainland. Unlike for Cubans and Cuban Americans who enjoy the confidence that arises from the right to political asylum afforded them by the Cuban Adjustment Act, for Puerto Ricans, political rights have not translated into economic success. The national poverty rate for Hispanics nationwide is about 21%, but for Puerto Ricans in New York, it is over 32%, higher than the poverty rates for African Americans.[22] Puerto Ricans are the poorest Caribbean Hispanics.

To these lower educational attainment levels and higher poverty rates, it is necessary to consider the familiar challenges of race: Puerto

172 The Hispanic Employee and the Organization's Future

Ricans who emigrate to the mainland, disproportionately, are people of color. Although there are many commentaries on this fact, the result is a distortion: Puerto Ricans of color are more likely to move to the mainland, while a disproportionate number of Caucasian Puerto Ricans remain on the island. Non-Hispanic Americans thus perceive Puerto Ricans to be primarily a people of color, who are less privileged than other groups, and who occupy blue-collar positions and the lower and middle ranks of an organization. This perception creates tensions between Puerto Ricans who become segregated by socioeconomic class, and how they are perceived *racially* by non-Hispanics.

Furthermore, as a group, they are looked upon with suspicion and resentment by other Hispanics, Latinos, and Latins; their lack of Spanish fluency creates impediments to their careers; lower educational attainment levels create obstacles to professional advancement, often reporting to Caucasian Cubans and Cuban Americans; and as a community they suffer from the stigma associated with being a people of color more likely to live in poverty and on public assistance. This is seen even among Puerto Ricans of achievement in the United States, where their insecurities undermine their ability to be effective on the public stage of civic life. Consider Anthony Romero, the Puerto Rican Executive Director of the ACLU, under whose tenure that organization was marginalized on the matter of the civil rights of Americans during the Bush administration's War on Terror. Another example is New York University professor Arlene Dávila who, when asked to participate in a panel discussion on Hispanic and Latino consumers, refused to sit on the panel after she realized that she would not be the only Latina present, but was confronted by other Latinas—one, naturally, Cuban, and the other, a Latin American from Mexico City.[23] These sorts of encounters are common enough where Puerto Ricans are concerned that organizers usually plan for backups to replace them, which happens more often than one would expect at conferences around the country.[24]

It is only natural to expect vast insecurities that swell within souls of Puerto Ricans, who are neither "fully" Hispanic, nor "entirely" American and subject to the disadvantages of communities living with higher poverty rates. The result is the emergence of lingering melancholy among mainland Puerto Ricans. The double rejection to which they are subjected—most Americans think of them as "foreigners" and Hispanics view them with ambivalence—informs their performance as employees. With this background, there are certain actions that are suited to cultivating the development and contributions of Puerto Rican employees within an organization, policies that are closely linked to management's cultural awareness. Specifically:

Specific Mentoring for Puerto Rican Employees: Although Puerto Ricans are Americans, they are among one of the culturally isolated groups that are not fully integrated into the mainstream of American life. Other groups in similar situations tend to be communities that choose to be self-segregated, primarily on religious grounds, such as the Amish or Hasidic Jews. Sociologists point to various factors for this, from racism, to the historical clusters of neighborhoods, or "ghettos," where Puerto Ricans have lived, to the consequences of generational poverty. The origins notwithstanding, Puerto Ricans benefit from mentoring programs that stress social and cultural norms: business dress and attire, and social norms and a general orientation on the cultural norms of the larger "Anglo American" society that characterizes the non-Hispanic American workplace.

Continuing Education: The failure of Puerto Ricans, as a community, to achieve higher educational attainment levels continues to relegate them to the ranks of limited career success, with Sonia Sotomayor's ascenscion to the Supreme Court being a notable exception. More than other Caribbean Hispanics, Puerto Ricans display insecurities about their ability to graduate from college, or pursue post-graduate degrees. With this in mind, management and human resources are advised to make a concerted effort to reach out to Puerto Rican employees about how to develop a realistic program to combine work and continuing education opportunities that allow them to pursue degrees during evening, part-time, or weekend instruction. For reasons that are not fully understood, Puerto Ricans do less well than other Caribbean Hispanics in these programs, and often require taking sabbaticals that allow them to enter into full-time programs.

Linguistic "Glass Ceiling": The inability to speak Spanish fluently, and the lack of familiarity with business Spanish, remains an impediment for Puerto Ricans. Already stigmatized by other Hispanics and throughout Latin America, it is imperative that Puerto Rican employees be able to discuss the limitations imposed by the inability to communicate properly in Spanish. As with U.S.-born Latinos, Puerto Rican employees are embarrassed about the need to "learn" Spanish, and there is often a reluctance to take courses to learn *business* Spanish, which is a difficult issue for management and human resources professionals alike. It is important to note that Puerto Ricans encounter an unusual linguistic obstacle: Puerto Ricans in Puerto Rico are fluent in Spanish, but may not be fluent in English; Puerto Ricans on the mainland may be fluent in English but not in Spanish. The result is that Puerto Ricans are an ethnic group separated by language, and this is a very disempowering reality of their identity.

Cultural Literacy: With one foot in Puerto Rico and the other firmly on the mainland, Puerto Ricans, already living under the cloud of "suspicion" in the eyes of their fellow Latin Americans, are at risk for losing "authenticity." This reflects not so much the process of assimilation, but of acculturation: Puerto Ricans "lose" basic Hispanic norms and idioms long before they are integrated into the mainstream of American life. The result is a psychological disconnect; Hispanics and Latins report difficulty in "identifying" with Puerto Ricans as "real" Hispanics. This discomfort leads some Puerto Ricans to "disguise" their identities: The Puerto Rican Policy Institute, for instance, changed its name to the Latino Policy Institute, although its mission concentrates on Puerto Rican affairs. In fact, this distancing has many factors that contribute to this cultural disorientation, and management should encourage Puerto Rican employees to counter the rejection they are subjected to by other Hispanics by developing their "pan-Hispanic" identities as a bold affirmation of self.[25] These factors together contribute to a melancholy in the Puerto Rican's identity in the United States, and are issues that management should take proactive steps to overcome.

Questions & Answers About Exempt Hispanic and Latino Employees

Why are Hispanics reluctant to relocate for work, even if it means career advancement or demonstrating they are a "team player"?

This is where the power of culture and tradition play an important role in shaping the decisions people make. The Hispanic worldview's emphasis on tradition, deferring to the family, the moral imperative of familial responsibility, and the nature of the individual's dependence on the family all conspire to make it reluctant for Hispanic, Latino, and Latin salaried employees to uproot their families and relocate great distances. It may seem contradictory—an immigrant from, say, Chile, leaves his or her hometown, family, and friends and travels more than 5,000 miles to work in the United States. This is true, but these are "hardship" cases—most Latin American immigrants make this journey out of economic necessity, and end up working in hourly positions, or as day laborers. For U.S. Hispanics, on the other hand, there are strong communities that anchor them to specific geographic regions: Cubans in south Florida and northern New Jersey, Puerto Ricans in New York's tri-state area; Mexicans in Texas and southern California. There is a reluctance to move out of these regions, and one finds that, in cases where executives do agree to relocate, that is a short-lived arrangement: most Cuban managers and executives, in due course, find their way back to Miami; few Caribbean Hispanics are willing to cross west of the Mississippi; and there is such a dearth of Mexican Hispanic management talent that they, literally, don't have to venture far from their residential zip code to find employers to pursue their careers. At times, the "tipping point" of Hispanic talent is deemed to be so crucial to an organization, and that talent is so concentrated in a specific location, that rather than having employees move to different offices, corporate America is realizing that it has to relocate its Hispanic division to where the labor force is found. This is how Dow Elanco decided that, in order to grow its business in Latin America, it would have to relocate its offices to Coral Gables, Florida, where middle- and upper-middle class Hispanic executives lived, and where they wanted to work. Occupying several floors in an office tower right off Miracle Mile, Dow Elanco's Latin American operations were forced to accommodate the unwillingness of Hispanic managers and executives to move to Midland, Michigan, where Dow Chemical Company was founded and where it is headquartered.[26]

Why are Hispanics reluctant to assimilate into the mainstream of American society?

The assumption in this question is that the mainstream of American life, which is understood to be "Anglo-Protestant" culture and the English language, is universally superior to other cultures and languages. Samuel Huntington famously phrased the question thusly: "Will the United States remain a country with a single national language and a core Anglo-Protestant culture? By ignoring this question, Americans acquiesce to their eventual transformation into two peoples with two cultures (Anglo and Hispanic) and two languages (English and Spanish)."[27] The reason this is a matter for discussion and reflection at all is because no human society is perfect, and Hispanics, once they arrive in the United States, realize that they can take a "cafeteria" approach: pick and choose the best values, traditions, and practices from Hispanic and Anglo-Protestant societies. They acculturate (meaning they are able to function successfully in Anglo-Protestant society), but they seldom fully assimilate (meaning abandoning their own culture and language to become "mainstream" Americans). For individual Hispanics, Latinos, and

Latins, again, the Hispanic worldview plays a crucial role. Here is one example: Hispanics value family to such a great extent that they reject the generational segregation of American society: nuclear families comprised of parents and children, where grandparents and adult siblings are apart and live away. Hispanic societies thus reflect this kind of organization: in Latin America entire industries common throughout the United States—self-contained "retirement" communities throughout the Sun Belt, assisted living centers that ring suburbs, nursing homes for the frail, and hospices for the terminal—are virtually unknown. Hispanics, as a demographic, reject the idea that grandparents will not have a day-to-day role in raising their grandchildren. They equally reject the idea that teenagers will not have a day-to-day role in helping with their elderly grandparents and great-grandparents. It is not uncommon among Hispanic and Latin families for parents to warn their children against adopting "false" practices—*valores anglosajones,* or Anglo-Saxon values—that will lead to the "destruction" of the family. For Hispanic communities, such as in Miami and San Antonio, entire communities reflect these Hispanic collectivistic ideals. "An entrepreneur who spoke no English could still, in Miami, buy, sell, negotiate, leverage assets, float bonds, and, if he were so inclined, attend galas twice a week, in black tie. . . . [And among] Anglos who did not perceive themselves as economically or socially threatened . . . there remained considerable uneasiness on the matter of language, perhaps because the inability or the disinclination to speak English tended to undermine their conviction that assimilation was an ideal universally shared by those who were to be assimilated," Joan Didion wrote of Miami in 1980.[28] Cubans have never been convinced that to succeed in the United States one has to assimilate into American society. To be sure, U.S. Hispanics are aware of the shortcomings of their own society (which offers limited opportunities to women or the failure to support a child's professional ambition strongly enough, for instance) and they are firm in their resistance to certain aspects of American life (such as the disrespect children show their parents and elders), but also are attempting, successfully or not, to not be seduced by the "false" promises of Anglo-Protestant society (sacrificing their family's well-being for the sake of a career). If the business of America is business, as Calvin Coolidge said, Hispanics are aware of the paradox that, in English the saying goes, "No one on their deathbed ever wished they had spent more time in the office." There's no Spanish-language equivalent for that saying.[29]

Why do Hispanic, Latino, and Latin employees prefer a vertical organizational structure rather than a horizontal one?

This, again, reflects the collectivistic worldview through which Hispanics see the universe and their place in it. Inherent in the ideas of communalism, passive resolve, and self-improvement are formal structures and lines of command. The notion of "empowerment" of the workplace through "horizontal" organizations may work in some industries, such as advertising agencies, entertainment, and software development, but clear and distinct lines of command are better suited for others, such as manufacturing, assembly plants, and the military. Apart from the creative genius of writers, artists, filmmakers, and playwrights, Hispanic societies seldom have significant business enterprises that can benefit from the "horizontal" structures required in creative enterprises and in the "creative destruction" process required for innovation.[30] In other words, Hispanics are consumers of video games, not the creators of video games; Hispanics buy iPhones from Apple, but few are hired as the software engineers to design the next generation software to develop next year's high-tech products that will take the market by storm. The practical result is that for the vast majority of Hispanics working in the United States today, there is a strong cultural preference for vertical organizational structure, where there is a clearly defined line of command, where titles are used throughout the organization, and where dress reflects either a company uniform (whether it is a Starbucks apron or a jacket-and-tie policy at the office), and the expectation that authority is to be respected is itself a value that is respected.

Why are there conflicts between Spanish and non-Spanish speaking Hispanics?

There are more than 395 million Hispanics in the world, and there are approximately 7–8 million "Latinos" in the United States who do not speak Spanish fluently.[31] This, more than anything, creates a linguistic divide among U.S. Hispanics that fuels rivalries and recriminations. For U.S. Hispanics who "played by rule," assimilated into the mainstream of American life, learned English flawlessly, and moved away from their culture, just as generations of other immigrants have done before them, they confront the no-win situation that the United States has changed, and it has become a bilingual consumer economy where fluency in Spanish, at least business Spanish, offers a competitive advantage. For U.S. Hispanics who acculturated—adopting Anglo-Protestant practices on a cafeteria pick-and-choose basis—but who remained bilingual and adhere to Hispanic culture and values, they now enjoy a distinct advantage, socially, professionally, and culturally. Consider two examples. The first centers on a colleague whose daughter was accepted to an Ivy League school in the Northeast. This colleague had insisted that her children learn Spanish by taking Spanish language classes during their high school years; her teenagers are able to read *Don Quixote* in the original Spanish Cervantes wrote it in. (How many non-Hispanic American high school students are able to read Medieval Tudor drama?) When her daughter was notified by the university of who her roommate would be during freshman year, she was delighted that it was another Hispanic young woman, from Texas. At this point it seems superfluous to point out that the colleague who insisted her children learn proper Spanish was . . . Cuban. She described to me how she took her daughter aside, sat her down, and explained that it was likely that her roommate, by virtue of being from Texas, would probably be a Mexican American, and almost certainly not be fluent in Spanish. "She was all excited, about having a roommate with whom she could speak Spanish, and remain current with Spanish films and music," she told me, shaking her head. "But sure enough, when we arrived on campus, her roommate was a wonderful and bright young lady, but she called herself a Tejana [Texan of Mexican ancestry], and confessed that her Spanish was terrible." Here you have two Latinas—one Cuban, the other Tejana—unable to cross the linguistic chasm that separates them. It doesn't take a rocket science to project a decade into the future and see which one has a more successful career trajectory. The other instant is instructive in shedding light on "Latinos" and the nature of identity politics in the United States. Each year the Miami Book Fair draws readers and writers from Latin America and there are numerous panels on all matters of subject. In 2005 an unusual controversy erupted when certain Latino writers, realizing they were scheduled to participate in panel discussions addressing the state of Hispanic literature that would be conducted in Spanish, objected, claiming that English was the "Latino" language of choice, and that because they wrote in English, it was the responsibility of participants to be conversant in English, even though their work was considered to be "Hispanic" literature. U.S. Latinos, who represent about 1.5% of all Hispanics in the world, set out to dictate to 98.5% of the Spanish-speaking world the conditions under which they would participate in the panels organized by the Miami Book Fair. It is not surprising that these demands ran their natural course: the organizers explained that English is not recognized as a language indigenous to the Iberian peninsula, and as such, English is not a "Hispanic" literary language, and that if they were unable to discuss their work in Spanish, perhaps one of the forums for English-language writing would be more appropriate. Some of the Latino writers scoffed at the suggestion that Latino writing in English be considered English-language literature, and then proceeded to boycott the Miami Book Fair. That is to say, there are tensions that arise when U.S. Latinos, to advance their specific political agendas, insist on dictating to that portion of humanity that celebrate the "Día de la Hispanidad" that they must capitulate to their demands and conditions.

Why is there a cultural gulf between Mexican Hispanics and Caribbean Hispanics?

Here is where nature and culture conspire to create obstacles. As discussed, Mexican Hispanics, racially, are overwhelmingly mestizo, a people that emerged from Europeans and the First Peoples of the New World, while Caribbean Hispanics follow a pattern more common to Americans: white (European descendants), black (sub-Saharan descendants), and mulatto (a mixture of black and white ancestry). There is, racially, a difference between Mexican Hispanics and Caribbean Hispanics. To this, although the common and shared bonds of Hispanic society go a long way to bridge the racial and cultural differences, it does not ameliorate all differences, and there are tensions that arise from lack of familiarity. For many Mexican Hispanics, their first contact with black Hispanics—usually from Puerto Rico, the Dominican Republic, or Cuba—occurs when they are in the United States, widely augmented by also living among African Americans. For most Caribbean Hispanics, the first time they encounter an "Indian" is when they encounter Native American immigrants from Mexico or Central America. These "encounters" between Mexican Hispanics and Caribbean Hispanics are more seamless than interactions between Hispanic Americans and non-Hispanic Americans, but it goes a long way in explaining the geographic "comfort" zones evidenced by Hispanic America: Mexican Hispanics primarily live west of the Mississippi and Caribbean Hispanics prefer to live east of the Mississippi. To this, there is another component that contributes to the cultural gulf between them, and it has to do with how Hispanics are viewed by non-Hispanics. Over the course of assisting various organizations in assembling staffs to pursue opportunities in the U.S. Hispanic market or in Latin America, there is a familiar pattern, often subconscious, in how Hispanics are seen and approached by non-Hispanics. Time and again, I am struck by a consistent pattern when discussing candidates for staffing, and it speaks to a lingering cultural bias that accentuates the positive for one group of candidates while focusing on the negative for another category of candidates. For Caucasian applicants, the discussion often begins with the positive: what does the candidate bring to the table? For Hispanic applicants, the discussion often begins with the negative: what does the candidate lack? Hispanics pick up on the code words used, or as Georgetown University professor in linguistics Deborah Tannen points out, there are distinct speaking styles ("message" versus "metamessage") between men and women that also apply between cultures. That is to say, there is a lingering resentment among Caribbean Hispanics that Hispanics, as a demographic group, are held back by the failure of Mexican Hispanics to succeed as America defines success. The anecdote provided earlier in this discussion, where I discussed Miami Cubans complaining about the "Latinolandia" agenda of Mexican Hispanics and Puerto Ricans who call themselves "Latino," are cases in point. That there are distinct economic expectations and achievement between Caribbean Hispanics and Mexican Hispanics is a greater contributing factor to the gulf between them than racial differences.

Why are there uneasy relations between black Hispanics and African Americans?

The United States is the only country in the Western Hemisphere that resorted to a civil war in order to end the institution of slavery. This was followed by a dismal century of forced segregation, creating two separate but unequal societies that seldom saw eye to eye on much of anything. "When white folk talk about justice, what they mean is 'just us,'" is one saying in black America to describe how the nation's laws, from Reconstruction through the early 1960s, were used as weapons to keep African Americans oppressed. That said, race relations in Hispanic societies have been less acrimonious, for a variety of reasons. Hispanic values, influenced by Roman Catholicism, are inclusive. In practical terms, through miscegenation, it's difficult to find families that don't have members, through blood or marriage, of various races and ethnic groups. The result is one where black Hispanics have less anger at their fellow Hispanics, which cannot be said of black America's attitudes toward white America. Consider a familiar example that is part of living in these United States. A year before this book was published, I agreed to meet a colleague at the information booth at Grand Central Station in New York. I arrived first and, while standing there, checking e-mail and voice mail messages while I waited, not far from me was an African American family, clearly tourists visiting the city. Their young son, about three or four looked up at me, and wandered in my direction. Then his mother looked over, and in a very forceful voice, said, "Don't you get near that white devil, you hear?" The boy stopped in his tracks and sheepishly walked away. There is such a thing as black America and such a thing as white America. So what does it mean to live in a society where black children are taught that whites are devils? How does this affect interactions and misunderstanding between black and white workers, and is it odd that black America resents the fact that black Hispanics do not share their anger and animosity toward white America? How do white Americans feel that their fellow citizens refer to them as devils? (If the reader is a white American who did not know that in black America, Caucasians are called "white devils," where have you been all your life?) It can be said that there is an instance in which Hispanics are right to refuse to "assimilate," because Hispanic culture has managed to reach a superior societal outcome in race relations—when Barack Obama was elected president, Mexican Hispanics could rightfully say that it really was no big deal, because the first black to be president of Mexico was Vicente Guerrero, back in 1829, and Cubans could point out that the dictator Fidel Castro overthrew, in 1959, was Fulgencio Batista, who, like Barack Obama, was a mulatto. At the core, black Hispanics share little empathy for the grievances of African Americans, because the cultural underpinnings of Hispanic and Anglo-Protestant societies have treated black people, however imperfectly and unjustly, so differently.

In Review

- The labor pool from which Hispanic, Latino, and Latin managers are drawn constitutes a distorted labor market.
  - Although they constitute 80% of all U.S. Hispanics, Mexican Hispanics represent only 20% of all U.S. Hispanic college graduates.
  - Fully 80% of all U.S. Hispanics with college degrees are Caribbean Hispanics.
  - Caribbean Hispanics are reluctant to move west of the Mississippi.
  - Mexican Hispanics resent and resist reporting to Caribbean Hispanics.
- Management needs to court Caribbean Hispanics with incentives to cultivate their potential contributions to the organization.

- Cuban Hispanics are the elite of U.S. Hispanics, whose cultural traditions and sensibilities inform, and distort, how non-Hispanic America approaches the Hispanic diaspora.
- Puerto Ricans, for peculiar cultural and political traditions, remain "stuck" in lower and middle management positions, creating obstacles to their advancement in the workplace.

• Latin immigrants who are Caucasian and college-educated catapult over U.S.-born Latinos creating tensions between native-born Hispanics and Latin immigrants who, if acculturated, are not assimilated into the mainstream of American life.

Training and Development: How Successful Managers Nurture Their Hispanic Workforce

Among the most critically important obstacles organizations face is retaining their Hispanic employees. Even during periods of economic contraction, the demand for Hispanic, Latino, and Latin employees is resilient. Indeed, during turbulent economic times, organizations need employees who can wear "multiple" hats, and as the United States consolidates its position as a bilingual consumer economy, employees who can wear the "English" customer service and "Spanish" customer service hats at the same time are coveted. In New York, as discussed in the next chapter, there is the phenomenon of Latino and Latin youth of color being preferred over African American job applicants in black neighborhoods because they are bilingual. This is consistent across the country: "For [State Farm Insurance], it's especially important because almost 60 percent of [our northern California] business is from the Latino community. I have three team members who are bilingual and [they] take pride in what they do, as well as providing excellent customer service," Mark Livingston, explains, reaffirming the competitive advantage that bilingual job applicants enjoy.[1]

The demand for bilingual and bicultural job applicants serves to stabilize the demand for Hispanic, Latino, and Latin job applicants. Given these facts of economic life, there are two distinct approaches to nurturing Hispanic, Latino, and Latin employees. To be sure, everyone is entitled to be treated with respect and in a fair manner, but it is also true that different categories of employees respond to different incentives. A simple example, which may come as a surprise to most non-Hispanic Americans, is that to Mexican Hispanics—almost 80% of all U.S. Hispanics—the cultural bonds to December 12 are stronger than they are to Thanksgiving Day. Although Thanksgiving ranks as perhaps the most important secular holiday in the United States, whose meaning has taken mythic proportions in American society, to Mexican Hispanics, the connection to this holiday is tenuous. Embracing Thanksgiving is a part of acculturation, one measure by which they can establish a connection to, and identify with, mainstream American life, even if the tradition of this secular holiday holds little resonance in Hispanic society. It is, in other words, an important "in-group" celebration for which there is little passion. December 12, on the other hand, is the Day of the Virgin of Guadalupe, the feast day of the patron saint of Mexico, a day that, to Mexicans and Hispanics of Mexican ancestry, rivals Christmas and Easter. In organizations where the labor consists almost exclusively of Mexican Hispanics it is not unheard of for management to offer these employees the opportunity to trade December 12 as a holiday in place of another, because honoring the Virgin of Guadalupe is culturally more important than Thanksgiving.

The significance, of course, remains that there are distinct approaches to nurturing training and development of the Hispanic, Latino, and Latin workforce. These approaches are philosophical and practical, consistent with the development of cultural intelligence. For nonexempt Hispanic, Latino, and Latin employees, it focuses on an approach, a way of managing and supervising that reflects specific cultural dimensions, and emphasizes recognition and respect for a job well done. For HSP employees, the focus is on mentoring, which allows organizations not only to develop talent internally, but also to be consistent with the acculturation and assimilation of these employees into the mainstream of American life. Both approaches, in essence, are ways of inculcating passion for Thanksgiving Day among the members of the Hispanic diaspora in the United States.

Nurturing "Cultural Dimensions" of Hispanic, Latino, and Latin Employees in Nonexempt Positions

There are certain management strategies that have proven to be more successful in working with Hispanic, Latino, and Latin employees engaged in nonexempt work. These approaches focus on cultural intelligence, and how to be mindful of the preferences of members of the Hispanic diaspora when it comes to fulfilling their obligations and meeting their responsibilities in the workplace. To understand how various cultural traits inform individual behavior, it's instructive to consider the work of the Dutch researcher Gerard Hofstede.[2] Hofstede's studies document consistent patterns in individual behavior shaped by cultural ideas and traditions. In studying national cultures and organizational cultures, Hofstede argues that "[c]ulture is more often a source of conflict than of synergy. Cultural differences are a nuisance at best and often a disaster."[3]

This is a reaffirmation that cultural differences create obstacles in the workplace that need to be met. To measure differences among human societies and organizations, Hofstede developed five "Cultural Dimensions" to rank individuals' attitudes, and how these beliefs and values shape their interactions with others in their organization, and in the societies in which they live.

One dimension is the Power Distance Index (PDI), which measures the extent to which the less powerful members of organizations and institutions (including family) accept and expect that power is distributed unequally. This, more or less, measures inequality in a society or organization. But as it is defined by lowest-ranking members, it suggests how an organization's or society's level of inequality is accepted by the least-powerful members as much as by the highest-ranking individuals.

Another dimension is Individualism (IDV) stands in sharp contrast to communalism or collectivism in how the individual sees his or her place in a group, whether it is the family, an organization, or society at large. In individualistic societies, there is the expectation that members are to look out for their own self-interest first and foremost; this is the basis of market-based economies where the individual's primary concern is his or her interests, and those of his or her immediate family. In communal/collectivist societies, on the other hand, individuals are tightly integrated into strong, cohesive "in-groups," often consisting of extended families (or clans), regions, and societies. The individual is expected to sacrifice personal ambitions for the well-being of the most immediate group. Although there is political connotation to the label "communal" or "collectivist," these are societies where a social, or socialist, approach to solving problems or meeting challenges is favored.

A third dimension is Masculinity (MAS), as opposed to femininity, refers to the division of roles between the sexes. As much a measure of sexism in society, this dimension explores a society's "assertiveness" or "meekness." Organizations that value individual assertiveness are deemed to be "masculine," while those that value modesty are classified as "feminine." Societies that are more "competitive" are masculine (U.S.); those that are more "cooperative" are feminine (Mexico, despite "macho" stereotypes coming out of Hollywood).

A fourth dimension Uncertainty Avoidance Index (UAI) measures society's tolerance for uncertainty and ambiguity. It is an indication to the degree to which members of a group, organization, or society feel uncomfortable or comfortable in unexpected or unstructured situations. This is closely linked to the idea of risk-taking and risk-avoidance among a group's members. Societies that are risk-averse favor rules, regulations, strict laws, and norms that establish predictability (think Latin America's nationalist-socialist tradition). Societies that encourage risk-taking are more unstructured, entrepreneurial, accepting of differences, and tolerant of diverging viewpoints, favoring fewer rules and regulations (think America's Wall Street cowboys and Western Wildcat traditions).

The final dimension is Long-Term Orientation (LTO) versus short-term orientation measures the attitudes of individuals as they look past the immediate situation. Ideas associated with Long-Term Orientation are perseverance and economy, while values identified with Short-Term Orientation are respect for traditions and the imperative to fulfill one's social and moral obligations to their group.

With this background, and in view that almost 80% of all U.S. Hispanics are of Mexican or Central American ancestry, how do the United States and Mexico rank on Hofstede's Cultural Dimensions comparison?

Hofstede Dimension	U.S.	Mexico
Power Distance Index (PDI)	40	81
Individualism (IDV)	91	30
Masculinity (MAS)	62	69
Uncertainty Avoidance Index (UAI)	46	82
Long-Term Orientation (LTO)	29	N/A

The social sciences, by virtue of dealing with human beings, do not utilize precise measurements. These disciplines do, however, use criteria that describe the broad, structural differences among groups of people along an individualism-collectivism spectrum. There are limits even to these attempts at measurement to allow for individual human differences. Comparing Mexico and the United States, using the UAI measurement, Mexico ranked eighty-two, and the United States ranked forty-six—quite a difference. According to Hofstede, Mexico is a society with "a low level of tolerance for uncertainty," and therefore, Mexicans favor a hierarchical structure in order "to minimize or reduce this level of uncertainty. . . . The ultimate goal of this population is to control everything in order to eliminate or avoid the unexpected. . . . [Such a] society does not readily accept change and is very risk adverse." In contrast, the low ranking of the United States "is indicative of a society that has fewer rules and does not attempt to control all outcomes and results. It also has a greater level of tolerance for a variety of ideas, thoughts, and beliefs."[4]

In comparing individualism, or IDV, Mexico ranks 30, which is higher than most other Latin American countries, but lower than Western ones. The United States ranks 91. Hofstede argues that Mexico's score is consistent with a society that favors collectivism. "This is manifest[ed] in a close long-term commitment to the member 'group,' be that a family, extended family, or extended relationships. Loyalty in a collectivist culture is paramount, and over-rides most other societal rules and regulations. The society fosters strong relationships where everyone takes responsibility for fellow members of their group." The American score, on the other hand, "indicates a society with a more individualistic attitude and relatively loose bonds with others. The populace is more self-reliant and looks out for themselves and their close family members."[5]

The more intriguing cross-cultural comparison, however, is the Power Distance (PDI), in which Mexico ranks 81 and the United States scores 40. Hofstede concludes that the differences between Mexican and American societies are significant in the matter of how power is dispersed throughout each culture. In Mexico, there is "a high level of inequality of power and wealth within the society. This condition is not necessarily subverted upon the population, but rather accepted by the culture as a whole." This is in sharp contrast to the United States, where power distribution is "indicative of a greater equality between societal levels, including government, organizations, and even within families. This orientation reinforces a cooperative interaction across power levels and creates a more stable cultural environment."[6]

This observation goes far in explaining why, for instance, Mexicans and Mexican Hispanics prefer top-down vertical organizations, where managers and supervisors are addressed with the honorifics ("Mr.," "Mrs.," and "Miss") rather than by their first names; where uniforms are the dress code, instead of "casual" attire; where there is a well-defined chain of command, rather than "informal" or "egalitarian" efforts to foster camaraderie; and where power is disbursed through formal bureaucratic structures for decision-making, which can take the form of a proactive human resources department, or a union. In contrast, Americans tend to operate under the belief that all are roughly "equal," that is to say, everyone is, more or less, in the "middle class," which, empirically, is not substantiated by statistics on income distribution. The facts notwithstanding, the perception among Americans that they belong to a democratic, egalitarian society of relative affluence does influence their behavior. It is not surprising that people feel comfortable addressing members of higher or lower rank by their first names; eschew the trappings of rank, other than for members of the armed forces or uniformed services (such as law enforcement, firefighters, postal service employees, etc.); and prefer casual work environments where democratic practices concerning decision-making, to the degree that is possible in any given profession or industry, is practiced.

If all this seems very academic, here is a straightforward takeaway: one of the most valuable lessons that non-Hispanic managers and supervisors can learn about working with Mexican Hispanics is empathizing with the "cultural wounds" that this community feels. In the same way that the discussion of reparations among African Americans is a way to give voice to the unfinished business of how American society can repay the moral debt it acquired through the institution of slavery, on a very different level, but emotionally analogous, is the Mexican Hispanic grievance against the hostility it continues to encounter from mainstream American society. Managers and supervisors intent on gaining the *confianza* of Mexican Hispanics can show their *simpatía* for this community in subtle ways that hold cultural resonance.

Yes, it isn't the fault of anyone alive today that the United States Government chose to violate the terms of the peace treaty ending the Mexican-American War. But the reality is that societies often have to make amends. The Germans, for instance, have to go out of their way to prove they're not anti-Semites, simply because of their nation's history of anti-Semitism. Non-Hispanic Americans, similarly, should be sensitive to the historic grievances from policies that date back to the passage of the Monroe Doctrine. Simply because non-Hispanic Americans are blissfully oblivious to these historic grievances, doesn't mean that they do not inform the attitudes of Mexican Hispanics and the perception among many Hispanics, which mirrors the beliefs of black America, is that the American government does not keep its word, does not always conduct itself in honorable ways, and cannot be fully trusted. Non-Hispanic managers and supervisors, in other words, should realize that their Hispanic, Latino, and Latin employees are skeptical, which is why earning *confianza* and building *simpatía* are of vital importance.

CASE STUDY

A Uniform Preference for Vertical Organizational Structure

In the enthusiasm unleashed by the implementation of the North American Free Trade Agreement, or NAFTA, in the mid-1990s, there was an explosion of investment and business activity in Mexico. Mexicans feared an "invasion" by corporate America as the U.S. companies—from McDonald's to Wal-Mart, Citibank to Home Depot—suddenly arrived, setting up businesses and opening franchising throughout the country. In the flurry of this activity, several companies that were setting up in-bond, or *maquiladora*, facilities encountered various challenges. One company, a partnership between American and Mexican investors, had significant contracts with important garment manufacturers in the United States. The operation was designed so that pre-cut pieces of cloth were shipped to Mexico, Mexican workers sewed the pieces of clothing into finished garments, which were then returned to the United States for distribution to retailers. The Mexican investors were silent, meaning their role did not include day-to-day management of the operations.

In the case of one client, the American managers, both from California, wanted to "introduce" a horizontal organizational structure. This meant that rather than having a top-down reporting structure, with the factory floor worker at the bottom, the foreman in the middle, and the American manager at the top, they wanted a horizontal structure, more informal and one in which all employees would be encouraged to make suggestions and offer recommendations. This approach included specific workplace decisions: dress was casual (denim jeans, open-button polo shirts, name tags with just the first name, white sneakers), titles were discarded (neither business titles, such as "Manager," or honorifics, such as "Mr.," were used), and there was an open-door policy (foremen and managers worked in cubicle spaces placed on the factory floor, with no walls or doors separating them from the assembly workers). However well intentioned, in a matter of months, productivity at this facility was down, absenteeism was up, and turnover was higher than at other facilities.

The problem, at its core, was a clash of cultural values. Whereas the American managers wanted to create a welcoming, egalitarian workplace that spoke to the sensitivities of cutting-edge management theories taught in U.S. business schools, for the Mexican workers, there were strong cultural preferences for a "vertical" workplace structure. Consistent with the more formal organization of Mexican society, which is seen in the emphasis on modesty, being polite, deferring to individuals in positions of authority, respect for elders, and pride in one's affiliations, the Mexican employees were uncomfortable at this facility. They were reluctant to call the managers by their first name; the Mexican foremen were resentful that they did not have offices that were raised above the factory floor so they could see the entire assembly operations; and the insistence on using first names made the employees feel self-conscious and awkward.

The solution was to reintroduce a vertical organizational structure, and the single most important step was to adopt uniforms. Khaki trousers replaced the denim, dark blue polo shirts with the company logo embroidered were brought in, casual leather shoes replaced the sneakers, and everyone's name tag had an honorific: "Mr.," "Ms.," "Manager," and "Supervisor." Other changes, such as relocating the foremen's offices took more time, but the managers insisted on keeping their cubicles on the plant floor, to encourage an "open-door" policy. In a matter of months, productivity increased, and this facility began to conform to standards at similar operations. More to the point, the employees self-reported greater satisfaction, and merit bonuses for quotas met improved.

Hispanic societies are not alone in their cultural preference for vertical organizational structures, of course. Among the Japanese and Koreans, for instance, it is not uncommon for a work shift to begin with group calisthenics and the singing of the company song. Hispanic societies can do without a company anthem, and in rare instances do workers at a company request group exercises or stretching. There are, however, specific cultural traditions, preferences and markers that don't translate well, and this is becoming increasingly important as U.S. companies balance the evolving needs of their workplace environments, especially where the cultural preferences between Hispanics and non-Hispanics are in conflict.

A characteristic of the collectivistic nature of Hispanic society, for instance, is emphasis on public recognition. In the Hispanic diaspora, there is the tradition of community, nonprofit, and volunteer organizations staging elaborate awards ceremonies for honorifics, such as "Outstanding Latino of the Year," "Community Role Model of the Year," "Excellence in Volunteering Award," and so on. These awards are not only public recognition of an individual's contribution to the communal goals of an organization, but also convey to members of an "outgroup" that they matter, that their work is recognized, and that it merits public recognition. In some organizations, "Employee of the Month" or "Associate of the Year" designations are not uncommon, and these are straightforward approaches that reverberate beyond the workplace for Hispanic, Latino, and Latin employees because they are powerful signifiers of accomplishment throughout the Hispanic diaspora.

A comprehensive program to nurture nonexempt Hispanic, Latino, and Latin employees should include:

Recognition: a program to acknowledge publicly the contributions of specific team members is important, especially if there is an off-site ceremony involved.

Choice of Holiday: allowing employees to reach consensus on whether, as a department, they would want December 12 (or another date that has cultural import to the majority of the workforce) as a holiday in lieu of another holiday, personal day, or vacation day, builds *simpatía* and empowers employees.

Affirm "Hierarchical" Unit Structure: the requirement of uniforms (similar to UPS, FedEx, or McDonald's) or dress codes (no denim jeans, shirts without collars, sneakers); the use of honorifics when addressing each other; and evaluations in which each member of a department or unit ranks the contributions of everyone else, all create group cohesion and are consistent with the collectivistic values of Hispanic society.

This is the background information that every line manager whose direct reports are Hispanic, Latino, and Latin employees in nonexempt positions should read, study, and understand. Being mindful of these cultural differences and nuances will make him or her more effective as a manager or supervisor. It is, of course, a general overview, and there are specific differences in each workplace. An organization in Los Angeles where almost all the Hispanic employees consist of Mexican Americans is different from one in New York where the majority of employees are of Puerto Rican or Dominican heritage.

With this in mind, in the previous chapter, we discussed the special concerns of two demographic groups: Cubans and Puerto Ricans. Now, we turn our attention to the obstacles posed by two recent phenomena, one affecting Caribbean Hispanics and the other Mexican Hispanics.

The Emergence of "Blatinos"

As the mosaic of Hispanic identities in the United States continues to evolve, the emergence of Caribbean Hispanic youth of color embracing hybrid labels is not to be unexpected. In metropolitan centers, such as New York and Miami, Caribbean youth of color, primarily of Dominican and Puerto Rican ancestry, have adopted a new label that reflects how they see themselves: black Latinos, or "Blatinos." This phenomenon is so recent that sociologists have only recently begun to study it; anthropologists are ahead of the curve. They have already turned their attention to Blatinos in the American workforce.[7] That Blatinos tend to be urban, young, and male means that they are disproportionately represented in the workforces of major metropolitan centers along the Eastern Seaboard. The fact that Blatinos are principally comprised of Puerto Rican and Dominican youth furthermore increases their "visibility" in contemporary culture; urban culture enjoys greater "street cred" among youth and hipster demographics.

These factors contribute to a disconcerting phenomenon: black entrepreneurs in metropolitan centers favor Blatinos over African American job applicants. The reasons for this are the fact that Blatinos are people of color, and they are bilingual. Blatinos can "pass" as black, while their command of Spanish vernacular allows them to communicate with Spanish-speaking customers. There is also the perception among black business owners that Blatinos are immigrants, and immigrants are widely presumed to be "better" workers than native-born job candidates. "[Black e]mployers have a favorable impression of immigrant labor. Even though they themselves are black, they often have a jaundiced view of the urban, or African-American labor force," Harvard anthropologist Katherine Newman reports, explaining why black businessmen in Harlem discriminate against African American job applicants. "They had very fine-grain preferences when it came to immigrant labor. . . . Latinos apply in smaller numbers than blacks but are much likelier to get hired [than native-born applicants]."[8]

This black-on-black discrimination fuels tensions between African American and Hispanic youth, and it creates a self-perpetuating cycle of challenges that center on the spread of Spanish in the nation's bilingual consumer economy; perceptions about disparities in the work ethics of immigrants versus native-born employees; and blurs the nature of race and diversity in the American workplace. There are no direct steps that can be taken to address these challenges, but management should be culturally intelligent about the conflicts Blatinos embody; embracing biracial identities and their bilingual skills creates a competitive advantage over monolingual African Americans, a considerable impediment to black youth, which suffers from higher unemployment rates during economic downturns.

The Pressure for Central Americans to "Mexicanize"

If Caribbean Hispanics are the forefront of racial identities east of the Mississippi, then Central Americans, particularly Salvadorans, are pioneering subsuming ethnic identities in the American West and California. The dominating, if not domineering, presence of Hispanics of Mexican ancestry, their U.S.-born Latino children, and waves of legal and illegal Latin immigrants from Mexico creates pressure for Central American immigrants to "Mexicanize" their public identities. This runs counter to the notion that immigrants will acculturate and then assimilate into the mainstream culture of the nation to which they emigrated. What we are experiencing, for the first time, is the reality that Mexican Hispanics, by virtue of higher fertility rates and immigration, created a tipping point for acculturation: it is easier for Latin immigrants to assimilate into a Mexican Hispanic identity than it is for them to move toward an Anglo American one.

"[T]housands of other Central and South American immigrants have left their native countries only to arrive in an American city dominated by Mexicans, who comprise L.A.'s largest Latino group and have access to most of the jobs sought by immigrants," Esmeralda Bermúdez writes. "The metropolis drives many to Mexicanize, to degrees big and small, often before they start to Americanize. Change comes gradually, particularly through speech, as different words take over, intonations fade and verbs are conjugated in new ways. Some immigrants begin to mimic *mejicanos* even before they leave their homeland. They toy with Mexican curse words and awkwardly bend their accents to blend in as they cross Mexico into the United States."[9]

This tendency creates its own set of distortions in the workplace, where the social and cultural character of the environment can become "Mexican dominant." In these instances, there is the subtle pressure, particularly for Latin employees, to adopt norms of the greater Mexican Hispanic society among them. This is a common response in diasporas, and it is an issue managers should be aware of, if only for their cultural awareness of the nuances and subtext that inform the work environment of distinct segments of the Mexican Hispanic workforce, primarily in areas west of the Mississippi.

CASE STUDY

The Dilemma at the *Los Angeles Times*

There are more Mexicans in Los Angeles than there are in Guadalajara. It stands to reason that there should be no difficulty for any organization to find a qualified candidate for any position given such a vast potential labor pool from which to draw. When the *Los Angeles Times,* the newspaper with the highest circulation in California, sought to be more inclusive in its coverage of southern California, particularly in view of the changing demographics of the constituencies and marketplaces it served, it sought to find a "Latino," meaning ideally, a "Mexican" voice to reflect the sensibilities of the Hispanic community. As this book shows, however, Mexican Hispanics are among the least-educated demographics in the United States, and finding a Mexican Hispanic who had the education, journalistic credentials, and work experience necessary proved an elusive task. Not unlike many other organizations before and since, the *Los Angeles Times* found itself having to dismiss U.S. Hispanics—and Latin American immigrants to southern California—to recruit a suitable candidate: Andres Martinez, a native of Mexico City.

Martinez, with an undergraduate degree from Yale, a master's degree from Stanford, and a law degree from Columbia, had a résumé that included reporting at the *Wall Street Journal* and editorial writing at the *New York Times*. Indeed, in 2004, he was a finalist for the Pulitzer Prize for his editorial writing at the *New York Times*. Although he subsequently resigned from the *Los Angeles Times* after an abbreviated tenure, this is a very public example of the challenge confronting every organization in the United States: whereas Mexican Hispanics constitute almost 80% of all U.S. Hispanics, they account for fewer than 20% of all college degrees awarded U.S. Hispanics in any given year. And for organizations that are proactive in hiring and promoting Mexican Hispanics, there is the stark reality that there are few who have the credentials and experience necessary to fill the ranks of upper-middle and upper management. This is the fundamental reason it is Cubans and Cuban Americans who swell the ranks of upper management positions, disproportionate to their demographic numbers, and inevitably creating a Cuban-nuanced sensibility where Hispanic issues, practices, and norms are adopted at the higher levels of organizations throughout the United States, creating cultural distortions in which the Cuban-minority perspective is projected on a Mexican-majority demographic.

CASE STUDY

Ask a Mexican Fraud at the *Orange County Weekly*

If the *Los Angeles Times* offers a classic case study of the challenges corporate America is encountering finding qualified Mexican Hispanics, then the *Orange County Weekly* is a lesson in the surreal. As the demographics changed dramatically in Orange

County, south of Los Angeles proper, local residents expressed curiosity about the ascendance of Mexicans in their community. The alternative newsweekly for the area, the *Orange County Weekly,* began to receive queries, and it responded by creating a column, "Ask a Mexican." The problem, of course, was familiar: Gustavo Arellano, the writer responsible for the column, was not a Mexican. He was a U.S.-born Latino, and to make matters worse, he was not fluent in either Spanish, or Mexican society. He summed up his Spanish as "atrocious," and when in Mexico, he entered as "tourist," who was disoriented in the norms of Mexican society.

This is an instance that is fraught with danger for organizations, because it speaks directly to the integrity, authenticity, and "street cred" among its customers. It's not difficult to see how a fraud was being perpetrated upon the reading public: it would have been honest to call the column "Ask a Latino," but if one is asking a "Mexican," one would expect that a Mexican is actually answering the questions. The other concern arises from how the author represents himself: pretending to be part of an "in-group" requires that one be part of that group. Arellano, who would be, when physically in Mexico, an American tourist on holiday in that country, was as disingenuous in representing himself as a Mexican. A greater concern, however, was the time in which this was taking place: James Frey had infuriated the public by publishing a nonfiction account of his life, *A Million Little Pieces,* which turned out to be a fabrication. In a similar vein, Arellano was falsely representing himself as a Mexican. To make matters worse, a jury had found Laura Albert, who wrote under the pseudonym, "JT LeRoy," guilty of fraud, and not a fictional "creation," as she claimed. By misrepresenting her identity to her publisher, Laura Albert was engaging in fraud. In the case of Arellano, Scribner published a collection of his columns under the title of *Ask a Mexican,* raising the question of why Scribner decided, it could be argued, to perpetrate a fraud upon the book-buying public.[10]

The scarcity of competent Mexican Hispanics, again, underscores how fraught with peril is the landscape organizations throughout the United States encounter in their proactive efforts to be more inclusive and have their workplace reflect the changing demographics of American society. The *Orange County Weekly* should be commended for attempting to address the questions and concerns their readers were raising, as the community changed around them. That they chose to play fast and loose with how they represented their column and their columnist—perhaps exemplifying the continuing problems of recruiting qualified Mexican Hispanics and Latin immigrants from Mexico—symbolizes more than a deliberate effort to deceive their readerships, but Arellano's posing as a Mexican did prove problematic: "Ask a Mexican" ended in March 2008, because even in southern California there are authentic limits to the inauthentic.

Mentoring Program for Hispanic, Latino, and Latin Employees in Exempt Positions

The *Los Angeles Times,* in search for a Latino, ended up with a Mexican. The *Orange County Weekly,* looking for a Mexican, settled on a Latino. Neither choice proved satisfactory, which is one reason mentoring programs continue to offer insights into identifying and cultivating talent within the various "Hispanic" constituencies. HSP professionals tend to hold leadership roles outside work, often serving as pillars of their communities, engaged in perceived obligations to ameliorate the obstacles the Hispanic diaspora faces locally. This, almost always, involves some form of mentoring, designed consistent with the collectivistic values of Hispanic culture. This represents an opportunity for HSP employees to *colaborar* and brings that experience to their employers, enhancing mentoring programs. Tapping this in-house HSP experience is a source of strength that can be channeled for the benefit of all employees, and the organization.

"For many minority professionals, involvement in such [mentoring] activities is an important, inherently satisfying part of their lives. For some, it's a way of giving back—or, more accurately, giving in turn the kind of help that benefited them early on. But it's also a fertile source of continued personal growth. In these myriad roles, minority professionals hone valuable leadership skills," Ann Hewlett, Carolyn Buck, and Cornel West write in the *Harvard Business Review.* "The problem is that those skills are not properly recognized by their employers. And no conscious attempt is made to transfer them into the corporate environment and develop them further. The disproportionate load of care that minority professionals bear in their extended families is also invisible to employers, and neither acknowledged nor supported by corporate benefits packages. The result: too many high-potential employees end up feeling ignored and diminished, overextended and burned out. At the same time, organizations are being deprived of the strong and diverse leadership they could so easily draw upon."[11]

There are several ways of implementing mentoring programs that nurture the HSP employee within the organization, preparing him or her for career advancement. The one described here is the one that consistently shows superior results. It focuses on the role and importance of *culturally aware* mentoring programs, simply because this is one of the more cost-effective ways to convey to the Hispanic, Latino, and Latin employee that they are valued, and the organization displays *simpatía* for the realities of the Hispanic diaspora. One of the "realities" that reverberates with greater force is the political awareness that, by virtue of demographic numbers, cultural claims to vast stretches of U.S. territory, and the emergence of a bilingual consumer economy, Hispanics are the only immigrant group that defies "assimilation" in the traditional American sense, and will continue to do so throughout this century. No other immigrant group has been able to have two national television networks—Telemundo and Univision—broadcast around the entire nation, and be commercially successful.

This means that "Hispanics" may acculturate, or assimilate, but they straddle two cultures and are the only segment of Americans that are truly bicultural. Through demographics and economic wherewithal, Hispanics have created a tipping point, transforming the United States into a bilingual, bicultural consumer economy. The downside of this, however, is that unless a Hispanic, Latino, or Latin employee is fully fluent in the dominant Anglo American culture, there is a need for "mentoring." Thus, how is "orientation" different for the Hispanic employee? What are the educational and professional needs of the Hispanic employee as he or she builds seniority?

A solid mentoring program for Hispanic, Latino, and Latin employees:

- Demonstrates openness and sincerity;
- Avoids gestures and behaviors that convey power and authority;
- Discusses language as an opportunity and an obstacle;
- Describes culturally acceptable norms and helps protégés find ways of living with them;
- Is receptive, showing empathy and validating feelings;
- Becomes a role model and provides peer support; and
- Allows for a formal conclusion of the mentoring program.

To develop and implement a successful mentoring program for HSP employees, it is imperative to have the commitment of senior management. "The commitment of senior management was cited as an important corporate attribute in retaining minority employees by 85 percent of executives and 82 percent of professionals; the next most frequently mentioned attribute was 'making diversity an integral part of the business strategy,' cited by 66 percent of executives and 62 percent of professionals," the Korn/Ferry Best Practices for Diversity study reports. "There is significant disagreement on the effectiveness of programs and organizations. Corporate executives say that 'relationships with minority-oriented organizations' are the most effective programs for attracting minority employees (cited by 91 percent), but just 61 percent of professionals view such programs as effective. Professionals believe that internships (cited by 65 percent) are most effective in attracting minority employees. Skills training is considered by corporate managers to be the most effective program to retain minority employees (cited by 98 percent), but just 70 percent of professionals view such programs as effective. Eighty percent of managers believe that mentoring programs are effective programs for retention, but just 57 percent of professionals agree. Managers and professionals also disagree on how effective larger corporations are, in general, in achieving diversity goals."[12]

Armed with this commitment from senior management, managers and supervisors, alongside human resources staff, are better able to assess their internal capabilities for identifying and recruiting internally mentors and role models who can participate in the development of talented Hispanic, Latino, and Latin employees within the organization. The initial orientation process for mentoring programs set the tone, and when dealing with employees who are "out-group," it is important to have a program in place that offers guidance into acculturation into the specific norms within an organization. This is an expanded process of socialization into the organization's culture, familiarization with the employer's philosophical approach, and how the firm understands and fulfills its social responsibilities to the community in which it operates. *Orientation* refers to the process of introducing mentoring program participants into the program itself. *Socialization* refers to the process of teaching employees about corporate culture and philosophies. *Training* refers to the process of improving skills needed today or in the near future, and development refers to improving skills over the long term.

Orientation and socialization into a mentoring program is referred to as "Onboarding." It describes the process of performing all the company actions that support new hire assimilation and transitioning current employees into a mentoring program. Onboarding steps include:

- Ensure the fit is good—evaluate skills to create a solid match.
- Tailor the program to the participants and workplace culture.
- Ensure proper training and orientation of mentors.
- Separate mismatched employees under different mentors.
- Ensure the employee's socialization and acculturation is appropriate.

The onboarding process should begin before the employee is brought into a mentoring program. These seven steps can serve as a checklist.

Step 1: Pre-Mentoring. As a preparation step, this is often not so much forgotten as simply not given adequate attention to ensure the program's first day's success.

- Inform the staff that a new employee will be joining the department, or that a current employee will be participating in a mentoring program.

- Provide some background information (name, work experience, start date).

- Make sure the work station is ready, neat and clean, and that computers, telephone lines, and other critical equipment is up and running.

- Prepare a tentative schedule of first-day and first-week activities including daily and weekly "check-in times" for employee questions and feedback.

- Have work ready and waiting for the employee being mentored.

Step 2: Welcome to New Employees and Current Employees. Before mentoring begins it is advisable to take some time to get acquainted with the new employee and current employee that will be participating in the program. A good opportunity for this is with an orientation tour of the facility and department. Managers and supervisors should be mindful that, culturally, being attentive at the beginning of any new relationship or professional experience is greatly valued in Hispanic culture. Being mindful of offering refreshments, including coffee, tea, soft drinks, or mineral water is valued. Consistent with the company's policies on such gestures, for participants in mentoring programs for middle- and senior-level positions, gifts—such as sending a basket

of fruit or an arrangement of flowers to a candidate's home—
may be appropriate.

It is important to introduce the new employee, or reacquaint
a current employee, to as many others in the department as
possible. Demonstrating to the employee that the organization values him or her as a new member of that team is a
powerful form of recognition. As with mainstream American
society, the first impression is important. A personal welcome
from a manager and director conveys a "we care" attitude
that nurtures *confianza* down the road.

Step 3: Acclimation. This step consists of a number of practical suggestions that build *confianza* by conveying a caring
attitude.

- Provide a tour of the department.
- Introduce the individual to co-workers.
- Explain the duties of each person so the new employee can
  understand how each fits into the organization.
- Review the day's planned activities and provide the
  employee with a schedule.
- Review any forms that the employee might have to com-
  plete or understand.

**Step 4: Assignment of an experienced co-worker, preferably
another Hispanic, Latino, or Latin employee, to be a "counselor" or "guide."** Relationship-building is always an important issue among all members of a workforce. For cultures
that are collectivistic in outlook, the quality of human relationships among the members is closely related to *confianza,*
which, in the workplace, results in increased retention and
productivity. Distrust, resentments, and frustrations
decrease productivity and can seriously reduce an organization's ability to meet its objectives. Openness, friendli-
ness, and trust among members of a team or department,

on the other hand, contribute to cooperation, productivity, and long-term employment. When we addressed the social factors that contribute to members of the Hispanic diaspora being "at risk," researches have posited that being removed from their home societies contributes to stress that leads to chronic medical conditions. Despite efforts of various Hispanic, Latino, and Latin communities to increase the "social capital" here in the United States, Latino and Latin segments of the Hispanic diaspora continue to struggle to overcome language and cultural barriers in the United States. Starting a new job that has a mentoring program reduces the demanding situation for the Hispanic, Latino, and Latin employee.

An assigned mentor (preferably with a similar culture) can show the newcomer, or a current employee participating in a mentoring program, to "learn the ropes" of the organization's culture, answer basic "how to" questions, familiarize the employee with the habits and daily procedures of the staff, make staff introductions, show the new employee the location of facilities (restrooms, cafeteria, equipment, and supplies), take the new employee to lunch, and provide limited instruction in informal department rules and procedures.

Here are a few ways to select a "counselor" or "guide." You need someone who is:

- On a peer level with new employee
- Well-versed in the organization and department practices
- Experienced and with a good understanding of policies and procedures
- Someone with excellent work behaviors
- Friendly, enthusiastic
- A positive role model

Step 5: Orientation. The purpose of New Employee/Current Employee Orientation is to welcome and educate all new and transferring employees and provide them with critical information about the organization. Managers and supervisors have the obligation to communicate with each new worker in a way that he or she can understand. In many instances, this means having information that is provided in English also available in Spanish (see www.Hispanic-Workforce.com). This information is designed to maximize their safety, success, and commitment to the organization.

Goals of an orientation program include:

- Reducing first-day anxieties by helping new employees feel secure, welcome
- Instilling positive attitudes toward work
- Communicating what the organization offers, but also what it expects in the way of performance
- Providing basic information needed to perform effectively and efficiently

Supervisors are crucial to the orientation and integration process. The supervisor is the first person the new employee will be dealing with and the person who will be most influential in the newcomer's first impressions.

After general orientation, the supervisor should introduce the employee to their job duties and performance expectations. Department orientation includes:

- Organizational structure
- Department policies and operating procedures
- Department goals and priorities
- General expectations and standards
- Safety rules should be in Spanish as well, written and distributed

- Pay
- Hours of work
- Overtime requirements
- Breaks and meal periods
- Job description and responsibilities
- Opportunities for training and learning
- Where do I go if I need something clarified in Spanish?

Step 6: Job-Related Training. Structured training is a methodical approach to ensure competency of the employee, and allows for the careful supervision of the acculturation process. It is also used to determine the skills needed to perform the tasks and define minimum performance levels. The methods of instruction include demonstration, personal coaching, written instruction (procedure manuals, guides, etc.), and shadowing of other experienced employees.

Written standard operating procedures (SOPs) are an important part of an organization's ability to achieve its goals. Formal SOPs are essential for businesses that employ more than one or two workers. Manuals however, cannot replace effective "hands-on" instruction and training. Demonstration in a training setting and practice are critical to good retention and accurate work. Managers should supplement written SOPs with visual aids. Whenever possible, use diagrams, pictures, or photographs that help explain correct procedures.[13] Consult extension and industry advisors for help with these materials. There is a wealth of support material available for managers and supervisors to review.[14]

Step 7: Feedback/Communication. There are certain aspects of Hispanic culture that inhibit feedback, even among HSP employees. One consequence of being members of the Hispanic diaspora is that Hispanics, Latinos, and Latins, even those who are college educated, are often reluctant to ask questions when they don't understand some part of their training, which is consistent with the lack of confidence that is found among members of "out-groups" when dealing with members of "in-groups." There is also a very strong desire to be successful in their work and to please their immediate supervisors. This often leads many to feel very insecure about asking questions. This insecurity can be turned into a positive through a mentor that stresses asking questions, requesting clarification and voicing reservations as a successful way of building "social capital" with managers and supervisors. This approach circumvents the problem often seen: insecure employees let problems fester rather than reaching out to the manager for help. In many cases, minor problems or misunderstandings can lead to the loss of good workers, all due to poor communication. Sometimes, managers who understand the importance of feedback for workers hesitate to provide it because of language and cultural barriers.[15]

In order to hardwire the feedback process:

1. Schedule a periodic checkpoint meeting with co-workers and supervisors to track performance.

2. Provide an initial thirty-day review designed to ensure that individuals can do their jobs.

3. If the employee is doing well, ask if they need anything from their supervisor, or yourself, to help do their job. It is important to reinforce good performance.

4. If the employee is faltering, provide coaching and feedback on areas needing improvement and recommend how to improve.

An important part of feedback is checking in with the employee at the end of the first month. Here are some sample questions that may be useful for the thirty-day discussion:

- Have the employee's co-workers been friendly and helpful?
- Does the employee know where to find resources needed to perform his or her duties?

- Has the employee been properly introduced to other staff in the department?
- Is the employee satisfied with his or her schedule?
- Is the job what the employee expected?

In Review

- "Cultural Dimensions," as defined by Gerard Hofstede, offer insights into the cross-cultural programs for Employee Training and Development in the changed American workplace.

- Fragmentation of the Hispanic diaspora, with the emergence of "Blatinos" and the cultural pressure for Central American immigrants to "Mexicanize" their identities, creates new challenges for managers, supervisors, and other administrators.

- Mentoring remains the most effective way of developing Hispanic, Latino, and Latin employees, providing it is done in a way that facilitates their moving from being an "out-group" closer to the norms of the "in-group," promoting their acculturation.

Chapter 10

Empowering the Hispanic Employee and an Organization's Future

When I was once interviewed by CNN reporter Louise Schiavone, one producer, without any malice, casually asked me what could be done to keep "them"—Hispanics, Latinos, and Latins—from "taking over" the country. I smiled politely and gave my standard reply: "Go home and get pregnant." That's what Vladimir Putin is telling his countrymen: the government will pay ethnic Russians to have more ethnic Russian babies. The only way to "stop" Hispanics from "taking over" is for non-Hispanic Americans to have more non-Hispanic American babies.

What will your organization's workforce look like a decade from now? Management needs to take a look around and see, precisely, how the demographics of their workplace are changing, and their communities are evolving. A decade down the road, who will have retired or left? A decade from now, when the natural contractions of the business cycle will have long run its course, who currently working will be ready for greater responsibilities? In the years ahead, what demographics are affecting customers, vendors, colleagues, and the community?

Managers need to understand that their organization's future is closely linked to the success of Hispanic, Latino, and Latin employees. Management needs to implement programs that, in the same way that diversity training paves the role for women and African Americans to advance throughout an organization, the cultural obstacles that hold Hispanics, Latinos, and Latins back should be addressed. With the lessons from the previous chapters behind us, it is now possible to think strategically about the future, raising issues that speak directly to the demographics, the undeniable and irreversible trends that are transforming the United States from a "black and white" society into one in which "brown" stands to become the plurality by mid-century. For organizations throughout the nation, there are obstacles as the present and future workforce becomes a tsunami throughout the economy. Specifically, the questions below seek to address these obstacles.

How and why Hispanics are concentrated in nonsalaried professional, service occupations. *Where is the next generation of mid- and upper-level managers coming from if not from the ranks of Hispanics?*

Why the occupational status of Mexicans and Puerto Ricans lags the most in comparison with the status of whites. Cubans and whites are comparable in occupational status. *What can managers do to ensure that local schools and colleges prepare young Hispanic, Latino, and Latin youth to stay in school and earn college degrees?*

As candidates for upper management are recruited from Latin America, *how can tensions between native-born Hispanics and Latinos and foreign-born Hispanics and Latins be addressed?*

Often there are educational and cultural limits that impose a glass ceiling on U.S. Hispanics. *How can these limitations be removed? Why does education improve the occupational status of U.S.-born workers but is not as effective at doing so for foreign-born Hispanics?*

More recently arrived Latin immigrants have lower occupational status than previously arrived immigrants, even if they have the same level of education and experience. *What mentoring or acculturation programs can an organization have to foster greater assimilation and career advancement?*

Hispanics report that they are frustrated by the lack of *confianza* they feel from their managers and the limited opportunities they have to *superarse* in their current work. As a result, they "have a very high probability of switching occupations within five years," the Pew Hispanic Center reports.[1] *What can be done to foster greater loyalty to the organization?*

It's a brave new world, where the changed American workplace represents new challenges. Organizations need to understand that it is market driven—no law requires companies to have customer service toll free numbers that say, "Press 1 to continue in English, *Oprima 2 para español*," but they do so because the realities of the competitive marketplace make it necessary. In a similar vein, the emergence of a bilingual consumer economy and the Hispanization of the United States now require that, in the same way that women were incorporated into the workplace, Hispanics be fully integrated.

Strategic decisions about an organization's future often convey the narrative of history, with the promise of new opportunities over the horizon. This is especially true for established firms and organizations, where the sense of history is always present. Sam Walton's memory looms large over the corporate culture at Wal-Mart; John Muir's legacy informs how the Sierra Club sees its vision; the United States Postal Service reveres the mandate set forth by Benjamin Franklin; and Sophia Smith's vision of feminist empowerment guides the spirit of Smith College. This is the reality to which Samuel Huntington speaks when he expresses alarm at the emergence of two competing cultures in the United States, with the emergence of Hispanics as a direct cultural and historical challenge to the Anglo-Protestant tradition. His warnings, however, are not unfamiliar, and have often been sounded throughout American history. "The new immigration from Southern and Eastern Europe, with its lower standard of living and characteristic racial differences has intensified many existing social problems and created a number of new ones," Arthur M. Schlesinger warned in 1921.[2]

To a great extent, the conflict between the Hispanic diaspora and mainstream American society goes beyond the differences between "out-groups" and "in-groups," and the guilt non-Hispanics feel about the historical crimes against the First Peoples of this continent. It is more than "brown" intruding on the unfinished business between "black and white," specifically the politics of grievance that many African Americans feel toward white America. The truth at the core is the basic human desire to be given a fair hearing. Hispanics feel marginalized because they believe their concerns are not validated; that they, as individuals and as a community, are vilified; and that past wrongs are not discussed openly and honestly.

Everyone has grievance, and every group can make a claim against another. Consider this curious grievance: after the election of Barack Obama, many blacks in the United States expressed their opinions about this achievement with the sentiment that they thought that such a thing would not happen in their "lifetime." A week after the election, I was at dinner at the home of family friends, a very privileged family who lives on the Upper East Side in Manhattan. Over the course of the evening, the patrician of the family, a gentleman who could have walked straight out of central casting, and with more than a passing resemblance to the actor Christopher Plummer, expressed his "disappointment" in the African American admission that they thought Caucasians voting for a black presidential candidate would not occur in their "lifetime." "The suggestion is that we are all bigots," he said, "when the truth is that, given a better choice of candidates, anyone would vote for whom we thought would be better for the country, regardless of race." He then went on to point out that the only black candidates in *his* lifetime to run for the president were not, in his view, electable. "If I recall correctly, there was Chisholm in 1972, followed by Jesse Jackson's runs in 1984 and 1988, which were followed by Alan Keyes in 1996 and 2000, and most recently Carol Moseley Braun and Al Sharpton in 2004. Jackson and Sharpton are toxic, and the rest, while good people, were simply not qualified. Colin Powell never ran, but had he run in 2000, I am convinced he would have won." The reluctance of African Americans to believe that white America and the Hispanic diaspora could, as Martin Luther King Jr. envisioned, judge a presidential candidate on the basis of his or her character alone, has hurt the sensibilities of many non-black Americans.

The strategy that the healthy development of an organization's workforce is best accomplished through empowering and nurturing employees is a sound one. An integral component of this strategy is the practice of "fair hearings," where the concerns, as they evolve and change over time, and impact both the work and personal lives of employees, are sound. In the late 1990s companies that empowered their employees by supporting Hometown Associations (HTAs) were rewarded with committed workers, and one unintended consequence was a steady flow of referrals when vacancies had to be filled. Other organizations generated tremendous goodwill by working with foreign government consulates to inform Latin immigrants about services their nations' diplomatic representatives could offer them. Still other firms extended the courtesies of offering bilingual seminars to inform workers about the mundane chores of everyday life: how to register children for school; how to apply for library cards; how to fill out the forms for the motor vehicles office; or how to get information about vaccinations or prenatal care. It is not uncommon for companies in the service sector to reward exceptional work by giving away calling cards good for international phone calls.

These steps, as we have seen, are one way of reaching out and empowering Hispanics, Latino, and Latin employees in ways that are culturally sensitive. Employers are right to express concern about liabilities incurred in providing this information, or may be concerned about appearing to favor one group over another. A solution is to provide a "Welcome Wagon" type of handout to all employees, with information about where the libraries are located, how to register children at school, where government social services are located, the address of the department of motor vehicles, and so on, to help all employees become oriented about the community. Employees who are from the area may have walked by the library all their lives, but for new residents, the information can be helpful, and conveys their employer's concern for their successful adjustment to the community.

Another recommendation that is societal in scope, but which proactive organizations can begin to contemplate, centers on the unpleasant realities of human history. No one alive today had anything to do with the unfortunate decision to go ahead with the Atlantic slave trade, or to establish the Inquisition, or to authorize the forced relocation of the First Peoples in North America during the Trail of Tears, known as disambiguation. But in the same way, however, that we benefit from what we have inherited from generations before us (the alphabet, the printing press, the lightbulb, and everything else that makes our lives less brutish, nasty, and short), so should we acknowledge the obligation to, if nothing else, *validate the grievances* of those among us whose forebears were affected negatively by wrongs. This is why we have museums, where we can learn about the good things we inherited—masterpieces, like the *Mona Lisa*, or technological advances, such as photography—but also about the shameful chapters in human history, such as the Holocaust or the Belgian occupation of the Congo.

It was briefly discussed that the Hispanic diaspora in the United States fails to show adequate *simpatía* for the spiritual traumata race relations have inflicted on the American psyche. Another area where empathy is lacking is in assuaging the fears and anxieties that non-Hispanic Americans have about Hispanic ascendance, evident in Samuel Huntington's writings, in the hateful rhetoric on A.M. radio talk shows throughout the country, and in casual conversations with CNN producers who express their apprehensions in unfortunate phrases.

But the facts are the facts, and fertility rates in the United States are, as the Census Bureau reports, what they are: the onerous responsibility falls on non-Hispanic Americans to empathize, simply because they have more power than members of the Hispanic diaspora by virtue of being the dominant culture of the United States. The Anglo-Protestant American culture, the "in-group," however, is in decline, and the Hispanic diaspora, the "out-group," is in ascendance, and the changed American workforce is a harbinger of things to come. That said, there are two areas where managers, supervisors, and other administrators can take a proactive role in beginning dialogues that will inform how "brown" relations with "black" and "white" America emerge.

There are two areas of concern that are only now beginning to appear on the radar screen of the nation's life, and as these grow more prominent, they will shape the narrative of "diversity," "empowerment," and "fairness" in the changed American workplace. One area concerns primarily Mexican Hispanics and the other Caribbean Hispanics. Regardless of what one thinks of the merits of these issues—or grievances—it is, in the American spirit, imperative to give them a fair hearing, not only because it is the right thing to do, but also because it is a proactive way of engaging Hispanics, Latinos, and Latins in a conversation that bridges the distance between the "out-group" of the Hispanic diaspora and the "in-group" of mainstream American society. In short, it is an important way that the "in-group" in *decline* can reach out to the "out-group" that is in *ascendance,* building *confianza* through management's act of *simpatía.*

Mexican Hispanic Historical Grievance

In the discussion presented here a subject alluded to, but not addressed, has to do with the latent hostility from Hispanics. Although they are few in number, managers and supervisors need to understand the underlying reasons for passive aggressive attitudes among certain Hispanic, Latino, and Latin employees, and how these historical "grievances" can be disruptive in the workplace. It is not a secret, for instance, that American society continues to deal with the consequences of the unfinished business from slavery: many African Americans believe that reparations were not made to compensate those held in bondage, and those who had to endure a century of oppression during segregation. "Forty acres and a mule" remains the mantra of the broken promises of free Americans to those who were enslaved, and their descendants.

In a similar vein, certain groups of Hispanics hold, if not grudges, then historical complaints, which create a simmering level of hostility toward non-Hispanics. The reasons or historical details, their merits notwithstanding, are not material to the discussion at hand, but managers and supervisors need to be aware of the specific nature of certain attitudes. Many Hispanics of Cuban ancestry (Latin immigrants from Cuba or their U.S.-born children) harbor the grievance that the United States has not done what it promised to overthrow the Castro brothers' regimes in Cuba. Many point to the failure of the Kennedy administration to provide air cover during the Bay of Pigs invasion in 1961 for the failure of that attempt. Many others nurture complaints that subsequent administrations have done nothing to end Communist rule on that island nation. The result is a fostering dissatisfaction with American political society, and the lingering cynicism and disappointment in U.S. institutions.

Puerto Ricans who, as we have seen, live under a cloud of suspicion in the eyes of their fellow Latin Americans, nurture a longing for independence. While Puerto Ricans are grateful that their status as U.S. citizens exempts them from all manner of immigration concerns, there remains the widespread feeling among Puerto Ricans that American citizenship does not fully compensate for national independence. These are conflicted feelings, particularly for those born on the U.S. mainland, many of whom feel torn between their cultural heritage, and the communities where they were born and raised. There is always a regret when a community makes a Faustian bargain; Puerto Rican youth tend to adopt aggressive attitudes toward "the Man," as mainstream American society and authority figures are referred to, which can influence their attitudes in the workplace.

Latinos, the majority of whom are Americans of Mexican ancestry, express a lingering complaint that has an undeniable air of moral authority, and is fraught with complicated emotions. While it is not unknown that the Mexican-American War concluded with the Treaty of Guadalupe-Hidalgo in 1848, what is not widely known is that the United States violated the terms of the treaty. That treaty required the U.S. government to recognize property and land deeds held by Mexican and Spanish citizens, known as "Californios," and to provide a mechanism by which the residents of the territories transferred to the U.S. jurisdiction to become U.S. citizens. This is not an exceptional clause in a treaty of this nature, and the United States was well on its way to complying with the terms stipulated. Notice the year, however. The year after the treaty was signed, in 1849, gold was discovered in northern California.

At that moment, everything changed in Washington: before the discovery of gold, few in Washington were concerned about the few thousand Mexicans and Spanish citizens out West, scattered across a vast landscape, living in small towns and cities like Albuquerque, San Diego, Los Angeles, and San Francisco, most of whom were ranchers or shopkeepers. The discovery of gold changed the political equation: Washington was not prepared to have non-Anglos, who spoke Spanish, and whose lifelong allegiance had been to Mexico City or Madrid own properties that may have vast reserves of gold beneath them. The sentiment and consensus in Washington was that, by right, this mineral wealth should belong to English-speaking Americans. Within two years, legislation was passed to deny Mexicans and Californios (Spaniards) titles to their property, and systematically deny them citizenship, a unilateral violation of the peace treaty with Mexico.

As historian Douglas Monroy explains:

> The Land Act of 1851 wreaked havoc on the [Mexican and Californio] rancheros' claims. It created a three-person commission to which all titles of the Spanish and Mexican eras had to be submitted for validation. . . . The commission proceeded from the assumption that all titles were invalid until proved otherwise. . . . The Land Act effectively dispossessed Californios of approximately 40 percent of their lands held before 1846. In the contradictory American tradition of liberty, speculators with cash and shrewdness, not small farmers, usually grabbed the lands.
>
> Article 9 of the Treaty of Guadalupe-Hidalgo declared that Mexicans "shall be maintained and protected in the free enjoyment of their liberty and property." . . . The massive alienation of Californio lands, and their transfer to others, obviously fell outside the letter and spirit of the treaty and American respect for private property.[3]

The result was a double disenfranchisement. Here we had a people who didn't cross the border, but the border crossed them, and then they were, by law, deprived of their properties and civil rights.

In the nineteenth century, gold backed money, and money, as the song says, changes everything.

Consider what this historical grievance means for Mexican Hispanics. Consider the implications of the paradox that it's quite possible that a Mexican whose great-grandparents had their ranch seized by the U.S. government, moved to Mexico, and subsequently returns to her ancestral homeland is considered an "illegal" alien, while a Cuban, who has absolutely no connection to the United States, can throw himself into the Straits of Florida, washes ashore in Miami

Beach, and is automatically entitled to permanent residence and social security benefits. In a similar vein, it's possible to find a complaint from every other segment of the Hispanic community: Dominicans complain that they are "immigrants" while Puerto Ricans are not; Chileans gripe about the U.S. overthrow of Salvador Allende; Nicaraguans resent the failure of the United States to comply with orders from the World Court and compensate that nation for mining it harbors, and so on.

There is, of course, nothing that any one of us can do about these historical grievances, but it is important to be aware of, and sensitive to, the nuanced tension that lies beneath the surface and affects labor relations. It's easy to dismiss these claims as immaterial to the workplace, but it is important to understand how they affect the "Latino" psyche of employees, another manifestation of the anguish of the Hispanic diaspora in the United States. If nothing else, awareness of these issues makes one a better manager or supervisor.

Staying current in the marketplace of ideas is also important, and for a generation, Mexican intellectuals have pondered the possibility of a "Greater Mexico"—the idea that Mexican immigration to the United States was so persistent and sustainable, that Mexican culture could "re-settle" lands lost to the United States at the conclusion of the Mexican-American War. This phrase was coined by Américo Paredes in his landmark work, "With His Pistol in His Hand," and it is an idea associated with his work and that of José E. Limón on the cultural conflicts along the Texas-Mexico border. Americans, clinging to the belief of a "melting pot," dismissed that notion, arguing that Mexican immigrants would follow historical norms and assimilate into mainstream American life, as previous generations of newcomers did before them.

A recent study by the Institute of Mexicans Abroad (IME), part of Mexico's Ministry of Foreign Relations, offers insight that answers this lingering question of how Mexicans who spend time working in the United States influence change in Mexico when they return. As Carlos González y Gutiérrez, IME's director, told Notimex, "To our surprise and unease, we realize that Greater Mexico isn't on the other side of the moon, but that more and more it looks like us, and that has many consequences. The principal one is that this new situation reflects, to a good degree, our divisions of class, background, language, ethnicity and educational attainment."

That is to say, there is a "perfect storm" in which middle-class ambition, immigration, and higher birth rates among Hispanics, is changing the face of Mexicans in the United States. Whereas in the past the bulk of Mexicans entering the United States has come from the economically marginalized—rural farmers, urban poor, undereducated, and unemployed—as part of NAFTA's unintended consequences, Mexican middle-class professionals are now establishing themselves on both sides of the border. Hundreds of thousands of non-*mestizos,* which is to say, Mexicans who are Caucasian and of European descent (like the initial waves of Cuban refugees and their U.S.-born children), are migrating to the United States; the idea of a "Greater Mexico" is becoming a reality, at least in terms of shaping the narrative of the Mexican Hispanic experience in the United States.

In recent years in fact, reaching out to Mexicans and their U.S.-born children has become a priority for Mexican intellectuals. "Americans reject them because they see them as Mexicans and Mexicans reject them precisely because they are not Mexicans," Elena Poniatowska, a Mexican writer, says, commenting on the identity politics that gave rise to the word "Latino" in the United States. "I have had young Chicana writers introduce themselves, and within two minutes declare to me that they are lesbians. I wouldn't come up to anyone and say, 'I am a heterosexual and a grandmother.' This happens only to people surrounded by a culture trying to destroy them and who have created themselves out of this destruction."[4]

What are the implications of the grievances Mexican Hispanics feel, their historic sense of entitlement to settle in the United States, and the idea of "Greater Mexico" for organizations? What are the socioeconomic, cultural, and political consequences of these subjects for the changed American workforce?

These are the questions that are bound to join discussions of "glass ceilings" and "affirmative action" in the next decade.

Caribbean Hispanic Racial Paradox

If Caribbean Hispanics have a racial history more analogous to the American experience, then it follows that they face similar issues when it comes to race as do non-Hispanic Americans. In the United States, it is generally understood that a person is "black" if there is any Negroid ancestry; in Latin America, there were many categories to distinguish complicated ancestry, so much so that it proved unworkable, because it gave everyone a headache trying to figure things out. What emerged was a consensus that "mulatto" would apply to a person who was of mixed ancestry, Caucasian and Negroid.[5] Barack Obama uses this term to describe himself, as knowing that other Americans saw him as a "mulatto trapped between two worlds" of black and white America. How many worlds is a person "trapped" between if he is a mulatto *who is also a Hispanic?*

Caribbean Hispanics can seldom be confined to the "racial" box of American life, where it is "black" or "white"—which box would singer and actress Jennifer López choose? So it is not surprising that Caribbean Hispanics encounter distinct racial tensions when "black," "white," and "brown" collide, living their lives in the Hispanic diaspora. Consider racial tensions among law enforcement officers in New York, where "Blatinos"—Hispanics who are black or mulatto and come primarily from Puerto Rico or the Dominican Republic—are part of the mosaic of New Yorkers. In a story on race relations in the New York City Police Department, Michael Winerip reported:

> Several years ago, before going undercover, [undercover police officer] Derrick recalls being in street clothes, on his way to work at the 63rd Precinct in Brooklyn, when he saw an elderly woman being robbed by two teenagers. He managed to get the woman into his car, subdue the attackers (though he had no handcuffs) and persuade a passer-by to call 911—an effort that would win him a hero's medal. But as he waited for backup, he was scared. Most officers at the 63rd were away at a funeral that day. He feared that the officers who showed up

would not know him, and that he would be in danger—a black man in street clothes with a gun. Seeing a patrol car approach, he waved his police ID over his head and kept screaming: "I'm a cop! I'm a cop!"

Race colors everything for Harlem narcotics detectives. It lies beneath the surface in a dispute over tactics between a white sergeant and a black undercover detective. Race is out there in the neighborhood where Sergeant Brogli's team pits African American informers against Dominican drug dealers. Race is in the police radio descriptions ("suspect is a dark-skinned Dominican, mid-20's . . ."), and race amplifies the anger on the street when the police drive up and arrest yet another dark-skinned man.[6]

In the course of doing their work, police officers who happen to be "Blatino" confront unique challenges:

Years ago, when Detective [Johnny] González [who is Dominican and black] was on uniformed housing patrol in Red Hook, Brooklyn, white officers couldn't tell what he was by looking at him and were guarded until reading his name tag. "Then they'd say, 'Oh, you're González—these blacks, aren't they like animals with all their kids?'"

"Now I'm in a Dominican neighborhood," he said. "I'll hear some sergeant, not knowing I'm around, talking about Domos this, Domos that."

"I had a white cop ask me, 'How many in your family are drug dealers?'" said Detective González, who doesn't drink alcohol. "I told him, in my family, nobody."

If the police can be too quick to label, Detective González says, they are only reflecting society.[7]

Imagine having to write job performance reviews on these three employees. For residents of the most diverse city in the nation, what can be said confidently about their cultural intelligence? How would a manager begin to approach the climate of hostility in which these officers work?

This is not so much about a "post-racial" America as it is about self-identification in a time when demographics are in flux, and there is a seismic shift. It is not difficult to see the complexities that emerge in the new workplace. This anecdote, which is replied in thousands of variations throughout the nation on any given work day, shows how "lookism" can undermine *confianza,* and how this, coupled with the tendency to internalize job performance, further erodes the Hispanic employee's confidence. It is, however, a person's self-esteem that informs his or her demeanor in the workplace, and in turn, it affects how others, including immediate supervisors, perceive him or her.

It is difficult to underscore the sensitivity of U.S.-born Hispanics, particularly English-dominant Latinos, to the social stigma attached to the idea of "walking while brown." Consider that U.S.-born Hispanics are among the most vocal opponents to any amnesty program for illegal aliens, and are the more enthusiastic supporters of the armed forces. To prove their patriotism, and prove their right to belong, they are among the most ardent supporters of tough immigration laws, and often express hostility toward new Latin immigrants.

How is "race" to be redefined in the changed American workplace? How is an interracial person of Hispanic ancestry to be classified for the purposes of diversity? How are tensions and resentments, such as those expressed by Detective González in the New York Police Department, to be addressed? How are Americans, whom Europeans consider to be all mongrels—to the European sensibility, an American such as Ronald Reagan who was a "mixture" of Irish and English, was a "half-breed"—to rethink what it means to transcend race and ethnicity?

To appreciate the vexing challenges of the ascendance of Hispanics in the workplace, consider that in other industries, management is employing anthropologists to make sense of it all. Merchandisers, for instance, routinely consult "retail anthropologists" to understand how consumers move and conduct themselves in retail stores. For the "changed" American workplace, which means "Hispanized" workplace, *confianza* is one of the "anthropological" keys to making sense of it all. If *confianza* is absent between employees, managers, or supervisors, many Hispanic, Latino, and Latin employees will "shut down" in how they see their managers or super-visors, and how their repertoire unfolds.[8]

This is especially the case when it comes to race, and the reason for this is cultural. It is also important to bear in mind that "look-ism" plays a role as well. A sophisticate, who was once a beauty queen in Latin America, dryly remarked that in the United States, the "Latino" community was filled with "short, fat, brown people who were angry they were not tall, thin and fair." If there are legit-imate issues with society's perception of beauty, which itself changes over time, as the plump and pale figures in pre-Raphaelite paintings attest, what is certain is that questions of "race" are being replaced by the issue of "lookism," and Hispanics, Latinos, and Latins are at the forefront of this emerging discussion. Not unlike the Amish who don't want you, but just want you to leave them alone, there will come a time when the rhetoric against Hispanics, Latinos, and Latins will be over, and when that day comes, they won't be miss-ing anyone.

This is further complicated by the linguistic barriers between His-panic Americans and non-Hispanic Americans. Consider the linguistic divide:

	Speaking at Home	Speaking at Work
Spanish	56%	31%
English	18%	51%
Both	26%	15%
No Answer	0	3%[9]

That 80% of Hispanics and Latinos speak Spanish at home, and almost a third are able to work full-time jobs without having to speak English suggests that 1) the United States has reached an irreversible "tipping point" in becoming a permanent bilingual consumer econ-omy; and 2) U.S. Hispanics have the critical mass necessary to sus-tain a separate community, one in which Hispanics will acculturate, but will not have to assimilate, into the mainstream of American life.

In consequence, what can be said with certainty is that strate-gic thinking that considers an organization's future, and how a Hispanized labor market can meet future goals, includes priorities that consider the following points.

The Hispanic diaspora requires diversity programs that integrate them into the changed American workplace. Management should develop diversity programs that speak to the specific linguistic, cultural, and family needs of Hispanic, Latino, and Latin employees. Managers, supervisors, and other administrators should support policies that allow for a seamless integration of the Hispanic, Latino, and Latin worker through diversity programs that make him or her feel welcome and comfortable, and then incorporates him or her into the organization's workplace.

Effectively communicating with members of the Hispanic diaspora is crucial to their success, vital in bridging the abyss that separates the "in-group" from the "out-group." Language remains a crucial concern as the nation evolves into a bilingual consumer economy. English as a Second Language (ESL), Accent Reduction/Elimination courses, and Introductory Spanish need to be provided, or facilitated, as part of a sound diversity program. In organizations with large numbers of nonexempt Hispanic, Latino, and Latin workers, English-language literature should be written in the passive voice.

Recognition of work well done and nonpecuniary rewards are important aspects of Hispanic cultural traditions. Management policies should reflect the value that Hispanic, Latino, and Latin employees place on continuing education as a "reward" for a job well done. Affinity programs that are endorsed, or facilitated, by the organization can strengthen the bonds between the organization and its Hispanic, Latino, and Latin workforce. Mentoring is a time-honored mechanism for rewarding Hispanic, Latino, and Latin employees. It is imperative to have a balanced approach to evaluating job performance, highlighting what the employee brings to the table, not simply reiterating what is lacking.

Hispanic, Latino, and Latin employees challenge management's concept of the "work-life" balance. Hispanic, Latino, and Latin employees add their voices to other constituencies in seeking to expand how organizations define "family." Hispanic, Latino, and Latin employees are more likely to choose to remain the primary caregivers for elderly parents, and seek to have health benefits extended to include these responsibilities. Hispanic, Latino, and Latin employees are four times more likely to leave the workforce in order to fulfill what they understand to be their obligations to family.

Workplace conflicts and dispute resolution center on the growing "black versus brown" tensions in American society, and "white" anxieties about being displaced as Hispanic Americans move toward becoming the nation's plurality by mid-century. Hispanic, Latino, and Latin working-age employees are fast displacing African Americans, a fact that is creating tension between the nation's two largest minorities. Management needs to understand this tension that is invading the workplace, and to develop seminars, workshops, and classroom instruction that fosters a "dialogue" between African American and Hispanic, Latino, and Latin employees. Managers, supervisors, and other administrators should also be aware of the peculiar phenomenon that, as Hispanic, Latino, and Latin employees become acculturated, they tend to adopt antiblack attitudes.

Supporting professional and trade organizations is an indispensable way for management to support their Hispanic, Latino, and Latin employees. Management should encourage Hispanic, Latino, and Latin employees to participate in professional and trade organizations that are appropriate to their professions or interests. Management policies should, for firms that have a significant number of nonsalaried Hispanic employees, endorse Hometown Associations (HTAs) in order to send a powerful signal to employees about the organization's commitment to their concerns. When Hispanic, Latino, and Latin employees leave the organization, management should elicit information that will strengthen their diversity program. Proper exit interviews are valuable tools to improve the working environment for the Hispanic, Latino, and Latin employees who remain. Exit interviews can provide managers and human resources staff with insights that are indispensable to strengthening the organization's diversity program, for the good of all employees.

Organizations should adopt proactive strategies that offer a "win-win" outcome, creating a sustainable competitive advantage in the emerging U.S. labor market.

In Review

- Demographics changes are unfolding at a faster rate than anticipated, creating a situation in which Hispanics, Latinos, and Latins are the demographic group from which the majority of management candidates will emerge beginning in the next decade.

- The concerns of the Hispanic diaspora, including historical Mexican Hispanic claims to the violation of the terms of the treaty ending the Mexican-American War and the reframing of race and race relations by Caribbean Hispanics of color, are replacing the familiar discussions of "glass ceilings" and "affirmative action" that were common between the 1970s and 2000s.

- The "Hispanization" of the changed American workplace is a precursor to social, cultural, and political developments that will emerge in this century, the Hispanic Century in the United States.

Conclusion

The information provided in this book can be overwhelming, simply because it addresses the complexity of the "mosaic" that constitutes the "Hispanic" identity in the United States. Non-Hispanic managers and professionals, who see the workplace change around them as Hispanics, Latinos, and Latins surge into the American workforce, have long voiced concerns about how to make sense of the changes around them. This has, sadly, been complicated by the uniformed nature of the U.S.-born "Latino" compatriots who, severed from their culture by virtue of living in the Hispanic diaspora, remain woefully uninformed; most Latinos do not know enough Spanish to translate "To Whom It May Concern" properly. The result has been that non-Hispanic managers who have availed themselves to Latinos in their organizations have been given incorrect, or incomplete, information, compounding the challenges inherent in marshaling the fastest-growing workforce demographic in the country.

To remedy this situation, this book constitutes a road map that offers guidance on how to approach the challenges the ascendance of Hispanics represents to organizations throughout the United States. If one of the unfinished tasks from the twentieth century remains how to give women complete equality and opportunity in the workplace, the new challenge this century is how the workplace is to reflect the nation's changing demographics—nine out of ten babies being born in New Orleans are Latino—as the nation's business and cultural life reflect the acceleration of our becoming a bilingual consumer economy.

This book is dedicated to two men, Gonzalo Guerrero and Patrick J. Buchanan. Guerrero was shipwrecked in 1511, washing ashore on the mainland of North America in what is now Mexico's Yucatán Peninsula. When Hernán Cortés arrived in Cozumel and learned of his stranded countryman, one of two shipwreck survivors, it was Guerrero who refused to return to his countrymen. He had married a Maya woman, formed a family, and saw his future residing with his family. "This will never do," Cortés is said to have lamented. Patrick J. Buchanan sees this as the first step in the "death of the West," the miscegenation that Guerrero initiated, and sees calamity. "The invasion rolls on," he writes. "America's once-sleepy two-thousand-mile Mexican border is now the scene of daily confrontations."[1]

This book has attempted to transcend this discussion, simply by pointing out that fertility rates and demographics leave no other option: without Hispanics, the population of the United States would begin to decline by mid-century, and we would be disappearing as a nation-state.

This reality can be a source of fear, or it can be an opportunity upon which to seize: *What can Brown do for you?*

It bears recalling Adam Smith's instruction: "We address ourselves, not to their humanity, but to their self-love, and never talk to them of our necessities, but of their advantages." It is the members of the Hispanic diaspora in the United States who are going to go to work every day, and have payroll taxes deducted from their wages in order to pay for the Social Security and related entitlement programs on which the retiring generations of non-Hispanic Americans depend for the foreseeable future.

This is the demographic group that is going to get the nation's work going forward, with workers that far outnumber their proportions to the general population. This is the constituency that is going to prevent the United States from suffering the fate of Italy and Russia, where depopulation is a reality, and where the future of both nation-states are diminished along with their respective populations. This is the future of the nation's economy simply because any society's future is seen in the faces of its children, which in the case of the United States become more "brown" with each passing day.

The ascendance of Hispanics is a struggle of national progress, where things are not discussed in the rhetoric of grievance, but in the displacement of that grievance. *The border crossed us, and our titles to the land were invalidated, but we are here: in numbers no one ever envisioned, and the land is ours, because we are here and we are greater in number.*

The discussion presented in this book has provided the reader with greater cultural intelligence to understand the mosaic of peoples, cultural norms, and societal expectations of the members of the Hispanic diaspora in the United States. In order to understand them as people, colleagues, co-workers, employees, and supervisors, and business partners, it is necessary to understand how they are alike, and what makes them different—from mainstream American society and from each other as well. The approach incorporates increasing the reader's cultural intelligence with specific policy recommendations, each designed to demystify the Hispanic diaspora and explain the nuances of the mosaic of Hispanic, Latino, and Latin identities in ways that few within the community can articulate to others.

In many ways, this discussion is a bold affirmation of America, because one of the greatest writers the nation has ever produced, Walt Whitman, anticipated these changes, when he wrote, "Of every hue and caste am I."

That, in one sentence, describes the mosaic of cultures and races that constitute the Hispanic diaspora in the United States. That is the challenge of the emerging American workforce as this century unfolds.

Notes

Introduction

1. To many Hispanics, the use of "Latino" by English-speakers is a form of mockery, the way, for instance, that English-speaking Canadians dismiss their French-speaking compatriots by calling them, with a smirk masquerading as a smile, "the Québécois."

2. Think of the similar evolution terms for Americans of Sub-Saharan Africa have undergone: from Negro to black, then to African-American and Afro-American.

3. "Everyone will bring his report to the conference room prepared to make her presentation," is a familiar, though odd, corporate linguistic conceit. Furthermore, such a sentence is only true for a male employee who, on the way to the conference room, has the epiphany that he is actually a pre-op male-to-female transsexual person.

4. When discussing the kind of dog his family would bring to the White House, Barack Obama suggested that perhaps his family should visit a shelter and pick out "a mutt like me." See "Obama Seeks Speedy Action on Economy," by Jeff Zeleny and Jackie Calmes, *The New York Times*, November 7, 2008.

5. Levitan, S. A. & Johnson, C. M. (1983). The survival of work. In Barbash, J., Lampman, R. J., Levitan, S. A., & Tyler, G. (Eds.), *The Work Ethic: A Critical Analysis* (pp. 1–25). Madison, Wisc.: Industrial Relations Research Association.

6. See, Stencel, S. (1981). Workers' changing expectations. In H. Gimlin (Ed.), *Editorial research reports on work life in the 1980s* (pp. 45–68). Washington, D.C.: *Congressional Quarterly*.

7. See, Naisbitt, J. (1984). *Megatrends: Ten New Directions Transforming Our Lives*. New York: Warner.

8. Naisbitt, J. & Aburdene, P. (1990). *Megatrends 2000*. New York: Morrow.

9. Sources: Bureau of Labor Statistics, HispanicEconomics.com.

10. Figures taken from the Census Bureau, Department of Labor Statistics, *Hispanic Business*, and International Credit Monitor.

Part I

1. See, www.un.org/esa/population/publications/migration/italy.pdf.

2. See, "Population Decline Set to Turn Venice into Italy's Disneyland," by John Hooper, *The Guardian*, August 26, 2006.

3. See, "Putin Calls for National Population Boost," by Judith Ingram, Associated Press, May 10, 2006.

4. See, "Fertility of American Women: 2006," U.S. Census Bureau, August 2008.

5. Ibid.

6. The U.S. Census estimates that, had the United States been closed to immigration beginning in 1970, the population of the country would have peaked at 255 million in 2020, and then begun a slow decline, similar to what other countries are now experiencing.

Chapter I

1. "Hispanics Now Largest Minority, Census Shows," by Lynette Clemetson, the *New York Times*, January 22, 2003.

2. Sources: Mexican Migration Project (University of Pennsylvania), HispanicEconomics.com, Instituto Nacional de Estadísticas y Geografía, or INEGI (Mexico City).

3. Facts compiled from various sources: U.S. Census Bureau, U.S. Bureau of Labor Statistics, Pew Hispanic Center, Instituto Cervantes, and Hispanic Economics.com.

4. Roberto Suro is quoted in "Hispanics Now Largest Minority, Census Shows," by Lynette Clemetson, the *New York Times*, January 22, 2003.

5. See, Samuel Huntington, "The Hispanic Challenge," *Foreign Affairs*, March/April 2004.

6. "Chicago Reverses 50 Years of Declining Population," by Pam Belluck, the *New York Times*, March 15, 2001. The same was true in other cities, including New York. See, for instance, "City's Population Tops 8 Million in Census Count for the First Time," by Susan Sachs, the *New York Times*, March 16, 2001, and "City's Population Changes Are on Vivid Display in Queens," by Dean E. Murphy, the *New York Times*, March 19, 2001.

7. See, "Katrina Begets a Baby Boom by Immigrants" by Eduardo Porter, the *New York Times*, December 11, 2006.

8. Ibid.

Chapter 2

1. By continent, these nations consist of the following: Asia and Oceania: Philippines; Africa: Equatorial Guinea, Western Sahara; Americas: Argentina, Bolivia, Chile, Colombia, Costa Rica, Cuba, Dominican Republic, Ecuador, El Salvador, Guatemala, Honduras, Mexico, Nicaragua, Panama, Paraguay, Peru, Puerto Rico, Uruguay, Venezuela. The other nation, of course, is Spain. In addition, given that significant portions of the United States were once governed by Spain, some advocates include the United States, given that it is now the fourth largest Spanish-speaking nation in the world. Others, to broaden the "Pan-Iberian" identity of the "Hispanic" family, also advocate including Portugal, Brazil, and its largest African colonies of Angola and Mozambique, because these nations also celebrate October 12 as a national holiday of cultural pride and identity.

2. See: Sheffer, Gabriel, *Diaspora Politics at Home Abroad*, Cambridge: Cambridge University Press, 2003.

3. "The Federal Bureau of Investigation Hate Crimes Statistics Report released today demonstrates the real societal impact of anti-immigrant campaigns launched over the airwaves and through anti-immigrant legislation. The report shows a sharp increase in the number of hate crimes reported against Hispanics based on their ethnicity or national origin to the highest levels since the reports were first mandated by the Hate Crimes Statistics Act," the Mexican American Legal Defense and Education Fund, or MALDEF, reported when the 2006 Hate Crimes Report was issued. "According to the report, in 2006, Hispanics comprised 62.8% of victims of crimes motivated by a bias toward the victims' ethnicity or national origin. In 2004, the comparable figure was 51.5%. Since 2004, the number of victims of anti-Hispanic crimes increased by 25%." The FBI reported that for 2006 there were 576 anti-Hispanic crimes against 819 victims. The Report is available at: http://www.fbi.gov/ucr/hc2006/index.html.

4. In the United States, minorities are not unknown to self-segregate from mainstream society from pure disgust: Hasidic Jews look on everyone else as reprehensible creatures, best avoided. Strict Hasidic women, for instance, have been known to refuse to speak to non-Hasidic men, even when the men in question are police officers, firemen, or emergency medical personnel.

5. Marie Arana, *American Chica: Two Worlds, One Childhood*, pages 171–173.

6. It is true that many people want to come to the United States, but many others are trying to escape something, whether it is Cubans fleeing Communism, Haitians fleeing poverty, or multitudes from around the world trying to escape lack of opportunities to pursue their ambitions.

7. *Once Upon a Quinceañera* by Julia Álvarez, page 4.

8. It should be noted that Hispanics of Asian ancestry are primarily of Cuban or South American heritage.

9. Kevin Starr is quoted in "California Census Confirms Whites Are a Minority," by Todd Purdum, the *New York Times*, March 30, 2001.

10. The sources are the U.S. Census Bureau, the U.S. Bureau of Labor Statistics, the Pew Hispanic Center, *Hispanic Business* magazine, and Hispanic Economics, Inc.

11. Angelina Jolie claims part Iroquois ancestry on her mother's side, an ancestor by the name of Marcheline Bertrand.

12. See, *Political Debates Between Lincoln and Douglas*, 1897, page 344.

13. Quoted in "The Roots of the I.Q. Debate: Eugenics and Social Control" by Margaret Quigley, *The Public Eye,* 1995.

14. The Supreme Court's ruling stated, in part, that: "Marriage is one of the 'basic civil rights of man,' fundamental to our very existence and survival. . . . To deny this fundamental freedom on so unsupportable a basis as the racial classifications embodied in these statutes, classifications so directly subversive of the principle of equality at the heart of the Fourteenth Amendment, is surely to deprive all the State's citizens of liberty without due process of law. The Fourteenth Amendment requires that the freedom of choice to marry not be restricted by invidious racial discrimination. Under our Constitution, the freedom to marry, or not marry, a person of another race resides with the individual and cannot be infringed by the State."

15. Western feminists who denounce the "oppression" of women in Muslim countries being required to wear a chador or other garment, fail to consider that, for many women, they find it "liberating" to be able to go out in public without having to fend off unwanted stares, or gazes. In some ways, Muslim women are freed from the dehumanizing process inherent in being objectified as a sex object.

16. "Ageism," discrimination against the old, for instance, has been analyzed in minute detail in *Ageism, the Aged and Aging in America: On Being Old in an Alienated Society*, by Ursula Adler Falk and Gerhard Falk.

17. Janet McDonald, *Project Girl*, page 91.

18. The impact of "lookism" can be insidious. In *Ghosts of Manila: The Fateful Blood Feud Between Muhammad Ali and Joe Frazier*, for instance, Mark Kram describes Joe Frazier's "anger at Muhammad Ali's attacks on him, attacks that often disparaged his looks, particularly hurtful since Ali was so often celebrated in the press for being exceptionally 'good' looking." In *Driving While Black*, Kenneth Meeks writes, "The statistics speak for themselves, eloquently. But this book is not a sermon; it does not preach. What it does—very effectively—is put information into the hands of those whose rights are violated, and provide them with the means to resist, to fight back, to promote themselves. It is a handbook more than a call to arms, a manual of instruction and self-help more than a political tract." (See *Driving While Black*, page xi.)

19. Anthony DePalma, *Here: A Biography of the New American Continent*, page 151.

20. Could it also be a question of decorum? In the United States, for instance, before "casual" dress overtook American society, it was not uncommon for clubs to insist on the enforcement of a certain dress code. The Chemists' Club on East 41st Street, like other clubs in midtown Manhattan, would not serve men who were not wearing coats and ties. On the occasions when members arrived without being properly attired, management had a selection of spare jackets and ties it would lend to them before they were seated in the dining room. The sight of some diners wearing somewhat ill-fitting jackets—or ties that looked a bit too worn—was not uncommon. For those diners at private clubs who "lacked discretion," there were remedies available. This is often the case in Mexico City, but public restaurants, unlike private clubs, do not have clothes to lend to diners who are dressed inappropriately.

21. In fact, Gonzalo Guerrero was demonized, accused of being a person of "low character" who had been "possessed" by Satan.

22. See, "At the Slaughterhouse, Some Things Never Die: Who Kills, Who Cuts, Who Bosses Can Depend on Race," by Charlie LeDuff, the *New York Times*, June 16, 2000.

23. See, "Sweet and Sour Sounds of Home," published by The Conference Board Review, available at: https://www.conference-board.org/articles/atb_article.cfm?id=59

24. For more information, see http://www.qar.com/index.php?option=com_content&view=article&id=70&Itemid=56

25. See HispanicEconomics.com for more information.

Chapter 3

1. See, Samuel Huntington, "The Hispanic Challenge," *Foreign Affairs*, March/April 2004.

2. For more information, see: http://www.census.gov/prod/2002pubs/c2kbr01-15.pdf

3. For a fascinating account, see *Maximilian and Carlota: A Tale of Romance and Tragedy*, by Gene Smith, Morrow, 1973.

4. "The Mozo," by D. H. Lawrence in *Mornings in Mexico*.

5. James Hamilton-Paterson is describing the Bajau people of the Philippines in this quotation, but the Bajau share a similar Stoic view of the world. See, *The Great Deep: The Sea and its Thresholds*. Random House, 1992, page 260.

6. John Steinbeck, *Grapes of Wrath*, Penguin Books, USA, 1992, page 315.

7. Robert Putnam, *Bowling Alone: The Collapse and Revival of American Community*, page 332.

8. Ibid

9. A sociological discussion about prevailing cultural norms among Hispanics, Latinos, and Latins in the workplace is found in *Latino Families in Therapy: A Guide to Multicultural Practice* by Celia Jaes Falicov published in 1998.

10. Robert Putnam, *Bowling Alone: The Collapse and Revival of American Community*, page 19.

11. "Another George Bush, P., on Political Stage," by Frank Bruni, the *New York Times*, April 18, 2000.

12. *The Other Face of America*, by Jorge Ramos, pages xxiv–xxv.

13. Robert Putnam, *Bowling Alone: The Collapse and Revival of American Community*, page 21.

14. See, "Educational Attainment in the United States: 2003," U.S. Census Bureau, June 2004.

15. See, "Educational Attainment and Median Household Income," U.S. Census Bureau, 2003.

16. "Henry B. González" by Pete Hamill, in *Profiles in Courage for Our Time*, Caroline Kennedy, Editor, pages 92–96.

17. An example: officials in Madrid ordered that a census in Chile be carried out during the month of June, but because the seasons are reversed in the southern hemisphere, officials cancelled the census because of inclement weather that month. A report would be sent to Madrid, stating that they "obeyed," meaning they intended to carry out orders received, but they were unable to "comply" because of prevailing circumstances. If this is translated to a contemporary work environment, it is not difficult to see how "local"

circumstances can at times lead Hispanic employees to disregard directions from supervisors or regional managers who are not "on the ground."

18. Non-Hispanic managers are dumbfounded by this reasoning, and so are Hispanic employees who cannot conceive of the idea that managers do not have family obligations on Sunday that always take precedence over work.

19. "An Entry Card for Immigrants," by Mary Beth Sheridan, the *Washington Post*, July 26, 2002.

Chapter 4.

1. When Bernard Madoff confessed to a Ponzi scheme in which, by his own estimate, $50 billion had been lost to investors around the world, there was such fear that Madoff's arrest would result in anti-Semitism based on historical stereotypes that have falsely accused Jews of financial dishonesty, that the Anti-Defamation League in New York went on a preemptive campaign to prevent anti-Semitic attacks. No Hispanic or Latino advocacy organization in the United States has been able to turn the tide on the negative speech directed against Hispanics. The National Council of La Raza's "Wave of Hope" campaign to address the hate speech and violence directed against Latin immigrants has been of limited success.

2. From an interview by Bob Baldock and Dennis Bernstein for "Skirting the Brink: America's Leading Thinkers and Activists Confide Their Views of Our Predicament," National Public Radio project in progress.

3. Communities have tried, often unsuccessfully, to have areas designated as places where workers and employers can meet, without creating a chaotic atmosphere for other residents and business owners, but there is a natural mistrust: workers fear their immigration status would be challenged and employers fear they might be caught up in a sting operation by immigration officials.

4. Source: Hispanic-Workforce.com, U.S. Equal Employment Opportunity Commission (EEOC), and in case studies. A "classic" case study centers on B&H Foto and Electronics Corporation, which agreed to pay $4.3 million to Hispanic employees who were systematically given weaker performance reviews to justify lower wages than given to non-Hispanic employees. See: http://compensation.blr.com/display.cfm/id/155741

5. "Arriba! A [Latin] Radio Scold Gets Out the Vote," by Dan Baum, *The New Yorker*, October 23, 2006.

6. See: http://www.yucatan.com.mx/noticia.asp?cx=9$0539010000 $3941076&f=20081025

7. *Crossing Over: A Mexican Family on the Migrant Trail*, by Rubén Martínez, p. 142.

8. "Immigrant Laborers Feel Stranded in Pacific Northwest as Day Jobs Dry Up," by Sam Howe Verhovek, the *New York Times*, January 27, 2002.

9. Xóchitl Bada, of the Sociology Department at the University of Notre Dame, has studied how HTAs are an important part of Latin employees' lives. She notes: "Contemporary Mexican HTAs represent values of commitment, solidarity, altruism, and patriotism. HTAs in the United States are heirs to the historical mutual aid societies and welfare organizations created in the late nineteenth and early twentieth century in order to provide sickness care and death benefits at a time when such services were unavailable for many immigrant groups. Although Mexican HTAs have the longest history and are the best known, an increasing number of Dominican, Guatemalan, and Salvadoran hometown associations have been formed in the last decade and are actively participating in the improvement of their communities both of origin and of residence. Mexican HTAs have a long history—the most prominent were established in the 1950s. In recent years, many additional small HTAs have emerged under the leadership of local immigrant leaders. In the last decade, these HTAs have received financial and technical support from the Mexican government through its consular offices. The growing profile of Mexican HTAs in Chicago is reflective of the steady increase of these organizations. Metropolitan Chicago has the second largest Mexican immigrant community in the United States, following Los Angeles. Current estimates place the area's Mexican and Mexican-ancestry population at between 800,000 and 1,000,000 people, of whom two-thirds were born in Mexico. The states of Guerrero, Jalisco, Zacatecas, Guanajuato, and Michoacán encompass nearly 80% of all Mexican migrants in the Chicago metropolitan area. The number of Chicago-based HTAs for these five states alone quintupled from about 20 to over 100 during the 1994 to 2002 period. There are currently more than 600 Mexican hometown clubs and associations registered in 30 cities in the United States. In Los Angeles alone, there are 218 Mexican HTAs."

10. This concern, of public humiliation, has to be addressed head-on: managers have to explain that part of the ESL course is designed to teach the student how *to be a student*, and then how to learn English.

11. John Kenneth Galbraith, *The Good Society*, page 8.

12. See, "Tyson Foods Indicted in Plan to Smuggle Illegal Workers," by David Barboza, the *New York Times*, December 20, 2001.

13. See, "At the Slaughterhouse, Some Things Never Die: Who Kills, Who Cuts, Who Bosses Can Depend on Race," by Charlie LeDuff, the *New York Times*, June 16, 2000.

14. Personal e-mail communication, February 9, 2004.

15. "This is a great victory for the Tar Heel workers," UFCW organizing director Pat O'Neill told reporters on December 11, 2008, after the vote was certified. "I know they are looking forward to sitting down at the bargaining table with Smithfield to negotiate a contract. The UFCW has constructive union contracts with Smithfield plants around the country."

16. See, http://www.bls.gov/news.release/pdf/forbrn.pdf

17. Personal e-mail communication, February 9, 2004.

18. See "Meatpackers' Profits Hinge on Pool of Immigrant Labor," the *New York Times*, December 21, 2001.

19. The Tyson executives were found not guilty in March 2003. "A federal jury acquitted Tyson Foods and three of its managers today of conspiring to bring illegal immigrants from Latin America to work in their poultry plants," Sherry Day reported. "The case was closely watched by immigration lawyers and labor leaders because it focused on the recruitment, employment and treatment of illegal immigrants, practices in which many large food processing companies are said to engage to meet staffing needs in low-wage jobs." See, "Jury Clears Tyson Foods in Use of Illegal Immigrants," by Sherry Day, the *New York Times*, March 27, 2003.

Chapter 5

1. Samuel Huntington, "The Hispanic Challenge," *Foreign Affairs*, March 2004.

2. "Truth and Myths of Work/Life Balance," by Fay Hansen, available at, http://www.workforce.com/section/02/feature/23/36/99/

3. See *Cultural Intelligence: People Skills for Global Business* by David C. Thomas and Kerr Inkson, page 15.

4. See, "At the Slaughterhouse, Some Things Never Die: Who Kills, Who Cuts, Who Bosses Can Depend on Race," by Charlie LeDuff, the *New York Times*, June 16, 2000.

5. See *Cultural Intelligence: People Skills for Global Business* by David C. Thomas and Kerr Inkson, page 62.

6. See, "Hispanic Attitudes and Perceptions of the Election of Barack Obama as President of the United States," Hispanic Economics, Inc.

7. See, "Finishing Our Work" by Thomas Friedman, the *New York Times*, November 5, 2008.

8. See, "Business Traits, Market Characteristics, and Employment Patterns of Large Latino-Owned Firms in Southern California," by Waldo López Aqueres, Tomas Rivera Policy Institute, 1999.

9. A comprehensive introduction to the challenges confronting America's working poor is found in *Nickel and Dimed: On (Not) Getting By in America*, by Barbara Ehrenreich, which discusses the lives of millions of Americans who work full-time for poverty-level wages with almost no opportunity for advancement.

10. As a result of the sustained devaluation of the U.S. dollar, some companies—particularly Canadian, German, and Swiss—have begun to shift production to the United States to take advantage of significantly lower labor costs associated with the historic collapse in the value of American dollar on world markets in the 2000s.

11. See, "Sweet and Sour Sounds of Home," published by The Conference Board Review, available at: https://www.conference-board.org/articles/atb_article.cfm?id=59

12. For more information, see the Pew Hispanic Center studies, available at PewResearch.org.

13. *Here: A Biography of the New American Continent*, by Anthony DePalma, page 256.

14. Canada does not comply with the U.S. trade embargo against Cuba, for instance.

15. A partial listing of legal documents that are readily available in Spanish for HRM to make available to Hispanic employees include:

- Discrimination (Title VII, Civil Rights Act of 1964)
- Hiring (Title VII) and termination
- Wages and hours (Fair Labor Standards Act, minimum wage, child labor)
- Employee benefits (healthcare, 401(k), IRS, ERISA requirements)
- Family and medical leave (FMLA, return to work protection)
- Health and safety (OSHA regulations, workers' compensation)
- Workers with disabilities (Americans With Disabilities Act)
- Types of workers: permanent and contractors
- Unions (National Labor Relations Act)
- Internal human resources practices (e.g., taxes, personnel practices/documentation)

16. Continuing education courses are reasonably priced. Other alternatives are language courses on CDs that are commercially available, and

a good way of practicing is by watching the evening news in Spanish, because the anchors speak proper Spanish and, because the day's news is already familiar to the viewer, it helps following along.

17. In Mexico, the national retirement program is the Sistema de Ahorro para el Retiro, known as the S.A.R.

18. See, "Comparative Wages and Benefits in Mexico versus the United States," Hispanic Economics, 2007.

Chapter 6

1. Tajfel, H., & Turner, J. C. (1986). The Social Identity Theory of Inter-Group Behaviour. In S. Worchel and W. G. Austin (Eds.), *Psychology of Intergroup Relations*, vol. 2: 7–24. Chicago: Nelson-Hall.

2. "HR's New Mandate: Be a Strategic Player, " by Dave Ulrich and Wayne Brockbank, Harvard Business Review, June 2005, see: http://hbswk.hbs.edu/archive/4861.html

3. More information on this is provided at Hispanic-Workforce.com, where links to various federal agencies are provided.

4. This anecdote is a composite based on personal communication from three Cuban executives in Miami who routinely attend Latino conferences, as part of their organizations' corporate governance commitments. It is also based on personal observations at various conferences when I have brought up the matter over dinner with Cuban professionals.

5. The only cases are in Miami, where Mexicans commute from Mexico City to supervise their operations in the United States, and in these cases, what we have are Latins, not Latinos, supervising the work of Hispanics (Cubans).

6. Marilyn Halter, *Shopping for Identity: The Marketing of Ethnicity* (New York: Schocken, 2000), page 50.

7. Historian Mark Reisler is quoted in *By the Sweat of Their Brow: Mexican Immigrant Labor in the United States, 1900–1940*, (Westport, Connecticut: Greenwood Press, 1976).

8. To read the entire article, see: http://www.puertorico-herald.org/issues/2004/vol8n19/HispWorkForce.html

9. "500,000 Pack Streets to Protest Immigration Bills," by Teresa Watanabe and Hector Becerra, *Los Angeles Times*, March 26, 2006.

10. See, "Mexico Leftist's Backers Aim for Massive Protest," by the Associated Press, July 31, 2006.

11. "Mexico Leftist to Create Parallel Government," by Mark Stevenson, the *Washington Post*, August 29, 2006.

12. Ibid.

13. *Macbeth,* Act V, Scene 5.
14. See, "Thinking Outside the Big Box," by Jeff Chu and Kate Rockwood, *Fast Company,* November 2008.
15. http://www.pbs.org/itvs/storewars/stores3.html.
16. See, "Unions and Upward Mobility for Latino Workers," by John Schmitt, Senior Economist, Center for Economic and Policy Research in Washington, D.C., September 2008.
17. Karega Har is a member of the Bay Area Black Radical Congress, which indicates the growing recognition among African American activists that the concerns of Hispanics should be incorporated into their programs, given the demographic realities this century. See: www.blackcommentator.com/210/210_unions_immigrant_rights_hart_guest.html
18. Robert Frank, *Choosing the Right Pond: Human Behavior and the Quest for Status,* pages 224–225.
19. John Kenneth Galbraith, *The Good Society,* page 11.
20. Ibid.

Chapter 7

1. "Henry B. González" by Pete Hamill, in *Profiles in Courage for Our Time,* Caroline Kennedy, Editor, pages 92–96.
2. "Latinos Optimistic about the Future, Feel Candidates Ignore their Issues, and Have a Shared Policy Agenda, Poll Finds," National Council of La Raza, June 27, 2004, see: http://www.nclr.org/content/news/detail/25333/
3. For further information, see, "Spanish for Spanish Speakers: Developing Dual Language Proficiency," by Joy Kreeft Peyton, Vickie W. Lewelling, & Paula Winke, ERIC Clearinghouse on Languages and Linguistics, December 2001, available at: www.cal.org/resources/digest/spanish_native.html
4. See, "English-Only Latinos Face 'The Shame' of Not Speaking Spanish," by David Madrid, New America Media, October 4, 2005.
5. Source: HispanicEconomics.com, consistent with surveys conducted by other organizations, including the Pew Hispanic Center and *People en Español* Hispanic Opinion Tracking (HOT) Study.
6. "The Multicultural Military: Military service and the acculturation of Latinos and Anglos," by David Leal, in *Armed Forces & Society,* Volume 29, Number 2, Winter 2003.
7. See, http://www.naleo.org/Education_Summit2008.html
8. The Mexican Migration Project (MMP) was created in 1982 by an interdisciplinary team of researchers to further our understanding of the complex process of Mexican migration to the United States. The proj-

ect is a binational research effort codirected by Jorge Durand, professor of Social Anthropology at the University of Guadalajara (Mexico), and Douglas S. Massey, professor of Sociology and Public Affairs at Princeton University (U.S.).

9. Source: HispanicEconomics.com and U.S. Census, see: http://www.census.gov/income/cdrom/cdrom98/perinc/p0160.lst

10. See, "Latina Teenagers Have Nation's Highest Rate of Suicide Attempts," by Christina Hernandez, Columbia News Service, May 8, 2007, http://jscms.jrn.columbia.edu/cns/2007-05-08/hernandez-Latinasuicide

11. "Acculturation and Latino Health in the United States," by Marielena Lara, Christina Gamboa, M. Iya Kahramanian, Leo S. Morales, David E. Hayes Bautista, Rand Corporation, 2005. Available at: http://www.rand.org/pubs/reprints/RP1177/index.html

12. See, "Differences in Personal Models Among Latinos and European Americans," by Catherine Chesla, Marilyn Skaff, Robert Bartz, Joseph Mullan and Lawrence Fisher, in *Diabetes Care*, Volume 23, Number 12, December 2000.

13. "The Role of Acculturation in Nutrition, Lifestyle, and Incidence of Type 2 Diabetes among Latinos," by Rafael Pérez-Escamilla and Predrag Putnik, *Journal of Nutrition*, April 2007. See: http://jn.nutrition.org/cgi/content/full/137/4/860

14. See, "Physical Activity Patterns Among Latinos in the United States: Putting the Pieces Together," by Sandra A. Ham, MS, Michelle M. Yore, MPH, Judy Kruger, PhD, Gregory W. Heath, DHSc, MPH, Refilwe Moeti, MA, Centers for Disease Control and Prevention, Volume 4, Number 4, October 2007. Available at: http://www.cdc.gov/pcd/issues/2007/oct/06_0187.htm?s_cid=pcd44a92_x

15. See, "More Alzheimer's Risk for Hispanics, Studies Find," by Pam Belluck, *The New York Times*, October 20, 2008.

16. Ibid.

Chapter 8

1. Joan Didion, *Miami*, pages 63–64.

2. See, http://www.csrwire.com/News/11927.html

3. See: James N. Baron, Michael T. Hannan, M. Diane Burton, "Determinants of Managerial Intensity in the Early Years of Organizations," Research Paper 1550, Graduate School of Business, Stanford University.

4. The studies controlled for various factors, including industry, public versus private status, and occupational mix.

5. For an intriguing discussion of HRM as a management strategy, see Jeffrey Pfeffer, *Competitive Advantage Through People* (Boston: Harvard Business School Press, 1994).

6. An analysis of the Delta and American Airlines experience in the Miami-Dade County labor market is found at www.Hispanic-Workforce .com.

7. "Tapping the Hispanic Labor Pool," Rodriguez, Robert, *SHRM* magazine, April 2004, Vol. 49, No. 4.

8. Carla Joinson, "Strength in Numbers?" *HR Magazine* (November 2000).

9. The exact statement on accents is: "A. Accent Discrimination: Because linguistic characteristics are a component of national origin, employers should carefully scrutinize employment decisions that are based on accent to ensure that they do not violate Title VII. An employment decision based on foreign accent does not violate Title VII if an individual's accent materially interferes with the ability to perform job duties. This assessment depends upon the specific duties of the position in question and the extent to which the individual's accent affects his or her ability to perform job duties. Employers should distinguish between a merely discernible foreign accent and one that interferes with communication skills necessary to perform job duties. Generally, an employer may only base an employment decision on accent if effective oral communication in English is required to perform job duties and the individual's foreign accent materially interferes with his or her ability to communicate orally in English. Positions for which effective oral communication in English may be required include teaching, customer service, and telemarketing. Even for these positions, an employer should still determine whether the particular individual's accent interferes with the ability to perform job duties."

10. One exception is native French speakers who learn English: many Americans are drawn by that accent, and are enamored by how it sounds.

11. Whether it was art imitating life, or vice versa, in real life, Desi Arnaz, who portrayed Ricky Ricardo, was often seen as being the lesser of the business team that he and his wife, Lucille Ball, comprised. That it was Arnaz who was the mastermind behind Desilu Productions' ascent in Hollywood remains discounted, in part because of the reruns reinforcing his accent as something worthy of ridicule.

12. Dianne Markley is quoted in "Strength in Numbers?—Hispanic American Employment Recruitment," by Carla Joinson, Society for Human Resource Management, 2000.

13. Andrew Lam, *Perfume Dreams: Reflections on the Vietnamese Diaspora* (Berkeley, California: Heyday Books, 2005), pp. 113–114.

14. Llagas, C. (2003). *Status and Trends in the Education of Hispanics* (NCES 2003-008), Washington, D.C.: U.S. Department of Education, National Center for Education Statistics.

15. Manlove, J. (1998). The Influence of High School Dropout and Social Disengagement on the Risk of School-Age Pregnancy. *Journal of Research on Adolescence*, 8(2): p. 187–220.

16. Hoffman, S.D. (2006). *By the Numbers: The Public Costs of Adolescent Childbearing*. Washington, D.C.: The National Campaign to Prevent Teen Pregnancy.

17. "Hispanic Youth Dropping Out of U.S. Schools: Measuring the Challenge," by Richard Fry, available at www.pewhispanic.org.

18. Information on becoming involved in preventing students from dropping out of high school is found at www.dropoutprevention.org

19. That a Cuban was hired to launch a division that would speak to the Hispanic experience in the United States, when Americans of Mexican ancestry comprise almost 80% of that experience, created tensions between Mexican Hispanics and the Smithsonian. As a result, "The Official Mexican and Mexican American Fine Art Museum of Texas" was founded in 1984, as part of Mexican Hispanics' rebuke of the Smithsonian for this perceived insensitivity.

20. Source: Hispanic Economics, Inc.

21. See *Divided Borders: Essays of Puerto Rican Identity* by Juan Flores.

22. See "City Variation in the Socioeconomic Status of Latinos in New York State: A 2006 Policy Brief for the New York State Assembly Puerto Rican/Hispanic Task Force" by Christine E. Bose, http://assembly.state.ny.us/comm/PRHisp/20070110/

23. The ACLU proved ineffective in defending the nation's traditional civil liberties against the administration of George W. Bush's "national" security program. Similarly, Arlene Davila was gripped by such anxieties during the launch of a Hispanic division by NPA, LLC in January 2009, that she literally walked off the stage as she was about to take her seat.

24. According to HispanicEconomics.com, Puerto Ricans are three times more likely to cancel or be no-shows at conferences than other Hispanics or Latinos.

25. This cultural disconnect also occurs with other groups. African Americans who travel to Africa to reconnect with their roots often encounter frus-

trations that they have little connection to their ancestral homeland, and these trips often become melancholy journeys of loss rather than of self-discovery.

26. In due course, reflecting how fast the world changes, opportunities in Latin America became so significant, that Dow Elanco's operations moved further south—to Brazil, where it relocated its Latin American offices to Sao Paulo.

27. See, Samuel Huntington, "The Hispanic Challenge," *Foreign Affairs*, March 2004.

28. Joan Didion, *Miami*, pages 63–64.

29. This isn't to say that Hispanics may not have parallel thoughts: on their deathbeds I'm sure many Hispanics reflect on the fact that, at long last, they will be able to be free from their families.

30. A thorough discussion of creative destruction is found in *Prophet of Innovation: Joseph Schumpeter and Creative Destruction by* Thomas K. McCraw, Harvard University Press, 2007.

31. Source: Census Bureau, HispanicEconomics.com

Chapter 9

1. See, "Business Potential Boosts Demand for Bilingual Applicants" by Julia Hollister, California Job Journal, April 22, 2007, available at: http://www.jobjournal.com/thisweek.asp?artid=1989

2. Hofstede's two most influential books are *Culture's Consequences* (2nd, fully revised edition, 2001) and *Cultures and Organizations, Software of the Mind* (2nd, revised edition 2005, with his son Gert Jan Hofstede).

3. See, http://www.geert-hofstede.com

4. See http://www.geert-hofstede.com/hofstede_dimensions.php

5. See http://www.geert-hofstede.com/hofstede_dimensions.php

6. See http://www.geert-hofstede.com/hofstede_dimensions.php

7. As a general rule, European anthropologists have treated the emergence of "Latinos" in the United States as a subject of serious academic study.

8. See, "Burger Barn blues," by Daryl Lindsey, Salon.com

9. See, "Central American Immigrants Adopt Mexican Ways in U.S.," by Esmeralda Bermudez, *Los Angeles Times*, November 3, 2008.

10. For more information, see "Jury Finds 'JT LeRoy' Was Fraud," by Alan Feuer, the *New York Times*, June 23, 2007. This raises the question of whether or not Scribner perpetrated a fraud upon the public by publishing a collection of Arellano's columns in a book: *Ask a Mexican*, written by an American pretending to be a Mexican.

11. "Leadership in Your Midst: Tapping the Hidden Strengths of Minority Executives," by Sylvia Ann Hewlett, Carolyn Buck and Cornel West, *Harvard Business Review*, November 2005.

12. See, Korn/Ferry's "Best Practices for Diversity: Corporate & Candidate Perspectives" study, available at http://www.kornferry.com/Library/Process.asp?P=Pubs_Detail&CID=297&LID=1

13. "A relatively high degree of order seems to be the key factor underlying the characteristics inherent in the representation of a graphic symbol; and it is this factor that differentiates it from other forms of representation," Ravi Poovaiah writes in "Graphic Symbols for Environmental Signage: A Design Perspective," available at: http://www.designofsignage.com/theory/paper/index.html

14. Speicher, Doug & Stup, Richard, "Successfully Training Hispanic Workers," *Managing a Hispanic Workforce*, January 2001.

15. Speicher, Doug & Stup, Richard, "Successfully Training Hispanic Workers," *Managing a Hispanic Workforce*, January 2001.

Chapter 10

1. For more information, see the Pew Hispanic Center studies, available at PewResearch.org.

2. See, Daniel W. Drezner, 2004. "Hash of Civilizations," *The New Republic Online*.

3. Douglas Monroy, *Thrown Among Strangers: The Making of Mexican Culture in Frontier California*, pages 203–204.

4. "Literary Candor, Straight from Latin America," by Tim Rutten, *Los Angeles Times*, April 9, 2001.

5. A partial list of categories used in colonial Mexico, apart from Caucasian and black, included Criollo, Mestizo, Mulatto, Zambo, Castizo, Morisco, Albino, Albarazado, Coyote, Chamizo, Chino, Cholo, Grifo, Lobo Barcino, Cambujo, Zambaigo, and so on. Try to design a Census Bureau form for this.

6. "Why Harlem Drug Cops Don't Discuss Race: Color Can Give Anonymity Undercover, But Looking Like a Suspect Has Its Risks," by Michael Winerip, the *New York Times*, July 9, 2000.

7. "Why Harlem Drug Cops Don't Discuss Race: Color Can Give Anonymity Undercover, But Looking Like a Suspect Has Its Risks," by Michael Winerip, the *New York Times*, July 9, 2000.

8. See, "Business Traits, Market Characteristics, and Employment Patterns of Large Latino-Owned Firms in Southern California," by Waldo López Aqueres, Tomas Rivera Policy Institute, 1999.

9. Source: Census Bureau, 2005 statistics.

Conclusion

1. See, *The Death of the West*, by Patrick J. Buchanan, page 131.

Index

About the Author

photo by Johnathan Conklin

Louis E. Varela Nevaer is considered one of the nation's leading authorities on Hispanics and Latinos. As director of Hispanic Economics, he has written extensively on Hispanic consumer behavior in the United States and consulted to Fortune 100 companies who, since the passage of the North American Free Trade Agreement, or NAFTA, have worked on integrating the economies of the three North American nations. With more than a quarter century of expertise, Nevaer offers a unique perspective that reflects his varied background.

With family in Mexico, the United States, and Spain, Nevaer spends significant time in all three countries, able to move in these three distinct and disparate societies as a "native" in each, particularly germane to the content of this book, because Spain, as a member of the European Union, is a rival to the NAFTA nations. This perspective allows the author to empathize with the concerns and perspectives that Americans, Mexicans, and Spaniards have, particularly as they view each other and try to work together. To be sure, coming of age in southern Florida, it was impossible for Nevaer to escape the palpable influence of the Cuban exile community, and how a sudden influx of educated, professional (and Caucasian) Hispanics transformed a medium-sized city into an international tourist and business destination. The determination of Cuban exiles to succeed as America defined success, their constant longing for their lost homeland, and their educational wherewithal that allowed them to reshape the terms of trade with the greater mainstream American society—the minutes to the public hearings held by the City of Miami requires one to be fully bilingual to read them without the need of an English-Spanish dictionary—were instructive. In contrast, the quiet dignity of Mexican migrant workers, whose ranks constitute the most disenfranchised and less privileged segments of Mexican society in California, who endure humiliations and maintain that "this land" was once their forebears', offers a very distinct lesson.

Nevaer's professional life reflects the necessary framework to reconcile the disparate elements of what constitutes "Hispanidad" in the United States. His approach incorporates an interdisciplinary approach, one that draws from a wealth of experience—academic, professional, hands-on, and international—to offer solutions to the changing American workforce. It is thoroughly researched and documented, and readers are encouraged to make use of the information provided in the Notes. The description portions are conversational and breezy, while the proscriptive sections conform to familiar business-book structure. The two approaches reflect a journalistic approach to describing a subject and then an academic one in offering strategies and solutions.

Educated at Cornell University, Nevaer's professional writing includes several critically acclaimed business books, such as *HR and the New Hispanic Workforce,* Spring 2007, Davies-Black, San Jose, California; *The Rise of the Hispanic Market in the United Sates,* Fall 2003, M.E. Sharpe, Armonk, New York; *NAFTA's Second Decade,* Winter 2003, South-Western Books, Mason, Ohio; and *The Dot-Com Debacle and the Return to Reason,* 2002, Quorum Books, Westport, Connecticut, which was named one of the "Recommended" business books of 2002 by the Harvard Business School. In addition to books, he is a prolific journalist. Since the mid-1980s, Nevaer has been a contributor to Pacific News Service and the New America Media, which has syndicated his reporting and Op-Ed pieces for more than two decades; these pieces are available online at NewAmericaMedia.org.

Of equal importance is his philanthropic work, which includes such divergent interests as being on the board of Mesoamerica Foundation (mesoamerica-foundation.org) when it was created to support the work of the Sanctuary Movement in California in the 1980s, to being one of the founding directors of the Animal Cancer Foundation (acfoundation.org) in the 1990s. After the attacks of September 11, 2001, Nevaer was asked to curate "MISSING: Last Seen at the World Trade Center," an exhibition of the "missing" persons fliers created by friends and loved ones of those who perished when the Twin Towers collapsed, which traveled to seventeen cities around the country and was seen by almost two million Americans. In the 2000s, he has focused on issues affecting youth and Hispanics. These concerns have resulted in the publication of two books: *Illustrations from the Inside: The Beat Within,* Spring 2008, Mark Batty Publisher, New York, New York; and *Protest Graffiti Mexico: Oaxaca,* Spring 2009, Mark Batty Publisher, New York, New York.

A dedicated Web site for this book, Hispanic-Workforce.com, provides additional information that could not be included in this book.

He divides his time between the United States, Mexico, and Spain.

About Berrett-Koehler Publishers

Berrett-Koehler is an independent publisher dedicated to an ambitious mission: Creating a World That Works for All.

We believe that to truly create a better world, action is needed at all levels — individual, organizational, and societal. At the individual level, our publications help people align their lives with their values and with their aspirations for a better world. At the organizational level, our publications promote progressive leadership and management practices, socially responsible approaches to business, and humane and effective organizations. At the societal level, our publications advance social and economic justice, shared prosperity, sustainability, and new solutions to national and global issues.

A major theme of our publications is "Opening Up New Space." They challenge conventional thinking, introduce new ideas, and foster positive change. Their common quest is changing the underlying beliefs, mindsets, institutions, and structures that keep generating the same cycles of problems, no matter who our leaders are or what improvement programs we adopt.

We strive to practice what we preach — to operate our publishing company in line with the ideas in our books. At the core of our approach is stewardship, which we define as a deep sense of responsibility to administer the company for the benefit of all of our "stakeholder" groups: authors, customers, employees, investors, service providers, and the communities and environment around us.

We are grateful to the thousands of readers, authors, and other friends of the company who consider themselves to be part of the "BK Community." We hope that you, too, will join us in our mission.

Be Connected

Visit Our Website

Go to www.bkconnection.com to read exclusive previews and excerpts of new books, find detailed information on all Berrett-Koehler titles and authors, browse subject-area libraries of books, and get special discounts.

Subscribe to Our Free E-Newsletter

Be the first to hear about new publications, special discount offers, exclusive articles, news about bestsellers, and more! Get on the list for our free e-newsletter by going to www.bkconnection.com.

Get Quantity Discounts

Berrett-Koehler books are available at quantity discounts for orders of ten or more copies. Please call us toll-free at (800) 929-2929 or email us at bkp.orders@aidcvt.com.

Host a Reading Group

For tips on how to form and carry on a book reading group in your workplace or community, see our website at www.bkconnection.com.

Join the BK Community

Thousands of readers of our books have become part of the "BK Community" by participating in events featuring our authors, reviewing draft manuscripts of forthcoming books, spreading the word about their favorite books, and supporting our publishing program in other ways. If you would like to join the BK Community, please contact us at bkcommunity@bkpub.com.